RUM AND REGGAE

Jonathan Runge

Rum and Reggae

Harrap-Columbus

London

For Malcolm and Evelyn Cann

First published in 1988 by St Martin's Press, 175 Fifth Avenue, New York, NY 10010

First published in Great Britain 1990 by Harrap Columbus (a division of the Harrap Publishing Group), Chelsea House, 26 Market Square, Bromley, Kent, BR1 1NA.

All illustrations and lettering by David M. W. Greer
All maps by Jonathan Runge
All photographs by Jonathan Runge except pages 114 and 119, which are courtesy of the Jamaica Tourist Board.
Book design by Jennifer Dossin
Cover illustration by Karen Barbour

ISBN 0-7471 0207-4

PLEASE NOTE:
While every effort has been made to provide accurate information, prices, places, and people do change rather frequently in the Caribbean. Thus, please keep in mind that there may be discrepancies between what you find and what is reported here. In addition, some of the recommendations have been given by individuals interviewed by the author and may not represent the opinion of the author or of either the American or British publishers. The reader assumes all responsibility when participating in the activities or excursions described in this book.

Printed in Great Britain at The Bath Press, Avon

Contents

TOBAGO

Acknowledgments

Contrary to what you might think, writing a book on the Caribbean is not very glamorous. I did not spend my days on the beach or in the water. Well, sometimes I did. But most of the time I was running around checking out this and that and complaining about the heat. Just when I felt at home on an island, it was time to uproot and start all over again. Try doing that at least twenty-five times and you'll begin to know what I mean.

Fortunately, some wonderful people helped me along the way. I'd like to take this opportunity to gratefully thank those who did. In no particular order, they are: Brendan Hickey and Judith Wright (my Carnival buddies), Cynthia Allen (Kariwak Village—Tobago), Dr. Terry John, Anne-Marie Marecheau (Grenada Tourist Board), Dennis Henry, Ed Pope, Ray Bayley, Derek Lee-Pack, the Barbados Board of Tourism, Lee and Anne Katzenbach (Prospect Lodge—Carriacou), Sylvia and Karen—my Swiss sweethearts, Phil Allen, Paula and Andy Pampero, Jane Tipson (Edgewater Beach Hotel—St. Lucia), Paul Butler (St. Lucia Forestry Dept.), Joyce Noble (Fairholme Hotel—Barbados), John Chandler (Oceanview Hotel—Barbados), Andy Voss (Barbados Windsurfing Club), Rebecca Kronlage, Ylva Lundgren, Mr. and Mrs. Lundgren, Ed Rosner and Tom Troendle, Jerilyn Caesar, Bruce and Arny (Sea Park—St. Croix), David Alexander (Carambola Golf Club—St. Croix), Yves Priam, Anne Grey Jean-Baptiste (Papillote—Dominica), Irvin, Felix Gregoire (Dominica Forestry Department), Corinna Edwards, Charlotte Berglund (Rainbow Reef Villas), Serge, Danielle and Jean-Jean, Ed Arnold (Saba Deep), Glenn Holm (Saba Tourist Board), Sam McCook (Jamaica Tourist Board), Tony Ray (Jamaica Tourist Board), Bari Weissman (Greycom International), Nadia, and Air Jamaica.

There were also several people up north shivering through the winter who provided support and assistance while I was in the land of the sun. I would like to specially thank my parents, Eunice and Albert Runge, for their continued support and enthusiasm for this project. And thanks go to Nan Garland, David Greer, Martin Merle, Warren Jacobus, and Manuel Martínez-Llorián for their efforts on my behalf.

Finally, I would like to thank my agent, Sallie Gouverneur, and my editor, Brian DeFiore, for having both the faith in me to go it alone and a sense of humor.

To all who helped, many thanks—ya mon!

Introduction

Have you ever wondered what it would be like to swim in a large tank of dark rum? It feels like rubbing yourself from head to toe with Vicks Vaporub. My friend Katie used to do it all the time at a rum mill—to remain unnamed—in the islands. She would swim laps, pausing after each for a high-octane sip of liquid gold. She'd prefer swimming in rum to a swimming pool: unlike chlorine, the rum didn't cast a green tint to her naturally blond hair. After her swim, Katie would drive into town to her favorite bar to jam on some reggae music. The bartender, whose name was Tyrone, would prepare a wonderfully nasty rum punch especially for her. He called her "Wassy" (pronounced waz-zy), which roughly translates from Caribbean patois to *wild fun*—for Katie knew how to have a good time.

Perhaps you may not have had the privilege of a rum dip. Don't worry, for there are many other adventures and activities awaiting you in the tropics. Just be assured that you have bought the right book, for *Rum and Reggae* will show you how to find your own wassy fun, with a twist.

This is not your typical Caribbean tourist guide. It is organized by theme or activity instead of by island. Why? Because *Rum and Reggae* is written for people like you who want more out of a vacation than the standard tourist fare. You're more active—you like scuba, windsurfing, hiking, cruising, golf, or tennis. Or you're more particular, in search of secluded, hedonistic, cerebral, or hip places.

This book also differs from other guidebooks in another way. Instead of telling you that everything is "nice"—nice, that is, for the average tourist—*Rum and Reggae* offers definite opinions. I will tell you what is fantastic and what isn't, from the point of view of someone who loathes the tourist label.

So mix yourself a stiff rum punch (don't forget the bitters and fresh grated nutmeg), put on some Bob Marley, and sit back and let *Rum and Reggae* take you on your own private Caribbean trip.

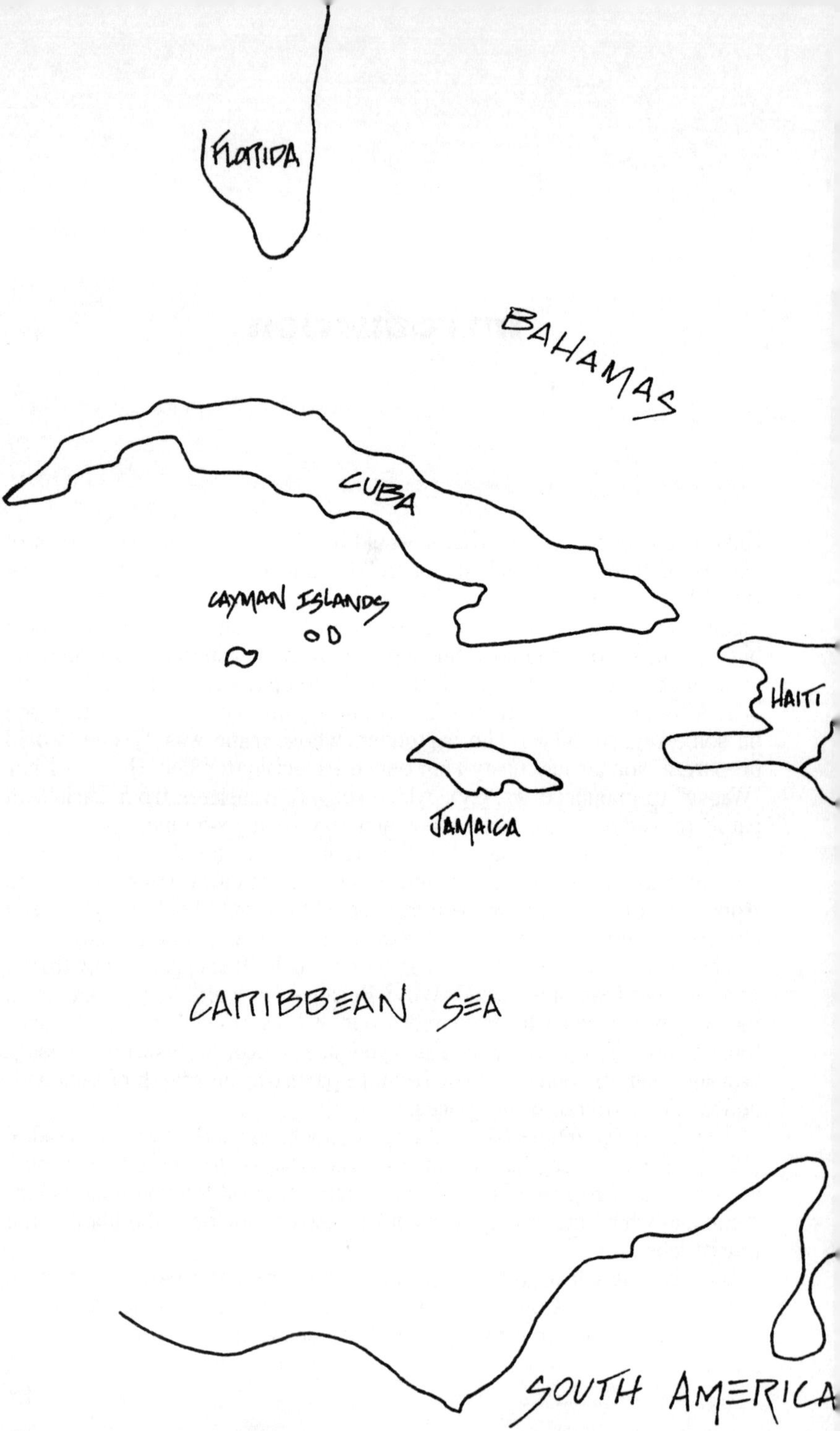
FLORIDA
BAHAMAS
CUBA
CAYMAN ISLANDS
HAITI
JAMAICA
CARIBBEAN SEA
SOUTH AMERICA

RUM & REGGAE'S CARIBBEAN

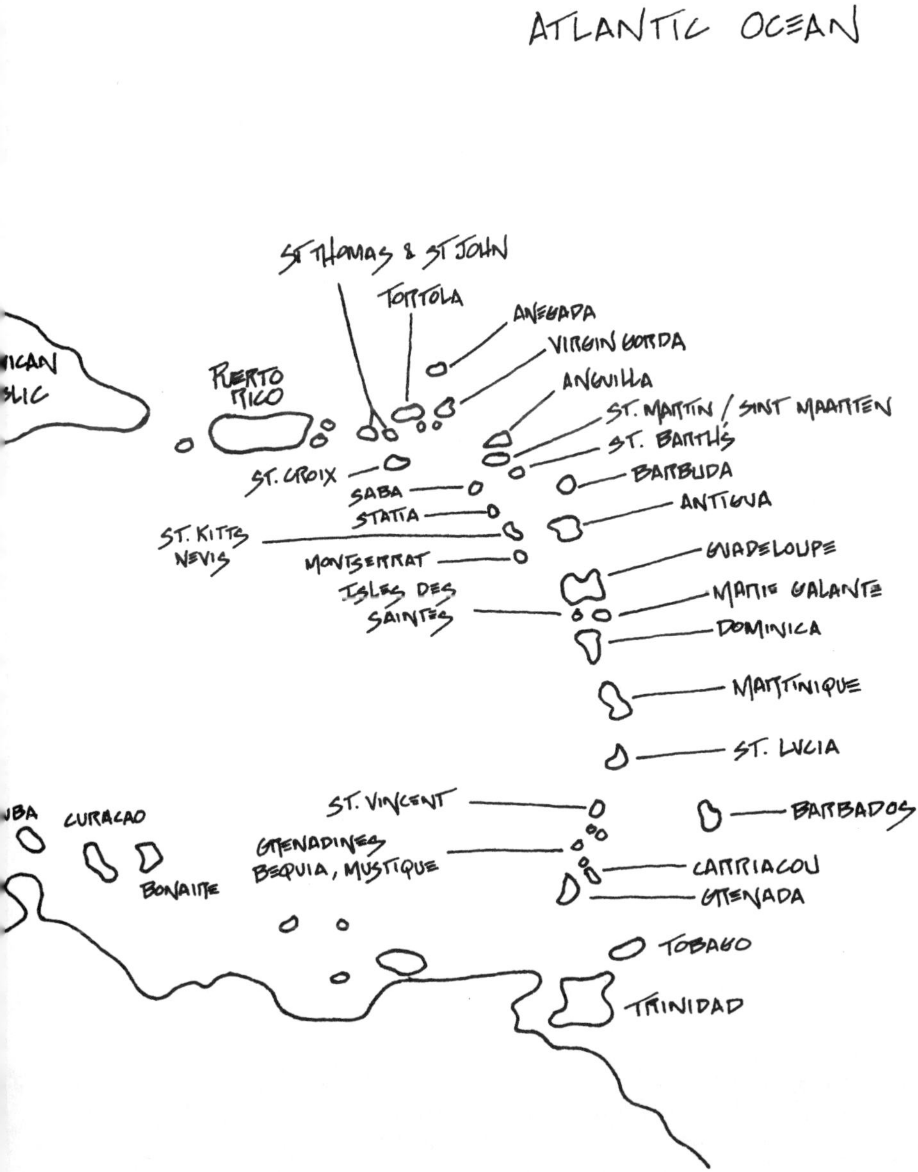

BEFORE
YOU GO

At the time of going to press the conversion rate was £1 = $1.75.

RESTAURANT PRICES

Prices represent per-person costs for the average meal from soup to nuts.

$—$0–10	(0–5.63 Sterling)
$$—$11–20	(6.20–11.27 Sterling)
$$$—$21–30	(11.83–16.90 Sterling)
$$$$—$31–40	(17.46–22.53 Sterling)
$$$$$—over $40	(over 22.53)

LODGING RATES

*Rates are for *high season* unless otherwise noted.
*Rates are for a single (noted as "Singles" in this book) or double (noted as "Doubles" in this book) room, EP unless otherwise noted.
*Expect a service and tax charge of about 15% added to your bill.
*Be sure to ask about credit cards when making your reservations if you intend to use them as payment. Many places, even expensive ones, do not accept credit cards.

DIRT CHEAP—$10–20 U.S.	(5.63–11.27 Sterling)
CHEAP—$21–40 U.S.	(11.83–22.54 Sterling)
NOT SO CHEAP—$41–80 U.S.	(23.10–45.07 Sterling)
PRICEY—$81–120 U.S.	(45.63–67.61 Sterling)
VERY PRICEY—$121–180 U.S.	(68.17–101.41 Sterling)
WICKED PRICEY—$181–240 U.S.	(101.97–135.21 Sterling)
RIDICULOUS—$241–300 U.S.	(135.77–169.01 Sterling)
OUTRAGEOUS—$300 and up!	(169.01–169.01 Plus)

MEAL CODES

EP (European Plan)—No meals included
CP (Continental Plan)—Continental breakfast included
MAP (Modified American Plan)—Full breakfast and dinner included
FAP (Full American Plan)—Full breakfast, lunch, and dinner included (sometimes with an afternoon "tea" or snack)

CLIMATES OF THE CARIBBEAN

The weather in the Caribbean is about as close to perfect as anywhere on earth. The temperature rarely dips below 70° or above 90° (at sea level). It can get cooler at night in the mountains of some of the islands, making it ideal for sleeping. The sun shines almost every day. Rainfall comes in the form of brief, intense cloudbursts, quickly followed by sun. It's pretty hard not to get a tan.

The reasons for this ideal climate are the constant temperature of the ocean—about 80° year round—and the steady trade winds from Africa. The Caribbean is not susceptible to the harsh weather patterns of the middle latitudes. The only weather peril to a Caribbean vacation is an occasional summer tropical depression or hurricane, which can make life very exciting.

There are three basic climate categories: arid (hot and dry), lush (hot, somewhat humid, with lots of rainfall), and those islands that have a little of both (the windward side being the wetter and greener) or that fall somewhere in the middle. The larger, mountainous islands almost always fall in the latter two categories. Conversely, the flatter, smaller ones are almost exclusively arid. All are warm to hot, depending on the season and the extent of the trade winds. Summers, while only about five degrees hotter than winter, feel a lot warmer due to the increased humidity and decreased wind. The one constant is the sun. It is always *strong,* and will swiftly fry unprotected pale faces—and bodies—to a glowing shade of lobster red.

There is also another climate down here, one I measure by the "friendliness barometer." This "barometer" reveals the attitude of the local people toward tourists. Some of the island nations of the Caribbean are wonderfully warm and positive while others are fairly antagonistic. The determining factors are the amount of tourist traffic and the degree to which local governments have educated the populace as to the economic importance of tourism. For example, both St. Thomas and Barbados are flooded with tourists every season, yet the atmosphere of the former is hostile while the latter is remarkably warm—a result of education. Other islands, because tourism is a recent phenomenon, are open and friendly to the point of innocence.

How do you find which "climates" are best for you? Simple, check out the chart on the next page.

CLIMATES CHART

FRIENDLINESS BAROMETER	ARID	LUSH	BOTH
VERY FRIENDLY	Tobago Bequia	Dominica Saba Jamaica	Trinidad
WARM	Barbados Carriacou	Montserrat Jamaica	St. Martin Virgin Gorda Jost Van Dyke Anegada
NEUTRAL	Mustique Anguilla St. Bart's	Grenada Puerto Rico Jamaica	St. Croix St. John Tortola
COOL	Antigua	St. Vincent St. Lucia Martinique Guadeloupe Jamaica	Nevis St. Kitts
NASTY		Jamaica	St. Thomas

BUILDING A BASE FOR TANNING

Since the advent of electric beaches (tanning machines) and pretanning accelerators, there is absolutely no reason to get burned on your first day out in the tropical sun. With some advance attention, you can stay outside for *hours* on your first day, and let's face it, what you want to do when you step off the plane is hit the beach.

Just about every town has a tanning center with clever and cutesy names like Tanarama, Tanfastic, A Touch of Bronze, Endless Sunner, Sunsational, and Tanfasia. Most health clubs usually have one or two tanning "coffins" lying around, beckoning pasty skins to look healthier and more attractive in a matter of *minutes*. Ultraviolet tanning is quite safe when used properly, as the UVB light doesn't have the burning rays of earlier sun lamps and, of course, the sun.

Many of these tanning centers have tanning-prep packages of ten sessions: you start with about five minutes of "sunning" and work up to twenty or thirty. Spread out over the two weeks prior to your departure, this should give you an excellent head start on a great Caribbean tan.

Recent years have also seen the development of pretan accelerators. These marvelous creams, pioneered by Estée Lauder and now available from a wide variety of manufacturers, chemically stimulate the manufacture of melanin, the pigment that darkens your skin. (Normally it takes direct exposure to the sun to start its production.) A pretan accelerator doesn't change your color (or dye your skin like QT). Rather, it prepares the skin with extra melanin so that you tan the first time rather than burn, and much faster, too.

WHAT TO WEAR AND TAKE ALONG

Less is more. That's the motto to remember when packing to go to the Caribbean. Bring only what you can carry for ten minutes at a good clip, because you'll often be schlepping your luggage for at least that time, and it's *hot.*

What you *really* need to take along are a bathing suit, shorts, T-shirts, cotton sweater, a pair of sandals, sunglasses, and a Walkman. After all, you *are* on vacation. However, these are the eighties and people tend to dress up for no reason, so you may want to bring some extra togs to look presentable at the dinner table. To help you be totally prepared (and to make your packing a lot easier), I've assembled a list of essentials for a week.

THE PACKING LIST

CLOTHES

bathing suit
T-shirts (4)—you'll end up buying at least one
polo shirts (2)
shorts (2)
nice, compatible lightweight trousers (you can wear them on the plane)
sandals
cotton sweater
undergarments
sneakers or topsiders

If you must have them, wear the following (with appropriate shoes) on the plane:
Men: lightweight jacket, tie
Women: lightweight dress

ESSENTIALS

toiletries
sunscreens (SPF 15+, 8, 4 [oil] and lip protector)
moisturizers (Noxema is still the old standard for sunburn)
some good books
Cutter's or Woodsman's insect repellent (oh those nasty bugs)
sunglasses
hat/visor

HARDWARE

Walkman and tapes
camcorder or pocket camera
"credit-card" calculator (for exchange rates)

SPORTS ACCESSORIES (when applicable)

tennis racquet
golf clubs
hiking shoes
fins, mask, snorkel, regulator

PAPERWORK

passport
traveler's cheques

THE DEAL OF THE SKIES

For those of you with some time on your hands (and a sense of adventure), LIAT, the "Caribbean Airline," has a deal called the Explorer Fare. It costs (at press time) $327 U.S. and allows you to fly virtually everywhere that LIAT flies for thirty days. This is roughly all the islands from Puerto Rico south to Trinidad. The major restrictions are that you can't stop at the same place twice (unless you are in transit) and that you can't change the itinerary once ticketed (a $20 U.S. surcharge every time you do) or get a refund. This is a great way to see several islands on an extended holiday.

Remember that LIAT, and other small island airlines, fly small planes, from the nineteen-seat DeHavilland Twin Otter to the forty-four-seat Dash-8. Having flown LIAT extensively, I've developed some golden rules for stress-free flying when in the friendly but not so efficient skies of the Caribbean.

- ***Always have a reservation.***
- ***Reconfirm seventy-two hours before departure.***
- ***Get to the airport at least an hour before departure*—overbooking is a problem.**
- ***Never fly standby,* especially during peak periods—you won't get on.**
- ***Go immediately to the gate once you've checked in.* I was left behind when the plane arrived early and took off without me.**
- ***Avoid flying on Sundays.* Everything, including reservation lines and ticket counters, closes down in some places.**
- ***Keep luggage to a minimum.* Carrying a lot in the heat is unpleasant. Also, carry all valuables with you—don't check them in.**

PUBLISHER'S NOTE

Throughout this book there is advice on 'How To Get There'. Such advice is aimed at travellers from the USA. It is possible to fly direct to the Caribbean from the UK, or to take a cruise. Please consult your travel agent.

THE **PRIVACY** OPTION

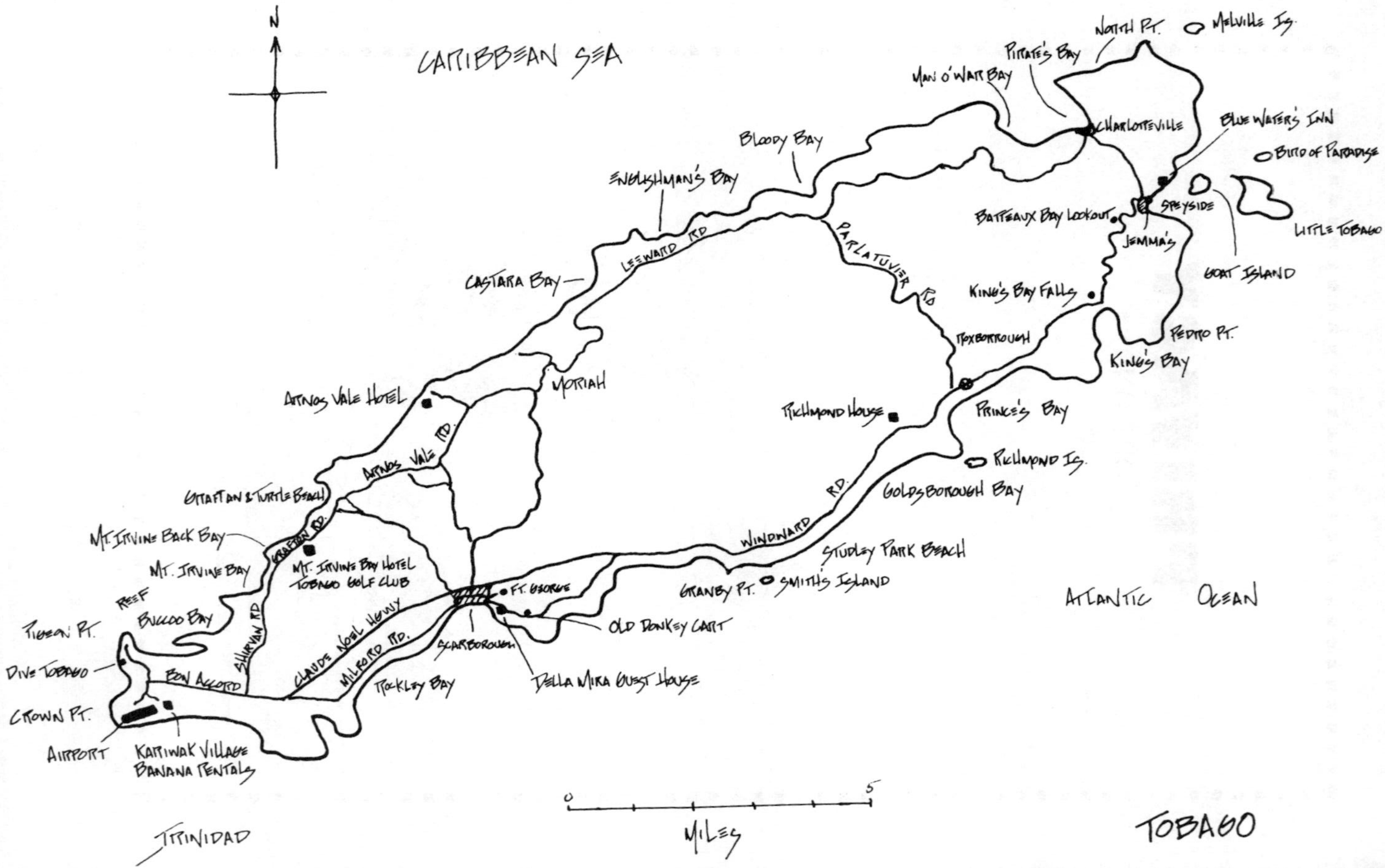
N
CARIBBEAN SEA
North Pt.
Melville Is.
Pirate's Bay
Man o' War Bay
Charlotteville
Blue Waters Inn
Bird of Paradise
Bloody Bay
Englishman's Bay
Speyside
Batteaux Bay Lookout
Little Tobago
Jemma's
Leeward Rd
Parlatuvier Rd
Castara Bay
King's Bay Falls
Goat Island
Roxborough
Pedro Pt.
King's Bay
Moriah
Arnos Vale Hotel
Richmond House
Prince's Bay
Arnos Vale Rd.
Richmond Is.
Grafton & Turtle Beach
Goldsborough Bay
Windward Rd.
Mt. Irvine Back Bay
Grafton Rd.
Mt. Irvine Bay Hotel
Tobago Golf Club
Studley Park Beach
Mt. Irvine Bay
Granby Pt.
Smith's Island
Ft. George
Atlantic Ocean
Reef
Buccoo Bay
Claude Noel Hwy
Old Donkey Cart
Pigeon Pt.
Shirvan Rd
Milford Rd.
Scarborough
Dive Tobago
Bon Accord
Rockley Bay
Della Mira Guest House
Crown Pt.
Airport
Kariwak Village
Banana Rentals
0
5
Miles
Trinidad
TOBAGO

EXPLORING TOBAGO

They don't make 'em like this anymore. Deserted beaches, cheap hotels, great snorkeling and scuba, lots of unspoiled places to explore, and the most friendly, smiling people (it sounds like a cliché but it's true) I've ever met anywhere. You have to pinch yourself to believe it—could a place like this really exist or am I having a flashback from the sixties?

Tobago has yet to be "discovered" by the package-tour pariahs who eventually make Miami Beaches out of popular Caribbean destinations. There is little tourist hype here—most visitors are weekenders from sister island Trinidad. The possibility of running into someone you know is fairly remote, so you don't have to hide in an exclusive or expensive resort for privacy. Indeed, some of the smaller guest houses in the more remote locations on Tobago are probably more private than the larger hotels concentrated on the western end of the island. This is also a place that goes to bed early. There is virtually no nightlife, which makes it a wonderful spot to recuperate from the fast lane of Carnival (see pages 67-77).

The slow pace and mellow atmosphere don't mean that there is nothing to do. Au contraire. The best way to spend time on Tobago is to explore. While the island's western end at times resembles standard tourist fare found elsewhere in the Caribbean, the center and eastern end are magical. And the best way to explore is on a scooter. Not only does a scooter allow greater accessibility to out-of-the-way beaches and destinations, riding one is also a great deal of fun.

If you don't have much luggage and you arrive before five P.M., you can walk from the airport to Banana Rentals, (809) 639–8441, at Kariwak Village, rent a Honda 80 or 125, strap on your luggage, and be on your way. The charge for a Honda 80 is about $15 U.S. per day. (You'll end up saving quite a bit of money that would usually be spent on taxis.) A helmet is provided and Stephen—the manager—will tell you all you need to know about driving on Tobago. The speed limit is 30 MPH, there are no freeways, and driving is on the left. A valid U.S. license and credit card are all you need.

There are several excursions that will take you all over the island. Each is detailed in the following pages. They are best done early in your visit so that the places you really adore can be revisited. Also, there are other activities, such as scuba and snorkeling, that should find a way into your schedule. And of course there are the Tobago beaches, among the finest and least crowded in the Caribbean—even at the height of winter—that will command your body and soul.

EXCURSION #1—THE WINDWARD ROAD (all day)

Starting from Crown Point, head east on the Claude Noel Highway to Milford Road. Turn right and follow the road to Scarborough—the island capital. You'll pass a long beach at Rockley Bay with several spots to turn in and stop. When you reach Scarborough, check out Acadia Records on Castries Street, where you can buy premixed calypso tapes of your favorite hits (they do a brisk business right after Carnival). Then go up the hill to Fort George. Here you'll find beautifully landscaped grounds and some old buildings that are just screaming to be photographed. When you're ready, proceed on the Windward Road—there is little else to see in Scarborough.

Windward Road will be your course for the remainder of the day. There are many points along the way that are worth stopping for. Note that there is a gas station in Roxborough in case you need to fill up. Here are the possibilities:

- GRANBY POINT, Mt. St. George—A high-up vista view of Hillsborough Bay and Smith's Island.
- STUDLEY PARK BEACH, Studley Park—A very pretty, palm-lined, brown sand beach. Just beyond the new bridge.
- RICHMOND HOUSE, Belle Garden (see page 15)—Definitely worth checking out.
- KING'S BAY WATERFALL, Rosenwald Estate, Delaford—A good place for a fresh-water swim. Turn into the cocoa plantation at the 20-mile post and proceed to a car park.
- BATTEAUX BAY LOOKOUT, above Speyside—After a twisting and turning ascent through a landslide area and gorge, there is a lookout at the top of the road on your left. Extraordinary views of Little Tobago Island and the blue Atlantic beyond.
- SPEYSIDE, Speyside—Have a lunch at Jemma's (see page 17) and check out the Blue Waters Inn (see page 15).
- CHARLOTTEVILLE, Charlotteville—The end of the road belongs to this very interesting fishing village. There are good beaches on both Pirate's and Man-O-War Bays.

The best way back is the way you came. It will give you a chance to stop and linger at favorite places.

EXCURSION #2—THE LEEWARD SIDE

This outing will be slower, more laid-back and beach-oriented. There will be many occasions when you will pass a road or path that leads to a beach not even mentioned here. By all means investigate. It may be just the secluded cove for an unscheduled tryst.

Beginning at Crown Point again, follow the signs for:

- PIGEON POINT—Acclaimed as the nicest beach on the island—forget it! It's crowded and small, but it *is* a good place to people-watch. There is a $5 TT (about $1.40 U.S.) admission fee. Dive Tobago is located at the entrance and will take you on snorkel trips to Buccoo Bay, Tobago's famous reef. For $25 TT (about $7 U.S.) you get gear, instruction if you need it, and a ride in a vessel about as stable as a canoe.

  If you skip Pigeon Point, head east on the Claude Noel Highway and turn left (the only major left) at the Milford-Shirvan Road. Follow Shirvan Road to Grafton Road to Arnos Vale Road. It sounds complicated but keep in mind that all you are doing is following the north coast road. Once you reach Bloody Bay you will probably want to turn around. The road beyond to Charlotteville is in bad shape. On the way to Bloody Bay, there are lots of points of interest and many deserted or secluded beaches. Half the fun is discovering your own. Here are a few suggestions:

- MT. IRVINE GOLF COURSE, Grafton Road (see "The Golf Option," page 151)—This is reputedly one of the fifty best courses in the world. You can't miss it as you drive by several fairways and greens before you get to the clubhouse. The pro shop sells Tobago Golf Club T-shirts.
- MT. IRVINE BEACH, Grafton Road—With public facilities set up by the Tourist Board, this beach is noteworthy as Tobago's only surfing beach. On some days the surf can break quite nicely. The best waves are found on the reef just to the right of the beach.
- MT. IRVINE BACK BAY, Grafton Road—After you pass Mt. Irvine Beach heading east, you'll notice Gleneagles Drive on your right. On your left will be a track through a field. Follow this to the end, park the scooter, and take the footpath down to one of the best beaches on Tobago.

- GRAFTON BEACH, Grafton Road—When you pass Gleneagles Drive, follow the first road (not track) on the left. This will take you to Grafton Beach.
- TURTLE BEACH, Grafton Road—Before you get to the Turtle Beach resort, you'll notice a small dirt road with white-and-black striped posts. Follow this road to this lovely beach. You'll be the only ones there.
- ARNOS VALE HOTEL, Arnos Vale Road—From Grafton Road, turn onto Arnos Vale and follow it to the Arnos Vale Hotel for a rum punch at the beach bar (see page 16).
- ENGLISHMAN'S BAY, Arnos Vale Road—After you pass Castra Bay, you'll see grazing cows in a pasture and will cross two bridges. Look for a large tree with a black barrel on your left. Park the bike and walk to Englishman's Bay for real seclusion.

TOBAGO: KEY FACTS

LOCATION	11°N by 60°W 22 miles northeast of Trinidad 2300 miles southeast of New York
SIZE	116 square miles 21 miles long by 7 miles wide
HIGHEST POINT	Pigeon Peak (1890 feet)
POPULATION	40,000
LANGUAGE	English
TIME	Atlantic Standard Time (one hour ahead of EST)
ELECTRICITY	AC/DC, depends on where you are—ask before plugging in
CURRENCY	The TT dollar ($3.60 TT = $1.00 U.S.)
DRIVING	On the left; valid driver's license okay
DOCUMENTS	Valid passport and ongoing ticket
BEER TO DRINK	Carib
RUM TO DRINK	Vat 19

GETTING THERE

While you can get a direct flight to Tobago from Miami, the fastest way is to fly BWIA, Pan Am, American, and Eastern nonstop to Piarco International Airport in Trinidad and connect with BWIA's Airbridge DC-9 service to Tobago ($75 TT/$21 U.S. round trip). If you're not in a rush and you happen to be in Port of Spain, you can sail on the ferry, which is a five-and-a-half-hour journey.

STAYING THERE

There are numerous accommodations on Tobago but only six that I'll bother mentioning. Two are guest houses, two are a little fancier, and the last are resorts. In no particular order:

KARIWAK VILLAGE (809) 639–8545
P.O. Box 27, Scarborough, Tobago, West Indies

Its location next to the aiport is suspect at first, but you will soon understand why so many people want to stay here. It's a very comfortable and casual place, with fourteen air-conditioned duplex cottages around an attractive pool and a thatched-roof loggia/hut arrangement housing the bar and restaurant. What makes Kariwak so popular is the food and service—all at a reasonable price. Owners Cynthia and Allan Clovis are very helpful and keep the Village running smoothly. It is also the in-vogue weekend retreat for Trinidadians. Breakfast here is the best on the island. The beach and airport are a five-minute walk away. Rates are NOT SO CHEAP for singles and doubles (MAP).

BLUE WATERS INN (809) 639–4341
Batteaux Bay, Speyside, Tobago, West Indies

This is an ideal place for a romantic tryst. The inn's location seems to be at the end of the world. Indeed, it's far—a two-hour drive from the airport along the Windward Rd. and then a semihairy climb and descent on a dirt road to the inn. The accommodations are simple, villa-style buildings with standard double rooms. What makes them special is that all eleven rooms face the bay and are only a few steps away from the beach. When the wind blows (almost steadily), the sound of the waves will lull you to sleep. The food is commendable and features fresh seafood. There is no printed menu and the fare changes daily. The dining room and bar remind me of a ski lodge on a beach—lots of padded chairs and a conversation pit. The inn has a tennis court, and birdwatchers and other naturalists can take a short boat trip from the beach in front of the inn to Little Tobago Island. Rates are NOT SO CHEAP for singles and doubles.

RICHMOND GUEST HOUSE (809) 639–4467
Belle Garden, Tobago, West Indies

Smack dab in the middle of nowhere sits the Richmond Guest House. Located in Belle Garden on the Windward Road, it is an old, recently renovated plantation house perched on top of a windy hill on a 1500-acre estate.

From the outside it looks ho-hum, but the interior is surprisingly stately with dark mahogany and high white ceilings. The furnishings are a funky reddish velvet and the rooms are *huge*—especially Room 4. The parlor is invitingly relaxing and beckons you to curl up with a good book. There is a bar and meals can and should be arranged as the closest good restaurant is an hour away. There is a beach nearby that, while pretty, can get rough. But you come here not for the beach but to emulate the long-lost life of the Tobago sugar planter. Rates are CHEAP for singles and doubles.

DELLA MIRA GUEST HOUSE (809) 639–2531
P.O. Box 203, Scarborough, Tobago, West Indies

Now *this* is a funky place. The water will stop flowing through the showerhead just as you've worked your hair into a lather. Then the hot-water knob (if you can call the water hot) will fall off, missing your big toe, but letting the water gush forth like something out of a Three Stooges rerun. Forget the pool furniture—it looks like it washed up during the last hurricane. And yet, the Della Mira has definite style—run-down, yes, but style nonetheless. It's very simple. I think my college dorm room was more sumptuous. However, it *is* cheap and beggars unfortunately can't be choosers. It's run and owned by Neville Miranda—a spunky older gentleman who holds the place together (barely). He is very friendly and will even do your laundry. There is a pool I wouldn't swim in and an overpriced restaurant that isn't worth it. When requesting a room, pay a little more to face the bay as the rooms are much bigger. Rates are DIRT CHEAP for singles and CHEAP for doubles.

THE MT. IRVINE BAY HOTEL (809) 639–8871
P.O. Box 222, Scarborough, Tobago, West Indies

You've seen this resort many times before, most likely at a convention or business meeting. Every island or state has at least one and this one came right out of the cookie cutter. But what makes this expensive hotel noteworthy is its championship golf course (see "The Golf Option," page 151), widely renowned as one of the best in the Caribbean. The hotel is big, especially for Tobago, with 110 rooms, two lighted tennis courts, and the standard amenities. But it lacks character, which is not surprising, and it only overlooks the water—no beachfront villas here. Rates are PRICEY for singles and VERY PRICEY for doubles.

ARNOS VALE HOTEL (809) 639–2881
P.O. Box 208, Scarborough, Tobago, West Indies

Once an old plantation estate, the Arnos Vale Hotel is a much smaller and tasteful version of what the Mt. Irvine should be. On a hill are a main house and cottages cooled by ceiling fans. The bulk of the accommodations are in more modern suites near the beach and are more expensive. There is a pool and a tennis court as well as lovely landscaped grounds. The reef at the beach offers excellent snorkeling. Rates are VERY PRICEY for singles and doubles (MAP).

EATING THERE

There are four places I'd recommend for your dining pleasure:

KARIWAK VILLAGE, Crown Pt. (639–8441)

Cynthia cooks and supervises a menu that concentrates on West Indian cuisine. Their callaloo soup and dolphin in spiced coconut sauce are excellent. $$$

THE OLD DONKEY CART, Scarborough (639–3551)

Owned and operated by a local woman named Gloria who also models in Germany. This explains the fine collection of somewhat overpriced German wines. The food is quite good and will particularly appeal to garlic addicts. Don't miss the garlic bread. Most of the dining is al fresco and the owner is friendly and efficient. $$$

JEMMA'S, Speyside (no phone)

Tucked away in a tiny shop on the beach at Speyside, Jemma's is a special place. The dining room has three lace-covered wooden tables of the old schoolhouse variety (matching chairs of course) with a window overlooking the sea. Outside there is a big tree that leans out over the beach with a built-in loveseat. The food is simple seafood but the taste of Jemma's fish and chips is forever etched in my memory. It was just great—a kingfish steak dipped in batter and served with a sweet and spicy sauce. Jemma was a little startled at how fast I ate it up. $

CORAL BEACH FOOD SHACKS (no phone)

If you really want good local food fast and cheap, this is where you'll find it. Probably the most celebrated is Miss Esmay's (no one, including Miss E., is sure of the spelling). The dish to get is crab and dumplings although the crab looked like a very large tarantula to me. She uses land crabs, which are big and hairy. Still, everyone loves 'em at $20 TT (about $5.50 U.S.) a pop. Moving down the road a bit, there's a green shack that sells Buss Up Shot (T & T's idea of pasta) with curried beef and chana (chick peas). To drink there's mauby—a spiced drink that's made from tree bark, looks like swamp water, and is definitely an acquired taste. You can also try sea moss—a seaweed milk shake that's supposed to put lead in your pencil, and tamarind nectar—a very tart juice made from the coating of the tamarind seed. Other favorites are roti (the Caribbean burrito), pelau (a seasoned rice dish), and fresh coconut. The latter is macheteed open for you as you cringe, terrified that the man will chop off his hand as well. The coconut milk is very tasty and the meat is scooped out with a piece of the shell.

CARRIACOU

A friend of mine told me once that just as her plane touched down on Carriacou, it suddenly lifted up with jarring swiftness. When she looked out the window, she saw a cow on the runway.

That is Carriacou. It's on its own wavelength. Everyone—and everything—moves at its own pace, as did the runway keeper. If you're an efficiency freak, this island isn't for you. But that's not the reason for coming to Carriacou in the first place. What makes Carriacou special—besides its natural beauty—is a unique sense of detachment.

In Carriacou you can have solitude without feeling lonely. There are enough people around to keep your sensibilities alive. But there's a mind-your-own-business philosophy bred by the big business of smuggling. Thus you can socialize only when you want to.

Located 20 miles north of Grenada, Carriacou is the largest of the Grenadine chain. It gets extremely dry, almost parched, as the winter progresses. It then begins to look like autumn in New England—give or take a few palm trees and other tropical props.

There is only one place at the moment that plays well with the scenario—The Prospect Lodge, (809) 443–7380, Carriacou, Grenada, W.I. Set on a bluff on the northwest corner of the island, it commands a stunning view of the hills and coastline of Hillsborough Bay all the way to Cistern Point. At night, there are only three lights visible on the harbor. That is a peaceful sight. In fact, the view in the moonlight is a "wow" experience.

Prospect served as the center for some vague Russian cult until it was bought in 1986 by Lee and Anne Katzenbach. New Englanders by style and disposition, they decided that Carriacou was the state of mind they wanted and opened the Prospect Lodge in December 1986. In their pre-

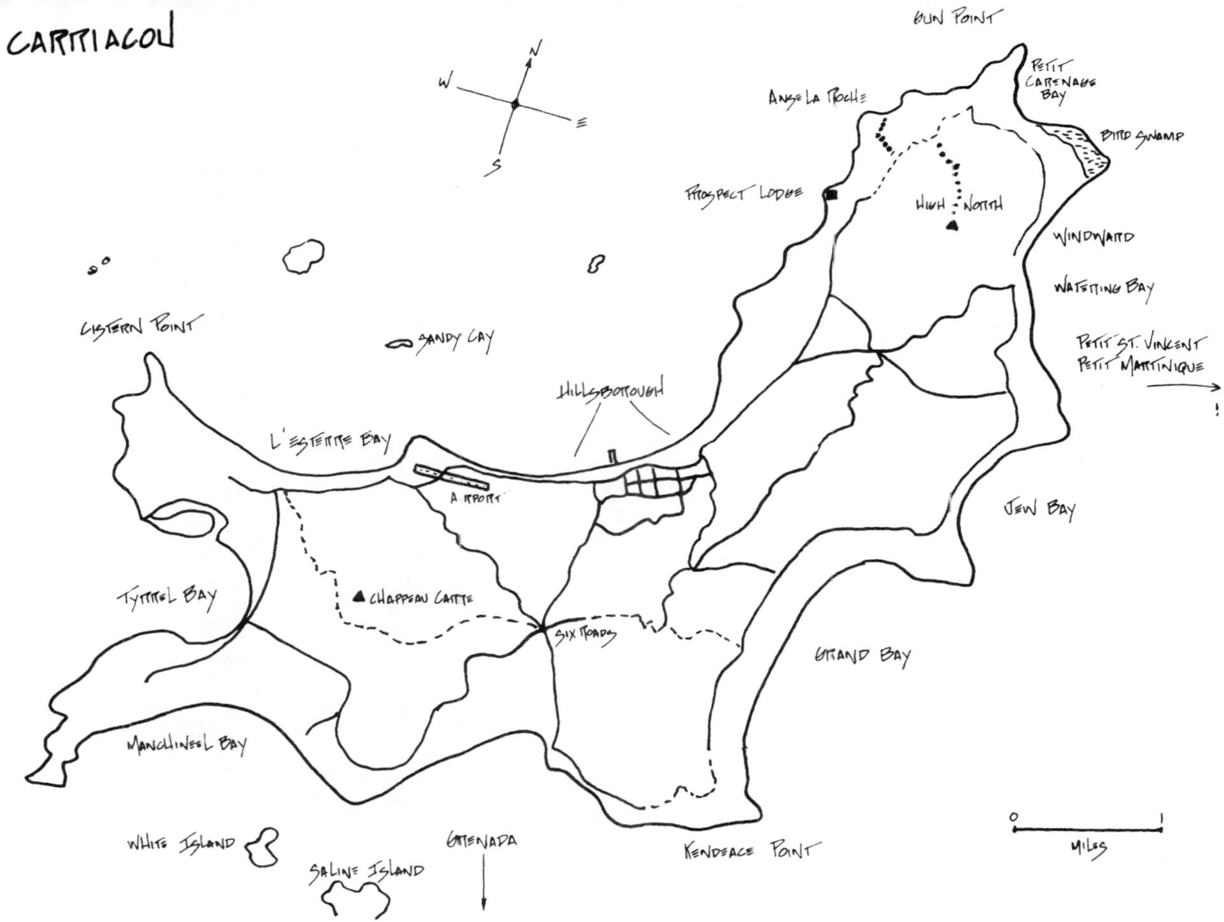
CARRIACOU
N
W
E
S
GUN POINT
PETIT CARENAGE BAY
ANSE LA ROCHE
BIRD SWAMP
PROSPECT LODGE
HIGH NORTH
WINDWARD
WATERING BAY
PETIT ST. VINCENT
PETIT MARTINIQUE
CISTERN POINT
SANDY CAY
HILLSBOROUGH
L'ESTERRE BAY
AIRPORT
JEW BAY
TYRREL BAY
CHAPPEAU CARRE
SIX ROADS
GRAND BAY
MANCHINEEL BAY
WHITE ISLAND
SALINE ISLAND
GRENADA
KENDEACE POINT
0
1
MILES

Anse La Roche
with Union Island in the distance.

vious incarnations, Lee was (and still is) an artist and Anne was a teacher-cum-entrepreneur.

The buildings themselves have a definite outdoorsy feel and flavor. Wood-louvered windows prop open like awnings to let in the outside. The rooms are painted light pastel shades or white, with white floors. The effect is very Cape Cod. There is artwork on the walls and the best library I've encountered in the Caribbean. Breakfast and dinner are served on white tables on one half of the large main loggia. The other half has a comfortable seating arrangement with a sofa bench to stretch out on and look at the stars. Outside a hammock swings invitingly under several palm trees. The porch of Anne and Lee's pink house is a mecca for sunset viewing. Rates are CHEAP for singles and doubles (MAP).

WALKING ON CARRIACOU

The lodge is ideally located on the edge of the still-pristine northwest corner of the island. A number of good walks originate here.

WALK #1—ANSE LA ROCHE (twenty-five minutes one way)

This walk takes you up a James Taylor country road shaded by machineel trees (don't touch the leaves or the apples—the machineel is like poison ivy). When you come to a tree leaning out over the road, turn left and go down the cowpath past calabash trees to the ruins of an old plantation. In front is a huge sloping pasture that opens out onto a secluded beach—the Petit Martinique Straits and Union Island loom in the distance. This view is so enjoyable you may not want to proceed further. If you do decide to move on, pass through the meadow and follow the trail (flagged by a white shell on a black rock) down to the beach. It is almost always deserted. If you want to walk naked from one end to the other you can. The northern end of the beach has a sandier bottom and is better for swimming. The other end has good snorkeling by the big rocks. The way back is a fairly easy but steady climb. Take your time, it gets hot fast.

WALK #2—WINDWARD (one hour one way)

Another walk will take you around High North to Gun Point and Petit Carenage Bay. There is also a very nice deserted beach and reef for snorkeling. At the right end of the beach is a mangrove swamp called the "bird swamp." Directly across the bay is Petit St. Vincent—better known as

PSV—the "trop chic et cher" resort on its own island, and Petit Martinique. The latter is part of the Grenada chain although its residents hardly think so. It has a much higher living standard than its neighbors due to its proudly held position as smuggling capital of the West Indies. It's very common to see Carriacou-built trading boats laden with VCRs and French wine. Forget St. Thomas. Petit Martinique is where the *real* bargains can be found.

Continuing on your walk, the road leads into Windward. This is still a major West Indian boat-building center. Brightly colored wooden boats can be seen everywhere in the Grenadines. (They are very photogenic, especially in the late-afternoon light.) It's likely there will be a few on the beach under construction or repair. Most residents of Windward are of Scottish and West Indian descent. The Scots came here to build a merchant fleet when Britain ruled the islands—and never left. They have Scottish surnames and lighter skin than the other Carriacou residents.

There are several rum shops and minimarkets to get much needed liquid refreshment as it's very hot and dry in Windward. Here you can hire a boat to take you to PSV or Petit Martinique. Just ask around the dock or at one of the shops.

WALK #3—HIGH NORTH (forty minutes one way)

This is a good late-afternoon walk: watch the sunset from the ridge just below High North. It's a good idea to take a thermos of rum punch (or ice water) along as it's hot climbing. Start on the road to Windward until you pass the leaning tree and come to a sharp bend in the road to the right. There will be a pasture leading up the ridge from the road. Take the short cowpath to the pasture and follow the path and pasture up the ridge. It will then turn into a regular path until you come to a clearing. There will be a grassy knoll up to the left, which is your objective. Have another rum punch and watch for the green flash (a phenomenon of the tropics that occurs when the tip of the sun sinks into the horizon). If you want to linger for all the sunset hues, bring a flashlight as half-light fades fast in the tropics.

WALK #4—KENDEACE POINT (all day)

For the serious stroller, the rest of the island can offer longer and more diverse walks. The best of these is the one to Kendeace Point. Prospect Lodge has maps for sale for $3 EC (about $1.00 U.S.) and it's fairly difficult to get lost. It's best to leave early in the morning (by nine A.M.) and walk until noon. Then the heat takes over. So find a shady spot on the beach and wait it out until three P.M. This is a good time to read, meditate, and enjoy a siesta. Energy and vitality restored, you should be able to make it back by six o'clock for sunset and sustenance. The tired and weary can hop a minibus or hitch.

CARRIACOU: KEY FACTS

LOCATION	12°N by 61°W 23 miles northeast of Grenada 2175 miles southeast of New York
SIZE	13 square miles 16 miles long by 5 miles wide
HIGHEST POINT	High North (955 ft.)
POPULATION	7000
LANGUAGE	English
TIME	Atlantic Standard Time (one hour ahead of EST, no Daylight Savings Time)
ELECTRICITY	220/240 volts (50 cycles)
CURRENCY	The Eastern Caribbean dollar (EC) ($2.64 EC = $1.00 U.S.)
DRIVING	On the left; local permit needed with valid driver's license
DOCUMENTS	Valid passport or proof of nationality (with photo) and ongoing ticket
BEER TO DRINK	Heineken
RUM TO DRINK	The "house" brand from the local rum shop

DON'T MISS

SANDY CAY

About a half-mile offshore, this tiny island of creamy sand and palm trees is a fabulous spot for a day's outing. There is also a fantastic reef for snorkeling off the northern end of the cay with huge coral heads and a good variety of fish. The sun gets very intense but there are palm groves for shade and relief. To get there, ask for Reggie. His green, yellow, and red boat named *Roots II* will pick you and your group up at Prospect's beach and return you when you wish for about $80 EC (about $30 U.S.). Unfortunately, the odds are you won't be alone on the beach. This is a regular pit stop for the cruise contingent and a popular spot for locals on Sundays.

CARNIVAL

Carriacou is also the scene of an off-beat Carnival celebration. The main

THE TEN MOST LUXURIOUS RESORTS IN THE CARIBBEAN

- **MALLIOUHANA—Anguilla, B.W.I. This is the crème de la crème of luxury and taste. The Haitian paintings even match the upholstery!**
- **TAIWANA—St. Bart's, F.W.I. It's so expensive and exclusive that if you have to ask how much, you don't belong here.**
- **ROUND HILL—Montego Bay, Jamaica, W.I. This is a celeb hangout, with wonderful bungalows obscured by lush vegetation (privacy the byword here).**
- **SANDY LANE—Barbados, W.I. The grande dame of the west coast hotels, it's the ideal place to throw a party. Double ballustrades enclose a terrace that would put the mansions of Newport to shame.**
- **TRIDENT—Port Antonio, Jamaica, W.I. This is the last word in opulence in the very lush and very tony Port Antonio (the villas are fabulous).**
- **LITTLE DIX BAY—Virgin Gorda, B.W.I. This is the best of the Rock resorts on the prettiest of the Virgins. The landscaping is beautiful. Certainly worth mentioning are the others, CANEEL BAY and the new CARAMBOLA Beach and Golf Club.**
- **PETIT ST. VINCENT—St. Vincent and the Grenadines, W.I. A remote, deluxe resort on its own island in the southern Grenadines. Choose a beach to call your own.**
- **LA SAMANNA—St. Martin, F.W.I. Jackie O. is a regular. This resort has the most beautiful beach on St. Martin/Maarten.**
- **COTTON HOUSE—Mustique, St. Vincent and the Grenadines, W.I. A haunt of the rich, famous, and infamous on this most exclusive of enclaves, it's the place to stay if you're not at one of the island's deluxe villa-compounds.**
- **MONTPELIER PLANTATION—Nevis, W.I. Experience the private life of the sugar planter on the pretty and sleepy island of Nevis.**

event here is Shakespearean recitals. Each village has their representatives (called "pierrots") who must recite flawlessly or get hit over the head with a stick or other blunt object. Fortunately, the contestants wear cardboard boxes over their heads and padding in their capes to prevent any real damage. When the recital/duel is finished, the whole party runs to the next village for the next round. Eventually, everyone winds up in Hillsborough for jump-up (the island term for party) in the streets.

REGATTA

Featuring boat races and even more onshore fun, Regatta is the big hoohah of the Grenadines. The racing is really secondary to the drinking and shenanigans characteristic of all Caribbean sailing regattas. It lasts for four days (around the first week of August) with frolicking summer camp activities like greased-pole, tug-of-war, and donkey races. For more info, contact the Grenada Tourist Office, Collingham Gardens, London, SW5, (01) 370-5164.

BIG DRUM

Fanciers of primitive music will love Big Drum. It's about the closest thing to tribal drums you'll hear. Also known as "nation dances," this percussive music derives from the African tribes sent to Carriacou in the eighteenth century. There are three drums made of rum kegs and goat skins. Big Drum is played at most important island occasions—boat launchings, house blessings, and tombstone dedications are the most common—where goats are sacrificed and a good time is had by all. You also may hear Big Drum at Regatta festivities or a *Blocko*—Carriacou's version of a block party.

PLANTATION LIFE ON NEVIS

Once upon a time, before Sweet 'n Low, Fit-for-Life diets, and Tab, sugar was king. A glimpse into the life of the Caribbean sugar plantation during the last century makes this point very clear: big manor houses, a sprawling sugar-mill complex, fields and fields of cane, and presumably overworked and underpaid workers scurrying around. Indeed, vestiges of the once-opulent plantations remain today. Windmill towers, mill foundations, and ruins of warehouses that once housed a fortune still stand on practically every island. Fortunately, the manor houses have fared much better, kept intact by the remnants of the plantation wealth that once was.

Recent interest in the glory days of the distant past has created a wave of acquisitions and renovations. Many of the interested are refugees from the north, pouring money into the Taras of yesteryear and turning them into gilded resorts for the unlanded aristocracy of the urban eighties. And nowhere is this trend more prevalent than on Nevis, a small island tucked away on the leeward side of the Leeward Islands.

In the Caribbean, airports are a fairly accurate barometer of how laid-back an island is. Nevis hit an all-time high on the mellow scale when the customs man checked my bags and then carried them to my cab. What we have here is an island that is incredibly low-key with several rehabbed plantations for hire—where you can re-create the idle life of the sugar planter. This setup is perfect for those frazzled corporate heavies who for a week are "out to lunch and cannot be reached." Here you can stay sequestered on your plantation—stroll the grounds, loll in the pool, sip rum punches to oblivion, catch up on all your Danielle Steele and Stephen King novels, and muse about how much longer you can maintain the staff, what with the price of sugar these days. You may even feel strong enough to hit the beach. One of the recommended cloisters is on the beach, the others maintain beach clubs on Nevis' best plage, Pinney's Beach.

Beyond the borders of the plantation of your choice, there really isn't much else to do or see. Some people climb Mt. Nevis (3232 feet) for diversion, although chances are the summit will be in the clouds. There is the town of Charlestown, which is good for a few hours in the morning or late afternoon (midday is too hot). A drive around this circular island is pleasant—you can always plantation-hop, and the windward side is very open and scenic.

For the relatively intrepid, there is St. Kitts, a forty-five-minute ferry ride away on the *MV Caribe Queen*. Ferries leave twice a day from Charlestown (except on Wednesdays when there are three departures. Generally, there is an early-morning and a late-afternoon departure—no service on Thursdays, Sundays, and holidays). Upon arrival, you can check out Basseterre—which I personally found rather unappealing. A better bet is to hire a car or scooter and drive around St. Kitts, where there are still sugar cane fields and working plantations in existence. There are also several plantations-cum-hotels of the same genre as the ones on Nevis—the most stylish and chi-chi of which is the Golden Lemon in Dieppe Bay, (809) 465–7260, furnished with antiques and decorated in pale tones to within an inch of its life by a former editor of *House and Garden.* Not quite as done up as the Golden Lemon is the Rawlins Plantation, (809) 465–6221, situated high up on the north coast with several outbuildings, good views, and an almost too-steady breeze. Not to be missed is Brimstone Hill, a once-massive fortress that earned the title of "Gibraltar of the West Indies"—until Mom Nature said, "Oh yeah, we'll see about

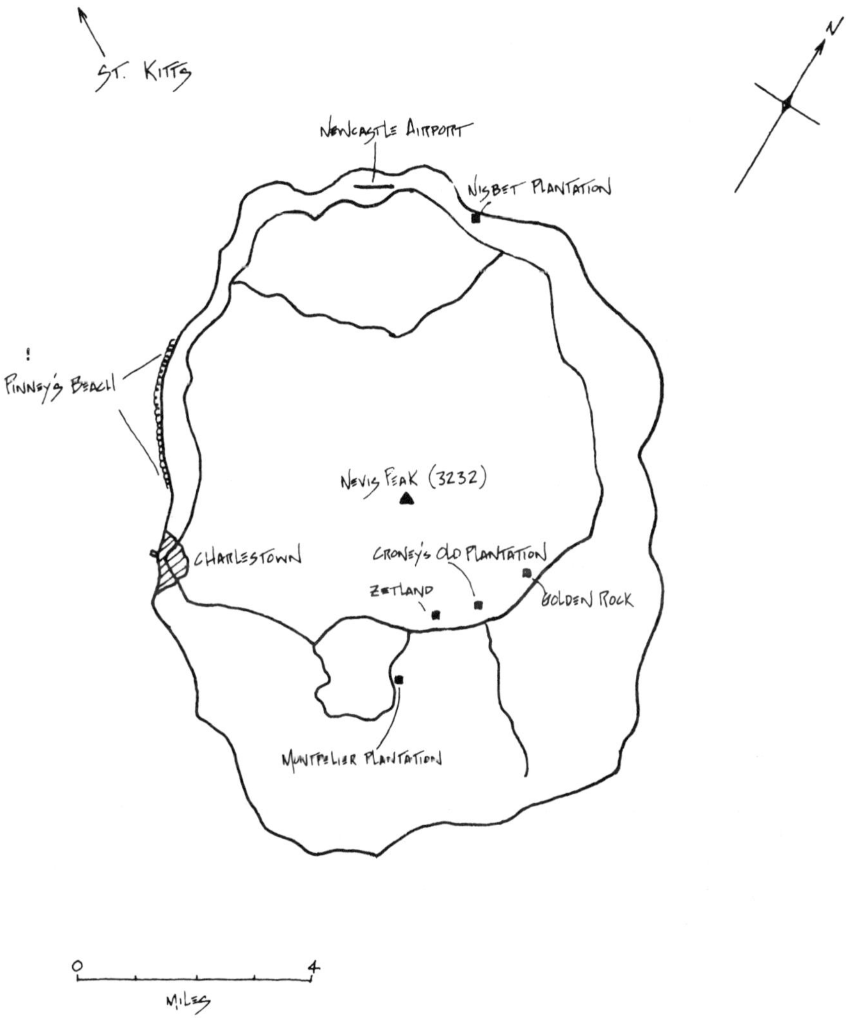

ST. KITTS
N
NEWCASTLE AIRPORT
NISBET PLANTATION
PINNEY'S BEACH
NEVIS PEAK (3232)
CHARLESTOWN
CRONEY'S OLD PLANTATION
ZETLAND
GOLDEN ROCK
MONTPELIER PLANTATION
0
4
MILES

NEVIS

that," and demo'd it in two hurricanes back in the 1800s. Today, it's a great spot for a picnic lunch to drink in the view and some stiff rum punch. You may decide to stay overnight at the Lemon or Rawlins, otherwise make sure you know the ferry-departure times or you'll be stuck without your dopp kit.

NEVIS: KEY FACTS

LOCATION	17°N by 62°W 2 miles south of St. Kitts 1800 miles southeast of New York
SIZE	8 miles long by 6 miles wide 36 square miles
HIGHEST POINT	Mt. Nevis (3232 ft.)
POPULATION	15,000
LANGUAGE	English
TIME	Atlantic Standard Time (one hour ahead of EST, same as EDT)
ELECTRICITY	220–240 volts/50 cycles
CURRENCY	The EC dollar ($2.64 EC = $1.00 U.S.)
DRIVING	On the left; local permit ($4 U.S.) and valid driver's license
DOCUMENTS	Passport or proof of nationality and ongoing ticket
BEER TO DRINK	Carib
RUM TO DRINK	The "house" overproof from the local rum shop

GETTING THERE

Newcastle Airport can handle only smaller-size planes, that is, nineteen-seaters on down. Thus you will have to connect with international flights from St. Kitts, Antigua, St. Maarten, St. Thomas, and St. Croix on LIAT, Winair, Coastal Air Transport, or Carib Aviation (charter). Plan to lose a full day each way for travel to and from the States.

STAYING THERE

This is what going to Nevis is all about—the "plantations." There are five on the island, two are superb, two are very good, and one is okay. All are expensive. It's a good idea to elect the MAP plan (restaurants are few and far between on this island). In order of preference:

MONTPELIER PLANTATION INN (809) 465–5462
P.O. Box 474, Nevis, West Indies
Stateside: (800) 243–9420/(212) 697–2340
Ray Morrow Associates, 360 Main St., Ridgefield, CT 06877

This is my favorite, although the Nisbet is a close second in appeal. What makes the Montpelier more attractive is its feeling of privacy and intimacy. If I were a famous movie star traveling incognito, I would stay here. There are lots of rooms, gardens, and secluded spots to lose oneself and snooping paparazzi.

An air of grandeur still permeates the Montpelier. The great house is a magnificent structure of stone with white-and-black trim. Inside, there are twin mahogany bars and four chintz-covered, sumptuous seating areas. Handsome, antique furniture dominates the interior and vintage paintings adorn the stone-and-wood walls that are capped by a high, vaulted ceiling. Off to one side, there is a library and card room, and a terrace ideal for viewing sunsets through tall coconut trees as well as for candlelight dining. Underneath the hall is a game room with pool and Ping-Pong tables (Bunny Bixly and Glory Upson take note). Upstairs in the back is a parquet-floor dance hall with Bose sound system and high-boys. Through the doors to the left of the great hall is an arched stone loggia leading to a covered terrace where breakfast and lunch are served. Adjacent to the terrace is a lap-sized swimming pool distinguished by its wall murals. There are comfortable chaise longues and a great pool cabana/bar with swinging sofa benches and more comfortable seating areas. I was very surprised to learn that the entire complex is only twenty-five years old, built on the ruins of the old estate. It looks authentic even to an old hack like myself. They did use the original stones from the ruins, so it's sort of real. And, of course, there is the requisite windmill tastefully landscaped with hibiscus and bougainvillea.

The sixteen guest rooms are well-appointed, with two firm double beds, large padded swivel chairs (and individual reading lights—very thoughtful), fresh flowers daily, and the biggest bathrooms I've ever seen in these parts. The rooms themselves are not huge but comfortable enough and there is a veranda with lounge chairs and views of the ocean. A family suite can also be rented for larger groups. Combined with the rest of the package, you will be very happy here for a week.

There are 60 acres on rising ground to meander around, including a 3-acre organic vegetable garden that supplies the produce on the dinner table. For exercise, there is a tennis court near the great house and a beach club on the northernmost and prettiest end of Pinney's Beach. A shuttle will take you there and pick you up. The inn also has a Boston Whaler with an 85 on it for waterskiing and excursions.

Rates are VERY PRICEY for singles and WICKED PRICEY for doubles (MAP only). Prices fall by almost 50% after April 15.

NISBET PLANTATION INN (809) 465–5325
Nevis, West Indies
Stateside: (218) 722–5059/5046
613 Missabe Bldg., Duluth, MN 55802

The overwhelming impression you get when seeing the Nisbet Plantation Inn for the first time is that of a fairway on the sea. The grounds are so spacious and well manicured that you almost expect a golf ball to land at your feet at any time. Very tall coconut trees form an airy canopy for the eclectic mix of cottages comfortably spaced across the lawn. And a very dramatic planting of palm trees creates a Champs Elysées effect from the great house to the sea. Very grand indeed.

The plantation house itself is very attractive and charming. Wide stone steps lead to a screened-in, sunny veranda with very comfortable seating areas, where you can stretch out with a book and spend hours undisturbed. And the bar is within finger-snapping distance for that occasional libation. There is an excellent library if you forgot your Jane Austen vacation reading. The dining veranda commands that majestic Champs Elysées vista I mentioned earlier, lending a regal air to the dramatic setting.

On the grounds are fifteen cottages of various styles, some octagonal, some in the Victorian/gingerbread mould, scattered about the premises. Each has two units, with veranda, twin beds, vaulted ceiling with fan, vanity, bookcase, rattan furnishings, and modern bath. Some of the older units have four-poster double beds and like decor for those seeking "character." There is also a deluxe three-bedroom house available for larger parties.

The Nisbet's big advantage is that it has its own beach. It's not the nicest beach on the island, but it is sand and salt water and you don't have to hop in a van to get there. An outlying reef keeps the water fairly calm for swimming. There is a beach bar (drinks are pricey) and an outdoor restaurant for lunch. Horseback riding is available nearby and there is a tennis and croquet court with raquets, mallets, and balls provided.

Rates are VERY PRICEY for singles and WICKED PRICEY for doubles (MAP only) but are reduced by almost half after April 15.

THE SECOND TIER

GOLDEN ROCK HOTEL (809) 469–5346
P.O. Box 493, Nevis, West Indies
Stateside: (800) 223–9815

The drive up to the Golden Rock is quite stunning—past stone walls and bougainvillea that set the stage for a truly magnificent great house to loom up in front of the car at any moment. So it's a letdown when you arrive and only see several buildings and an occasional windmill.

Not to say the place isn't special—in its own low-key way it's actually quite exquisite. The grounds, on 150 acres, are lush and verdant, with fantastic views of the windward side from over 1000 feet above sea level. The low stone buildings are attractive and overgrown with vegetation, particularly the bougainvillea-covered, 175-year-old Estate Long House—where a courtyard serves as the al fresco daytime dining area and is the place for afternoon tea. The interior of the Long House contains a neat bar and games room with nets and ivy on the ceiling. The old stone walls of the dining room once housed the plantation's kitchens.

There are fifteen rooms for guests in a cluster of cottages with verandas, king-sized (or twin) four-poster beds made of bamboo, dressing room, and bath. There is also a duplex suite available in the old windmill that the management promotes as the "honeymoon suite." It consists of an upstairs "playpen" with the centerpiece a king-size four-poster bed ("Oh sweet mystery of life, at last I've found you"). A circular staircase follows the stone walls around to the lower level, where two more double four-posters can accommodate whoever else wants to join the party.

There is a tennis court and spring-fed swimming pool on the grounds. The hotel maintains facilities at Pinney's Beach (with restaurant and water-sports facilities) and at their own beach down on the rough-and-tumble windward side—watch the undertow. The Pinney's Beach location is not nearly as prime as Montpelier's, being located further south nearer the crowds that come up from Charlestown.

Rates are VERY PRICEY for singles and WICKED PRICEY for doubles (MAP).

CRONEY'S OLD MANOR ESTATE (809) 469–5445
P.O. Box 70, Nevis, West Indies
Stateside: (800) 223–9815/(212) 840–6636/Canada (800) 468–0023
c/o International Travel & Resorts, Inc.
25 W. 39th St., New York, NY 10018

Run by a mother-son duo since 1981, this compact plantation will have tremendous appeal for character-seekers. There are restored buildings next to the soon-to-be-restored dilapidated original ones—the combination of which is marvelous. Renovations first began in the midsixties, when, according to the current owners, the place looked like London in 1945.

There are ten units built into the restored original structures, like the blacksmith's shop and carriage house, so each is unique in shape and style. There are rooms with touches of excellent wood craftsmanship, marble terrazzo floors, vaulted ceilings with fans, wide-board floors with carpeting, stone walls, and a Jacuzzi in their own garden. The honeymoon suite (it seems every place has to have one) has a 35-foot ceiling, a sleeping loft with king-sized, four-poster bed, a gallery above the living room for romantic strolls and a reenactment of the balcony scene in *Romeo and Juliet.* There is also a kitchen, wet bar, and dining room so you never have to leave or get dressed.

The pool is also unique, built out of volcanic stone that was originally the water-collection cistern for the mill boiler and steamer. It's 44 feet wide and 7 feet deep at the center (5 feet at the side). There is a cabana with a hammock and a view to die for. Just pastures with horses adorn the green cone of Mt. Nevis. Painters take note.

There is a patio grill and bar where on Friday nights a steak and lobster buffet is spread out to the tunes of pan (steel band) music. The bar and grill room is actually the old plantation kitchen—the ovens are still intact. The card and piano room was originally the birthing room for the slaves. The dining room is in the old cooperage room, the library was the old disco (just kidding), and so on.

Rates are VERY PRICEY for singles and WICKED PRICEY for doubles (MAP).

THE THIRD TIER

ZETLAND PLANTATION (809) 465–5454
P.O. Box 448, Nevis, West Indies

While the grounds are immense (350 acres) on high ground that is known for its steady winds, this place hardly resembles a plantation. It looks more like a sprawling family resort with various types of archi-torture. It has sliding glass doors instead of French windows, chalet units instead of old mill buildings. There is a pool in the center of the grounds and a beach facility on the less attractive part of Pinney's (next to the Golden Rock). The main house is new and just doesn't have the detail, charm, or character of the four other plantations. The rooms are modern and comfortably furnished in the Ramada/Hilton mode, and some of the deluxe suites have plunge pools. So if all else is full and you must stay on Nevis, this is an acceptable alternative.

Rates are VERY PRICEY for singles and doubles (MAP).

BEACHING IT ON ANGUILLA

There's an old Patti Page song that goes:

If you're fond of sand dunes and salty air
Quaint little villages here and there
You're sure to fall in love
With An-guil-la.

Hey, wait a minute! Isn't it "you're sure to fall in love with old Cape Cod"? Well yes, but Anguilla could easily fit into Patti's refrain. It's so reminiscent of the Cape and Nantucket twenty years ago that it hits you like a horsefly. Of course some adjustments have to be made—like adding palm trees, turquoise water, West Indians, that kind of thing. But the actual island itself, minus the accoutrements, has the dunes, shrubby vegetation, gentle terrain, and beautiful beaches of the aforementioned area on the forty-second parallel. Any time of the year in Anguilla feels like summer up north—minus the fog, bad weather, and cold water.

For the longest time Anguilla was really in low gear. In the shadow of St. Martin, which lies only 10 miles to the south, it remained the Caribbean's equivalent of a sleepy little town until about five years ago. Then travel writers started raving about the Caribbean's "best kept secret." Soon, the crowds on St. Martin started spilling over on ferry day trips. And the word got out—Anguilla has some of the finest beaches in the Caribbean. So now things here are in high gear. Development is happening everywhere. If you want to see the island before what happened to Cape Cod happens to it, better make your reservations now. Some of the best beaches are slated for construction. The proverbial deserted beach, here and elsewhere in the Caribbean, is definitely an endangered species and increasingly close to extinction. The almighty dollar is very persuasive in these parts.

Everything here is focused on the beach, and it's a perfect place to spend a whole week just swimming and sunning. Don't expect much else: there's the beach, a good book, and bed. But for some, that's just what the doctor ordered.

Maundays Bay and Pimm's.

THE BEACHES

Out of a total of more than thirty, there are ten outstanding beaches scattered throughout the island. You're never very far from a good one. All have some of the whitest sand in the Caribbean, a creamy-colored mixture of ground-up shells and coral. It's quite lovely. So starting from the west end of the island and working our way to Windward Point, here are the best beaches:

SHOAL BAY (WEST END)

(Located at the western end of the paved road)

This beach is the home of "Cove Castles," the obtrusive white structures that were written up in *Architectural Digest* and are totally out of harmony with the island's natural setting. But they're there and that's that. Unfortunately, another development is going up adjacent to it—so there goes the neighborhood. The beach, however, is quite nice and empty if you walk down to the eastern end (to the left).

MAUNDAYS BAY

(Follow the signs for Cap Juluca)

Alas, this is one of the top three beaches on Anguilla currently being developed. A few years ago there was nothing here except a half-moon arc of beach culminating in dunes and a sand wall on the western end. Now there's a very Arabesque and very white bar and restaurant called Pimm's that sits on the other end, a sign of things to come. It's a pleasant place to have a drink or lunch if you don't mind spending $10 U.S. for a hamburger. The area around Pimm's will become the Cap Juluca resort, in full swing by early 1989. Right now, there is a watersports center offering 12-foot sailboats and windsurfers for hire.

COVE BEACH

(Follow the signs for Cap Juluca, but don't turn right at the beach, go straight ahead and park.)

Just to the east of Maundays, the long sweep of beach on the western end is too rough and exposed, but the other side is calmer and deserted. A nice touch is the palm trees on the other side of the dunes, giving the illusion of tiny trees on top.

BARNES BAY

(Follow signs for Coccoloba Plantation)

Another nice stretch of beach that has had to endure development. Most unfortunate is what was built on the eastern end, a complex called Coccoloba Plantation that looks like a church built by Jim and Tammi Bakker. You can escape much of this, however, if you walk as far away as possible in the opposite direction.

MEADS BAY

(Follow signs for Carimar Beach Club)

There are definite plans to build a huge, 600-room hotel on this beautiful beach, to be called the Meads Bay Resort. This is obviously bad news for that delicate thing called ambience. It's also much to the chagrin of the management of the Malliouhana—the chi-chi resort that sits on a bluff on the eastern end of the beach. Fortunately for the privileged guests of that establishment, they have their own smaller, private beach. But for Meads Bay, it's curtains. So hurry up and see the beach before it's changed forever.

RENDEZVOUS BAY

(Directions below)

Now here's a superb and very long (almost two miles) stretch of beach. There's plenty of room and not much development—yet. The best way to access this beach is to enter on the dirt road on your left as you drive from The Valley (the capital and only commercial center on the island—if you can call a couple of intersections with some stores a center). Once you pass Connor's Car Rentals and Hertz, you will notice signs for Arlo's Place and Skiffle's on the right. Take the next dirt road on the left (about a quarter-mile from the signs). Stay to the left and go all the way to the end, park, and walk to the right—or west. Find a stretch of sand to call your own and enjoy.

LIMESTONE BAY

(North of The Valley)

This small, sandy cove is a local favorite. It is reached by taking a right turn just before the Cottage Hospital and following the road a few miles to Limestone Bay.

SHOAL BAY

(Follow signs to Shoal Bay)

The great snorkeling right off the reef, the calm water, and Happy Jack's restaurant make Shoal Bay a favorite of day-trippers from St. Martin. The

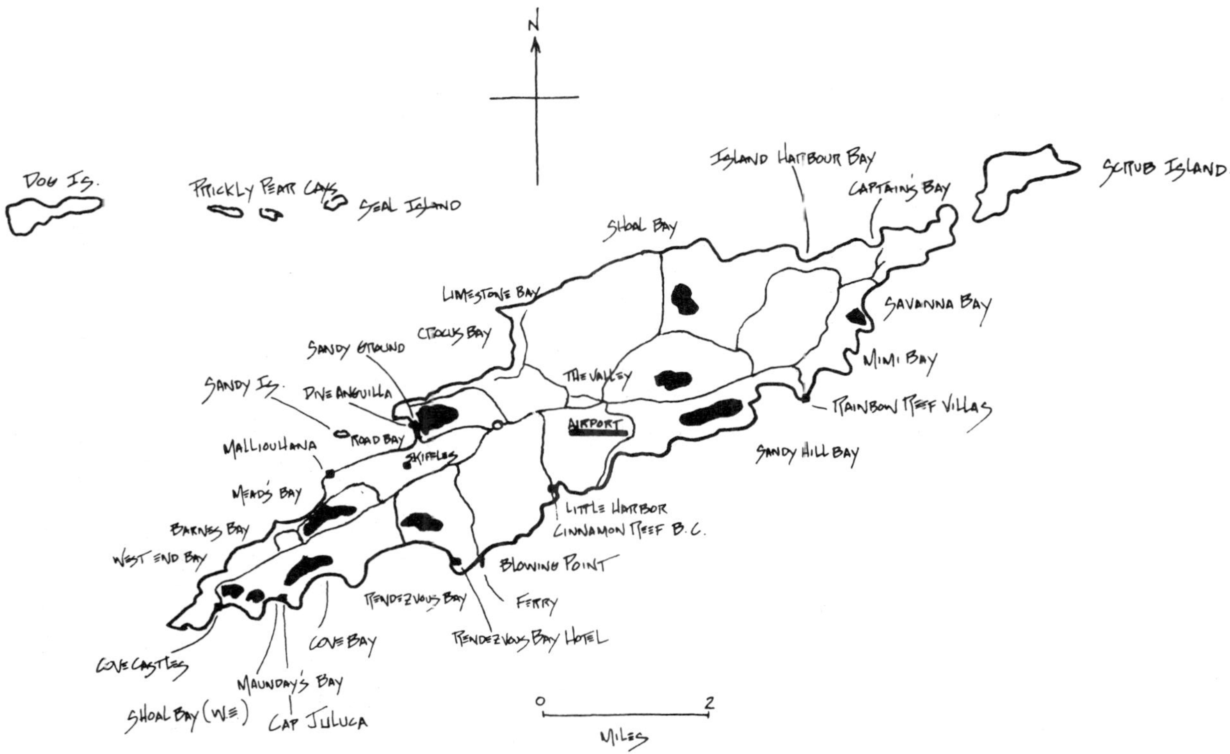
N
Dog Is.
Prickly Pear Cays
Seal Island
Island Harbour Bay
Captain's Bay
Scrub Island.
Shoal Bay
Limestone Bay
Savanna Bay
Crocus Bay
Sandy Ground
Mimi Bay
The Valley
Sandy Is.
Dive Anguilla
Rainbow Reef Villas
Airport
Road Bay
Mallіouhana
Skiffles
Sandy Hill Bay
Mead's Bay
Little Harbor
Cinnamon Reef B.C.
Barnes Bay
West End Bay
Blowing Point
Rendezvous Bay
Ferry
Rendezvous Bay Hotel
Cove Bay
Cove Castles
Maunday's Bay
Shoal Bay (W.E.)
Cap Juluca
0
2
Miles

ANGUILLA

Shoal Bay Villa development doesn't help matters any. Your best bet here is to go all the way down to either end of the beach—my preference is the eastern end (to your right). This is a great spot to watch sunset and fiddle about with a rum punch or Cape Codder from Uncle Ernie's, Trader Vic's, and Happy Jack's.

SAVANNA BAY

(Directions below)

This is a very pretty, long, and deserted beach on the still-undeveloped, quiet East End. It serves up some good surf and a steady onshore breeze. For calmer water, the coconut-tree–studded left side is best. The only drawback to this beach is that during heavy trade winds, the turbulent water tends to wash up debris that must have come all the way from Africa.

To get there, take the road to Island Harbor via East End. Once you've passed a semblance of a garage on your left, the road will go uphill and arc to the right. There is a small sign that says "Oil and Gas Available Here." Slow down. The road will bend to the left and you'll see a dirt road going downhill to the right—just opposite a white house with a black foundation and four wooden posts. Turn right and follow the road past the green house on the right with a stone wall and assorted trucks in the yard. The road here is rough but a standard rental car will make it (maybe with a few scrapes and loud thuds. But don't worry, it's a rental). After you pass the green house, take the right fork in the road and go straight to the beach.

CAPTAINS BAY

(Directions below)

The most secluded beach on Anguilla. This is a beauty—especially for basking in the buff. It's a small cove of creamy-white sand where privacy is virtually guaranteed because it's so hard to reach (the road is rough in spots). It's just you and the pygmy pelicans.

To get here, take the same dirt road that goes to Savanna Bay, but stay to your left for the entire way (about two miles). The road is broken up in places, and it's best traversed on a scooter but a car will make it. It's worth the effort.

ANGUILLA: KEY FACTS

LOCATION	18° N by 63° W
	10 miles north of St. Martin
	1675 miles southeast of New York
SIZE	34 square miles
	16 miles long by 3 miles wide

HIGHEST POINT	Crocus Hill (213 ft.)
POPULATION	7100
LANGUAGE	English
TIME	Atlantic Standard Time (one hour ahead of EST, same as EDT)
ELECTRICITY	110 AC
CURRENCY	The EC dollar ($2.64 EC = $1.00 U.S.)
DRIVING	On the left; need temporary permit—$6 U.S. with own valid license.
DOCUMENTS	Passport or proof of nationality w/photo and ongoing ticket
BEER TO DRINK	Heineken
RUM TO DRUNK	The "house" overproof

GETTING THERE

St. Maarten's Juliana Airport is the major gateway to Anguilla, with nonstops from the States on American, Eastern, Pan Am, and ALM and from Canada on Air Canada. From St. Maarten, Winair flies the ten-minute trip three times daily for $30. There is limited service from other Caribbean islands as follows: Antigua—LIAT; St. Thomas—Air BVI; St. Croix—Coastal Air Transport; St. Kitts—LIAT; San Juan—Air BVI; and Tortola—Air BVI.

A cheaper and fun alternative to flying in from St. Maarten is to take the ferry. From Juliana, hop a cab (about $8 U.S.) and head for Marigot where you can enjoy a delicious French repast in one of about five restaurants on the waterfront. Then hop a ferry to Blowing Point, Anguilla. There are several boats that do the trip and the heavy competition makes for an intense sales pitch at the dock. As the fares are identical ($6 U.S. one way, $10 U.S. round trip), choose the boat that allows you to sit outside (you can duck below should it get too wet). There are some boats that are totally enclosed—decidedly not as pleasant and definitely not for claustrophobes. Fortunately, if these boats are your only option, the trip only takes twenty minutes. Departures are about every hour and fifteen minutes beginning at 7:30 A.M. and running until 5:30 P.M. Upon arrival, you can rent a Peugeot scooter for $20 U.S. a day from Mitchell Connor (809) 497–6264 at his restaurant about 150 feet up the road on the left. If you don't have a lot of luggage, this is the best way to get around and will save you cab fare. Or, if there are none available, try Boo's Cycle Rental and Sales: (809) 497–2323.

STAYING THERE

The development of the past decade has opened up a much greater range of accommodations than was previously available. However, don't expect Anguilla's sleepy image to be matched by sleepy prices. It is expensive to stay here.

All of the accommodations recommended except one are on the water. Some have kitchens, which is advantage given the small number of good restaurants and the high cost of eating out.

RAINBOW REEF VILLAS (809) 497–2817
P.O. Box 130, Anguilla, West Indies
Stateside: (312) 325–2299

If you like the steady sound of breakers rolling in on the reef, then these comfortable and well-maintained villas are for you. Rather functional in appearance, they are situated on Seafeather's Point with spectacular views of the mountains of St. Martin and the distant hills of St. Bart's. There are two bedrooms, one bath, a long hall, a large living/dining/kitchen area, pantry, and covered veranda that provides optimal views and a stiff breeze. Each villa is situated to allow constant ventilation from the trades. There is daily maid service by a very friendly staff and owners Dave and Charlotte Bergland are very helpful. There is a shallow beach good for kids but not on a par with Anguilla's better beaches.

Rates are PRICEY for singles and doubles in season.

MALLIOUHANA (809) 497–2111
P.O. Box 173, Anguilla, West Indies
Stateside: (212) 696–1323
c/o David Mitchell & Co., 200 Madison Ave., New York, NY 10016

Like a celebrity traveling incognito, the Malliouhana doesn't disclose its whereabouts. You won't find any signs pointing the way—always a tip-off to an ultrachic resort. This is one of the Caribbean's poshest. Promising to "replenish the spirit of living," it will also most assuredly deplete your bank account. But if you have the money and want really sumptuous and tranquil surroundings, with nothing or no one else to harass you, then why not?

Everything here is carefully considered, from the tasteful color scheme of earth reds, forest greens, and sandy beiges to the small and multitiered layout of the many public loggias and alcoves. Throughout, there is a feeling of intimacy. You expect to see Jackie O. or Princess Stephanie sipping a lime squash under one of the countless oversized (and matching, of course)

Haitian or West Indian paintings. The bar is particularly attractive, with very comfortable sofas, piles of pillows, muted tones, and a terrific sound system.

Outside, there are two and a half free-form pools. The half-pool is a shallow model for tots. The other two are at different levels so that one spills into the next by means of a man-made stone waterfall. But far more appealing for swimming is the little-used, spectacular deep-water access down a series of steps from the pool. Some more steps and a landing have been carved into the rock. This allows you to dive into the crystal-clear water and swim around to either the resort's beach (about 100 yards to the right) or to an old ladder on the other side of the point (about a five-minute swim). Hopefully, the hotel will install a ladder right at the landing. You can also swim around to a very private beach right under the main building, with its own *very* private cave perfect for hanky-panky. All watersports activities and equipment (snorkeling, fishing, waterskiing, parasailing, out-island cruises, windsurfing, Sunfish and Hobies) are "complimentary," which is the least the resort can do considering the price you pay for a room!

And there's more: a superb and very expensive open-air restaurant overlooking the water and a pagoda-style exercise "hall" with Universal and aerobic machines, massage room, and the best view offered by any gym I've ever used. Three of the island's best tennis courts and the soon-to-be-spoiled Meads Bay beach round out the facilities. Oh yes, and the

The Exercise Hall at Malliouhana.

rooms—suffice it to say that they uphold the elegance of the rest of the resort. Each one has a terrace with ceiling fan, bamboo platform beds, and the same tasteful design scheme and furnishings. There's also a fabulous Japanese villa on the beach that costs buckets, but what style!

Rates are OUTRAGEOUS. NO CREDIT CARDS accepted (just Swiss bank account numbers—only kidding). Personal cheques are accepted with "prior arrangement."

CINNAMON REEF BEACH CLUB (809) 497–2727
Anguilla, West Indies
Stateside: (800) 223–1108/(212) 249–6840
c/o Ralph Locke Islands, 315 E. 72nd St., New York, NY 10021

A few pegs down from the luxury of the Malliouhana, but certainly still high on the comfort scale, is the Cinnamon Reef. Only four years old, this Spanish-cast resort is situated in its own protected bay named Little Harbor. Several rather oddly designed villas spin off from the main building—a long arched loggia of terra-cotta-tiled floors, heavy Mediterranean furnishings, and painted porcelain chandeliers. The restaurant, bar, boutique, and reception are also located here. The villas themselves have walled terraces with huge circular ports, a "designer" living area, and a raised bedroom space directly behind it. The villas are spaced far enough apart to be fairly private. The landscaping, however, needs work. Probably the best feature of Cinnamon Reef is the huge pool—featuring lanes—that's built on a terrace to allow for a breeze. Next to it are deco-turf tennis courts that are well maintained. The beach is okay and offers free use (for guests) of windsurfers, Sunfish, paddle boats, snorkel and fishing gear. Note: No children under twelve are allowed.

Rates are WICKED PRICEY for singles and doubles (EP). Add $40 U.S. per person for MAP.

CAP JULUCA (809) 497–6666/6779
P.O. Box 240, Maundays Bay, Anguilla, B.W.I.
Stateside: (800) 235–3505/(212) 308-3330

Many visitors to Anguilla have raved about Cap Juluca as the chicest and newest resort in the Caribbean. Certainly, it's worth recommending just for the spectacular beach in its front yard. Rates are RIDICULOUS to OUTRAGEOUS. NO CREDIT CARDS!

SKIFFLE'S VILLAS (809) 497–2619/2110
P.O. Box 82, Anguilla, West Indies

Beatles' fans will remember that the Fab Four started out as a skiffle band.

Who knows whether the owner had them in mind when he named this place. Anyway, these tastefully done villas, while not on the water, are fairly out of the way and private. They also offer good panoramas of the north (with a little, palm-studded cay known as Sandy Island front and center). There are five two-bedroom, two-bath units with bamboo furnishings, lots of tile, and good light. A small pool is located in the center though I wouldn't use it very much. Instead I'd hop on my scooter and head to one of the recommended beaches nearby.

Rates are PRICEY for singles and doubles.

RENDEZVOUS BAY HOTEL (809) 497–2549
Anguilla, West Indies
Stateside: c/o Una Gumbs, 5 Edgegrove St., Edison, NJ 08832

The original hotel on Anguilla and it looks it. The main building can be described as funky-borderline-rundown. The accommodations, however, have been recently renovated and are very clean and pleasant. The compound has a casual ambience that's wonderfully comfortable. As its name indicates, the hotel is on Rendezvous Bay beach, one of the island's best. It is run by an ample, bearded man named Jeremiah Gumbs, who manages to keep things running, as well as cook the family-style meals (renowned as quite good West Indian fare).

Rates are PRICEY for singles and doubles (EP). Add $20 per person (MAP).

EATING THERE

The choices are very few beyond the hotel restaurants. Your best bet is either to cook in and go out once or twice or elect the MAP at your hotel. Among the best the hotels have to offer is, as expected, Malliouhana ($$$$$). Its "cuisine gastronomique" is truly fabulous, while the price for such a treat is "astronomique." Another highly praised hotel restaurant is the Cul-De-Sac ($$$$). Its setting overlooking the lights of St. Martin is probably the most romantic on the island. The management has now changed so who knows what's going on there. As mentioned earlier, Pimm's ($$$$) at Cap Juluca has a wonderful setting, good service, and shows potential. Again, it's overpriced. The Mariner's ($$$) in Sandy Ground is popular with the yachty set since Road Bay is the only harbor on the island. They specialize in lobster for those craving the spiny Caribbean version.

Other good restaurants not affiliated with hotels and resorts are: Old

House ($$) on the main road, serving up good, inexpensive West Indian fare in a very casual and relaxed atmosphere, and the Fish Trap ($$$) in Island Harbor, a local favorite specializing in lobster and fresh seafood brought in from the fishing boats across the street.

Also not to be missed, particularly for those with kitchens, is the Fat Cat Gourmet. It features excellent packaged and frozen homemade dishes, such as chicken marbella, conch stew (guaranteed tender), and lobster quiche, that can be reheated whenever. Thus, you are relieved of shopping and cooking that would take up precious beach time. They make lots of desserts and will custom-bake a birthday cake or your favorite pie. Also available are pasta salads and daily specials for beach picnics as well as a catering service for any cocktail parties or dinner parties you may decide to toss. Servings for four will cost about $20 U.S., and they do deliver (phone 2752).

DON'T MISS

DIVE ANGUILLA WITH TAMARIAIN
WATERSPORTS, LTD. (809) 497–2020
P.O. Box 247, The Valley, Anguilla, West Indies

This is Anguilla's only full-service PADI dive facility and the only shop with a compressor on the island. Located in Sandy Ground on Road Bay, it has much to offer, including a resort course for the scuba curious that costs $55 U.S. for one open-water dive. Ian and Tom, the owners, also offer a PADI Open Water Certification course for enthusiasts. Most diving is done off the Prickly Pear reef, a 10-mile-long stretch of coral providing some excellent dive sights that is only a short boat ride away. For nondivers, waterskiing is available for $70 U.S. per hour and boats are available for hire to the out-islands, such as the very idyllic Sandy Island.

NUDE BEACHES IN THE CARIBBEAN

You might expect the Caribbean to be a paradise for nudists, or "naturists" as they prefer to be called. The fact is that there are surprisingly few official buff options—the proper British heritage of most islands takes a dim view of such "uncivilized" habits. Fortunately, most of the French and Dutch islands are more lenient. It's best to use your discretion at the more deserted beaches—keep your clothes close at hand in case of disapproving visitors. Women would be well advised not to sunbathe topless or nude alone, as local men are not accustomed to naked women on their turf.

Another option is to stay at a resort with its own private beach—many have sections that are clothes-optional (don't be shy to ask when making reservations). The Caribbean Information Office, (312) 296–2271, can provide information on these types of resorts, or consult Lee Baxandall's *World Guide to Nude Beaches.*

The following are some of the better-known nude beaches. In many cases, nude beaches exist without the blessing of local laws, so please remember to check out the scene with reliable local sources (like your hotel) before shedding your clothes and cares.

■ **NEGRIL BEACH—Jamaica**

This is the home of Hedonism II (see "The Hedonistic Option," pages 77–84) and is the land of anything goes. The buff area is in Bloody Bay—just east of Hedonism II.

■ **ANSE DE GRANDE SALINES—St. Bart's**

You'll feel weird if you don't take your clothes off here. This is one of St. Bart's best—ignore the weathered "Nudité Interdit" sign on the road to the beach.

■ **HAWKSBILL BEACH—Antigua**

A pretty beach and Antigua's only buff beach, it's located next to the Hawksbill Beach Hotel.

■ **ORIENT BAY BEACH—St. Martin**

One of the first "official" clothes-optional beaches in the Caribbean, it is also the home of Club Orient, a naturist resort.

■ **SALOMON BEACH—St. John, U.S. Virgin Islands**

Although there is a "No Nudity" sign posted here, most people at this beach obviously aren't paying attention. The trail to this beach is a little over a half-mile north of Cruz Bay on the left. About three miles from town is another clothes-optional alternative, JUMBIE BAY (trail on left).

■ **ANSE TRABAUD—Martinique**

The nicest beach on Martinique, located in the southeast corner of the island, is also quite "free."

■ **PLAGE CARAVELLE—Guadeloupe**

This is the primary buff beach on an island that put the "n" in *nudité*. Located at the Club Med Caravelle, the beach is open to the public.

■ **ANEGADA—British Virgin Islands**

Because this island is so remote to begin with (there is only one hotel—the Anegada Reefs Hotel), you will have miles of beach to yourself.

■ **THE GRENADINES**

There are many nudie options here, particularly at the island luxury resorts of Petit St. Vincent and Palm Island. Many of the other islands, such as Carriacou, Canouan, and Mayreau, offer discreet possibilities on deserted beaches. This is also very true of the "out-islands" reached by boat, such as the Tobago Cays (located east of Mayreau) and Sandy Cay off of Carriacou.

■ **TOBAGO (NORTH COAST)**

There are several deserted beaches here (see "Exploring Tobago," page 13) that could be used for discreet sunning.

THE SCUBA OPTION

ALWAYS BREATHE. That's the first rule of diving. Even when there is a 6-foot barracuda staring you in the face, maintain your composure and breathe regularly. If you don't, your lungs could explode. Besides, air costs about $1 for every minute you're underwater, so you're paying for it anyway!

NEVER RISE FASTER THAN YOUR BUBBLES. That is cardinal rule number two. If you do, you could very likely experience the "bends," which is not at all pleasant—not to mention that it can also paralyze and kill you.

BE PREPARED TO BECOME A SCUBA ADDICT. With 80-degree water, 100-feet-plus visibility, and an abundance of exotic tropical marine life to contemplate, chances are once you start, diving here will become an essential part of your life—right up there with your therapist and Sunday *Times*. It is an equipment-intensive sport, much like skiing, so soon you'll be shelling out tons of money for the latest in BCs, regulators, and fog-free face masks. Then there is the cost of transportation, accommodations, and the diving itself. This is very definitely, if you'll pardon the expression, an "upscale" sport.

There is no better reason to come to the tropics than to explore its tremendous marine resources by scuba (self-contained underwater breathing apparatus). You'll find some of the best diving in the world here and certainly the most accessible to the many potential divers on the Eastern Seaboard, Midwest, and Canada. Hundreds of programs and packages are available for all levels of divers—from total neophyte to the status levels of dive master and instructor.

What is it like to sink slowly to the bottom and look up and see the surface 60 feet above your head? It's wild—like being in a giant aquarium. What do you feel when you're neutrally buoyant and floating past fabulously colored fish and coral? Fantastic. It's another dimension, like being in a 3-D movie. The best word to describe the experience is "nirvana."

For those in search of a real mind-blowing experience, try diving at night. Imagine the thrill of jumping into total darkness with only the glow rings on the other divers' tanks and flashlights to guide you. Turn around and it's pitch black. Is the great white lurking somewhere behind you? This is the time where strict imagination control is in order. But don't worry, chances are Jaws is resting, waiting for the dawn feeding frenzy. Once you get to the bottom (which won't take long as night dives regularly don't go beyond a depth of 40 feet), you will observe the ocean asleep. Fish are so docile you can touch them. Coral comes alive, sending out delicate feelers to feed on plankton. Shine a light on a coral head and you'll see it close up within seconds. Colors become more brilliant than daytime, as the artificial white light brings out reds and yellows you can't see in sunlight. (As the water gets deeper, it "eats" the red and yellow light waves—giving everything a bluish cast.)

To keep up with the latest info on the sport, a subscription to *Skin Diver* magazine is considered a prerequisite for serious divers. It extensively covers the "big three" dive locations in the Caribbean—the Cayman Islands, Bonaire, and the BVIs (British Virgin Islands), and features dive operations and reports on special places around the world as well as the newest trends in equipment.

For novices, or those who don't want to be scuba-exclusive, there are some attractive options. The sensible choice is to first do a Resort Course, which allows you to complete a shallow dive (to 40 feet) in one day without any previous experience. It is the scuba sampler, will cost around $50 U.S., and is available on most islands. After this you'll know whether you'll want more, which is likely. Then you can sign up for certification—about five full days (four to five dives)—or just take more Resort Courses in between golf and the beach.

For those interested in doing some serious diving, it is imperative that you are certified or have completed your classwork for certification. In order to get tanks filled with air (or to rent scuba equipment), you must be a card-carrying (with photo) diver. Your certification is in effect your underwater driver's license—you must have one to dive. The course lasts about four to five full days if you wait to take it on your vacation. It's no fun paying lots of money to sit in a room for a week listening to lectures, while the sun and sea beckon. There are certification courses up north that will allow you to do your open-water dives down here—far preferable to the wet suits, cold water, and limited visibility of the Atlantic. Any dive shop in your area will be able to tell you about certification courses (usually given by PADI or NAUI—the two largest professional diving organizations) and where to find them. Many local YMCAs also offer a course that is widely recognized by most dive operators.

THE DIVE PACKAGES

Like other sports enthusiasts, divers like to be around each other. Camaraderie is a cherished commodity in the deep. A layman just won't be able to relate to the things you see and do at 80 feet below the surface. So it's fun to go on a "dive package" with its added social value of potential friendship. *And* it's cheaper.

Most of the packages go to one of the big three—the Caymans, Bonaire, or the BVIs. While these tend to be the cheapest, they are also the most crowded. In the business they call them "cattle boats." This is particularly true of Grand Cayman, where the reef off Seven Mile Beach is dotted with dive boats that let off thirty to forty divers at a pop. It's like being at Yellowstone during the height of summer. If you prefer more off-the-beaten-path places, then seek out the unexpected and the unusual—like Saba (see below).

The other choice is the live-aboard boat, of which there are two basic types. The first is a yacht charter, usually (but not always) a sailing yacht that has a resident dive master and either a good supply of tanks or a compressor onboard. Diving in this setting is normally an adjunct of the voyage and one of many onboard activities. This mode of travel/accommodations is very deluxe and service-oriented (see "The Cruising Option," page 85–101). The second form of live-aboard is the dive cruise, where you go from sight to sight, throw out the hook, and jump into the water. The focus onboard is generally more on diving than on luxury, as these are bigger boats and accommodate a lot more people than the yacht charters. They are like floating ski lodges, where everyone sits around and talks about the day's dives as they would discuss the slopes. Here, the reason for being is *beneath* the boat, not on it. This is great for those who love boats and diving and are not subject to claustrophobia.

WHERE TO DIVE

Since the Caribbean is huge and marine life is virtually everywhere, the options for diving are staggering. It is becoming increasingly popular to evaluate a destination not only for its dive potential but for other benefits as well. You may want to go somewhere that offers decent diving and has, for example, great food (see St. Bart's, page 200), great beaches (see Anguilla, page 33), or great karma (see Bequia, page 209). On the other hand, if it's superb underwater scenery you're after, there is an island called Saba that is basically just a volcanic cone that rises out of the sea—but oh, the diving!

SABA—DEEP UNDER THE SEA

Saba is probably best known for its airport, which not only has one of the shortest runways in the world (1312 ft.) but a landing strip clearly defined at both ends by precipitous cliffs, plunging over 100 feet into the crashing surf. Be sure to have a few cocktails in St. Maarten before making the twenty-minute flight. Watching the landing approach from the STOL aircraft will remind you of an old movie filmed in Cinerama—only *you're* in the plane heading directly for the rocky cliff, when at the last possible moment the aircraft banks to avert disaster. Fortunately, you are on the ground before you can get out a scream. The plane seems to land on a dime.

Saba is not well known for its diving—yet. It has been kept under wraps largely because of the island's uniqueness and its inability to accommodate big numbers of divers. But as more divers see what it has to offer—and the dive magazines pick up on it—it won't be long before the pristine undersea world of Saba loses its innocence. Fortunately, the government has recently declared most of the underwater territory around Saba a marine park—to prevent the looting and souvenir hunting that have ravaged the more popular dive sights elsewhere in the Caribbean.

Saba is certainly different from other islands in the West Indies. There are no permanent beaches, only a wandering one of black sand that exists for a few winter months at Wells Bay. The island is basically one big mountain with roads and villages clinging to its sides. Mt. Scenery is the highest point, over 3000 feet above sea level and usually in the clouds. There are four villages, Hell's Gate, Windwardside, St. John's, and Bottom, that are home to Saba's 1000 residents. The road that connects the villages has only been in existence for about forty years. When Dutch engineers declared the steep and mountainous terrain unfit for construction, a local man

Windwardside, Saba.

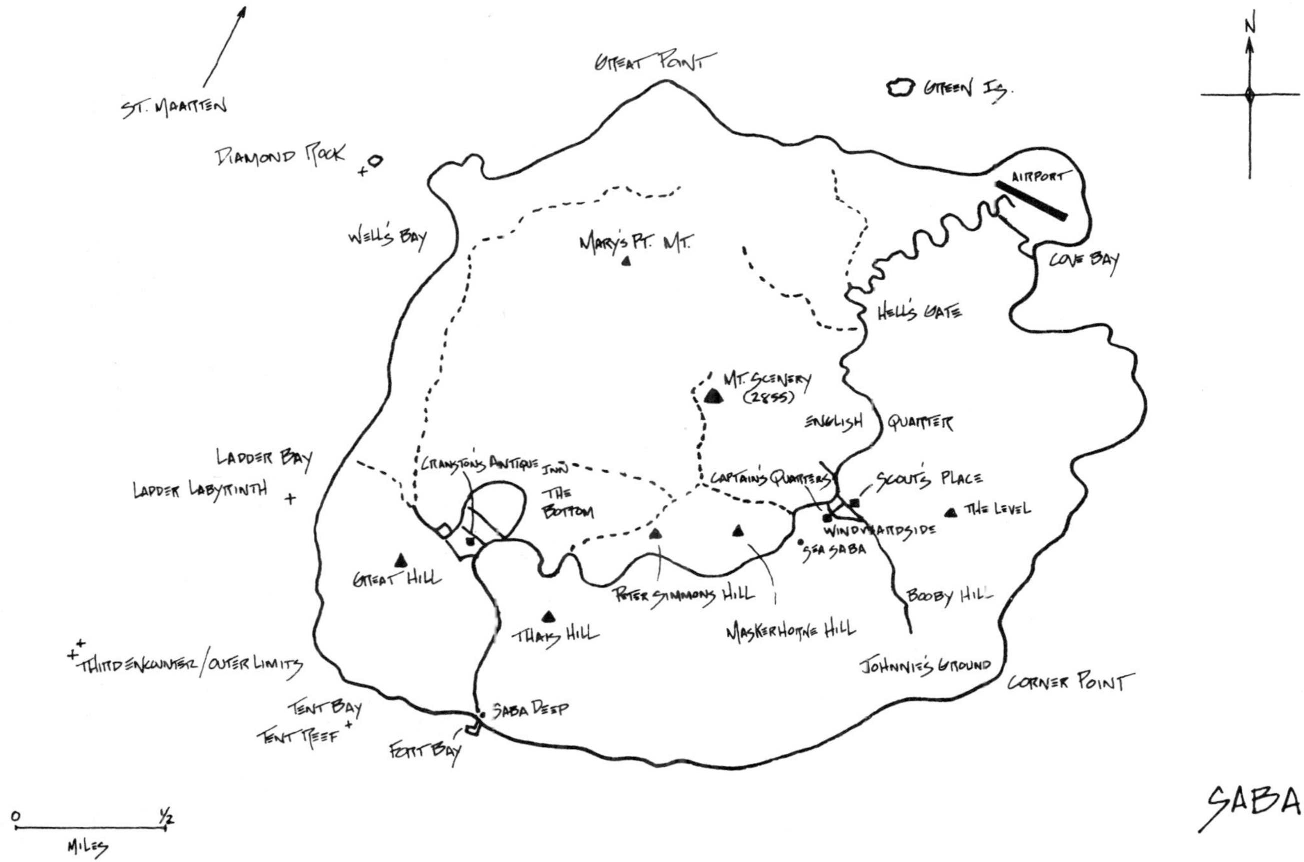

N
ST. MAARTEN
GREAT POINT
GREEN IS.
DIAMOND ROCK
AIRPORT
WELL'S BAY
MARY'S PT. MT.
COVE BAY
HELL'S GATE
MT. SCENERY
(2855)
ENGLISH QUARTER
LADDER BAY
LADDER LABYRINTH
CRANSTON'S ANTIQUE INN
THE BOTTOM
CAPTAIN'S QUARTERS
SCOUT'S PLACE
THE LEVEL
WINDWARDSIDE
SEA SABA
GREAT HILL
PETER SIMMONS HILL
BOOBY HILL
THAIS HILL
MASKERHORNE HILL
THIRD ENCOUNTER/OUTER LIMITS
JOHNNIE'S GROUND
CORNER POINT
TENT BAY
SABA DEEP
TENT REEF
FORT BAY
0
1/2
MILES
SABA

designed and built the roads with knowledge culled from a correspondence course.

It sounds pretty bleak, but the island is surprisingly lush and beautiful. The climate is ideal—the elevation of the villages keeps it comfortably cool and breezy in the evening, just right for sleeping. The days are warm but not hot, and the temperature of both air and water is around 80 degrees all year round. The vegetation is tropical and verdant—this is not a dry island. And the villages have the charm and appeal of a small town in coastal Maine. By tradition, most of the tidy houses are white with green trim and red roofs. It's very picturesque. It's also probably the cleanest island in the Caribbean. If it had a beach and a decent harbor it would quickly become the next St. Bart's. Thank God it doesn't!

There are three reasons to come to Saba. The first is for solitude and quiet: the deadline for your latest novel or screenplay is swiftly approaching and you need a place with few distractions and no one to call. The second is that you hate beaches, are scared of the sun, or just want a pleasant climate without boatloads of tourists and the hassle of Third World politics. The last is by far the best reason to come here—the diving. It is one of the last "virgin" dive sights and probably the finest you'll find in the Lesser Antilles (that is, Puerto Rico all the way down to Trinidad).

THE DIVING

There are two PADI dive operations on Saba, Saba Deep and Sea Saba. There was an intense rivalry between them when I was in Saba (the owners of the two shops were, at one time, partners). It was like a confrontation of two opposing battleships when the Deep and Sea boats met at Fort Bay, the island's one tiny man-made harbor. My sole complaint about diving in Saba is that this tension was a drag for us, the divers. I like the fraternity that going down deep creates, and it would have been nice to have met the people on the other boat.

Saba Deep is run by a real individual named Ed Arnold. One of the shop's founders, he is originally from the Ocean State (Rhode Island) and is the Magellan of the Saba undersea world. Ed has been a major force behind the expansion of diving here, and knows the dive sights probably better than anyone. Besides having a Zen-like style that is both comforting and entertaining, he's engaging and friendly. He's also a damn good instructor and a calming influence on predive jitters.

His shop is conveniently located at Fort Bay, the center of all boating activity on Saba. Unfortunately, the "harbor" is just plain ugly. There is no quaint village here, just a rock and cement pier that are also a breakwater. An upwind gravelcrusher (that grinds rocks into sand for other islands' beaches and cement) sends clouds of grayish-white powder into the air, coating everything in sight with layers of dust. That aside, there is a covered terrace that is a fun place to hang out with a Heineken and play dominoes or study dive tables. The shop has two decent-sized boats (18 feet and 20 feet), a compressor, and will rent out all necessary gear, including an underwater video camera to record your dive experience. A two-tank dive (the norm) costs $55 U.S. In keeping with Ed's low-key philosophy, he limits the number of divers to six. Ed also offers resort courses ($50) and with advance notice will conduct a PADI certification course ($225).

Sea Saba is the new kid in town, and it shows. Joan and Lou Bourque have gone all out to become *the* dive center of Saba, with a modern, attractive shop, new and well-maintained equipment, and a complete package worked out with the Captain's Quarters and Scout's Place. This includes dives, equipment, taxis (which can cost a lot when negotiated separately), all meals, accommodations, taxes, and service. The Bourques throw a rum punch party for their group and sponsor such things as slide shows, marine biology seminars, and lessons in underwater photography. Prices range from $470 to $673 per person (airfare extra), depending on accommodations and time of year. They also will assist in other recreational activities like hiking and fishing expeditions. If the above is not enough to lure you to Lou and Joan's operation, they offer a free package—on groups of six or more the seventh person goes free. So if you can pull a group of six friends together, you've got it made.

Sea Saba has a 21-foot outboard with twin Merc 90s for power. A two-tank dive costs $55 not including mask, fins, regulator, and BC. A Resort Course is $70 and certification $250; both prices include all gear.

There are twenty-five known dive sights that rim the Saba coastline and probably just as many yet to be discovered. Diving as a sport is very new to the island, so there is still territory to be explored. Also, the current spots are so good that the incentive to find more is low. Of particular interest are the deep dives, where you really feel like you've entered another realm. The ones named Diamond Rock, Third Encounter, and Outer Limits are the most spectacular. The shallow dives, while not quite as profound, are exceptional and longer. On my first shallow dive I saw a shark swimming right at me. Staying calm and thinking, "Oh, it's a shark," I turned to Ed Arnold, who wrote on his tablet, "Nurse shark—not dangerous." Somehow I already knew that, especially when he swam right by without showing slightest interest. (We later were able to swim within three feet of him while he was resting on the bottom, until he decided we were too close and swam away.)

There are so many great dives on Saba that it's hard to pick a favorite. But if I must, it would have to be Third Encounter. This dive takes you down 110 feet to a plateau about the size of a football field. Because of the depth, you can only stay down twenty minutes before needing decompression. The time passes much too quickly. As you descend, it doesn't seem like you've gone very far until a check of your depth gauge tells you otherwise. Once there, you feel that perhaps you've found Nirvana. Big groupers and bar jacks swim close—out of curiosity (and possibly hoping for a handout). A sea turtle swoops by giant sponges oblivious to the bubbling intruders. Then the guide motions you to swim off the plateau into the blue water, to the surprise of all. As you follow him you think, "Maybe he's got nitrogen narcosis"—"rapture of the deep" (caused by breathing compressed air—which is mostly nitrogen—at very high atmospheric-pressure levels). Then you see the reason. It seems like an apparition at first, a fuzzy spire of darkness against a light blue background. Images of Devil's Tower in Wyoming come to mind. (If you haven't seen it in person then you probably know it as "the shape" in the movie *Close Encounters of the Third Kind.*) Close up, you can see the pinnacle is covered with brilliantly colored coral. Keeping a watchful eye on the depth (if you go deeper than 110 feet it will alter your available time at the bottom), it's fun to explore this wonder of nature. Unfortunately, the beeps you suddenly hear are the signal from the guide's watch indicating twenty minutes are up and it's time to surface. But the memory of this experience will stay with you forever.

Other favorite sights include Diamond Rock, another pinnacle that juts out of the water about 100 feet. From a distance, the rock seems translucent, a grayish mass that lives up to its name. The illusion is shattered when you arrive to see that what you thought was beautiful is really just a rock covered with bird droppings. However, you won't be disappointed with what's 80 feet below the surface. Circumnavigating this large structure reveals schools of all kinds of fish; here I encountered the biggest barracuda (about 6 feet) I've ever seen.

Two other superb shallow dives are Tent Reef and Ladder Labyrinth. Tent Reef is a long overhang of coral that harbors all kinds of marine life, including spotted moray eel. This is also a preferred spot for night dives as it's close to port and in the dark has a dreamlike quality. Ladder Labyrinth has the look of a Tolkien or Lewis Carroll fantasy. Coral heads resemble giant mushrooms and the barrel sponges would be a perfect home for the White Rabbit. There is actually a mazelike network of sandy-floored passages, between the "Middle Earth"-looking piles of coral.

In between dives, the island of Saba offers a quiet calm that is very soothing. You can hike up Mt. Scenery (1064 steps that just won't quit!) from the village of Windwardside. Queen Beatrix of the Netherlands did it in forty-five minutes—a very steady clip indeed. Some guidebooks claim you can go up and down in an hour. Hah! *Running* up and down with a five-minute break at the top took me an hour and five minutes. Down on the coastline, the Ladder is another series of steps that at one time was how goods—even pianos—were hand-carried up to Bottom (it took twelve men to carry a Steinway).

Nightlife, like on any small island, consists of the local bars. Here it's the Captain's Quarters (pretty but not at all lively) and Cousin's, a funkier place with better music. Weekends light up Guido's disco ball as locals and tourists fall in on the dance floor. Don't expect a lot of people—fifteen is considered crowded here.

SABA: KEY FACTS

LOCATION	17°N by 63°W 28 miles south of St. Maarten 1680 miles southeast of New York
SIZE	5 square miles
HIGHEST POINT	Mt. Scenery (2855 ft.)
POPULATION	1000
LANGUAGE	English, although the official one is Dutch
TIME	Atlantic Standard Time (one hour ahead of EST, same as EDT)
ELECTRICITY	110 volts/60 cycles—same as U.S.
CURRENCY	Officially the Dutch Florin (FL) but U.S. dollars accepted everywhere
DRIVING	On the right; valid driver's license okay
DOCUMENTS	Proof of citizenship and ongoing ticket
BEER TO DRINK	Heineken
RUM TO DRINK	The "house" overproof

GETTING THERE

Winair, as described above, makes the flight three times a day from Juliana Airport on St. Maarten. Juliana is a major gateway to the Caribbean, with nonstops from New York on American, Pan Am, and ALM, and from Miami on Eastern. Several direct flights are available on a daily basis from other major cities in the U.S. and Canada.

STAYING THERE

There are two options available for lodging on Saba. You can stay at one of the three inns on the island or rent an efficiency apartment from Juliana's or one of several listings for homes and cottages managed by Glenn Holm at the Tourist Bureau (011–599–4–2231). If electing the former, it's a good idea to include meals on a MAP plan, as the best places to eat are the hotel restaurants. I prefer staying in Windwardside—it's prettier, cooler, and livelier (if liveliness is possible on Saba). Please note that credit cards are not accepted at the hotels and most places on the island.

CAPTAIN'S QUARTERS (011–599–4–2201)
Windwardside, Saba, Netherland Antilles
Stateside: (800) 223–9815/(212) 840–6636
Canada: (800) 468–0023

This is the best, most "upscale" hotel on the island. It also has Saba's only public swimming pool (for hotel guests and bar patrons). The accommodations are in several restored buildings at the bottom of the hill in Windwardside. The view from the pool is fabulous: blue water framed by the green mountains and valley below. The bar is compact but pleasant and comfortable. The dining pavilion is outdoors. Unfortunately, they replaced the old wooden furniture with white plastic, a big mistake. The food is probably the best on the island, however, so try to ignore the tacky decor. There are ten rooms with private bath and balcony; many of them have four-poster beds.

Rates are PRICEY for singles and doubles (MAP). Available as part of the Sea Saba package for less.

SCOUT'S PLACE (011) 599–4–2205
Windwardside, Saba, Netherland Antilles

Scout's motto is "Bed and Board, Cheap and Cheerful," which is an accurate description. It's a funky place, no doubt about that. The rooms are not squeaky clean but they're comfortable and adequate. Ten new ones were completed in 1988. There is a living room with VCR and an enclosed dining terrace that make the furnishings of the Captain's Quarters look like those of Louis XIV. But it's the cheapest alternative on the island.

Rates are CHEAP for singles and NOT SO CHEAP for doubles (MAP). Available with the Sea Saba dive package.

CRANSTON'S ANTIQUE INN (011) 599–4–3202
The Bottom, Saba, Netherland Antilles

A quaint two-story, shuttered house in the heart of Bottom. The building was once a Dutch guest house, and includes on its guest list Queen Juliana. Built about sixty years ago, there is a pleasant terrace in the front and a restaurant that specializes in West Indian fare.

Rates are NOT SO CHEAP for singles and doubles (MAP).

JULIANA'S APARTMENTS (011) 599–4–2269
Windwardside, Saba, Netherland Antilles

These are efficiency apartments that are just up the hill from the Captain's Quarters. Each unit has a private bath, balcony, and use of the facilities at the Quarters.

Rates are NOT SO CHEAP for singles and doubles (EP).

OTHER DIVE LOCATIONS AND OPERATIONS IN THE CARIBBEAN

There are hundreds of excellent places to scuba-dive in the Caribbean. The listing below highlights dive opportunities that may augment or even inspire your trip. For example, if you're planning to go to Dominica for hiking but wouldn't mind checking out the dive scene, you can check the following pages for dive operations on that island.

ANGUILLA

DIVE ANGUILLA WITH TAMARIAIN WATERSPORTS LTD. (PADI)
P.O. Box 247, The Valley, Anguilla, B.W.I.
(809) 497–2020

ANTIGUA

AQUANAUT DIVE SHOP (NASE)
St. James's Club, P.O. Box 63, St. John's, Antigua, W.I.
(809) 463–1430

DIVE ANTIGUA
Halcyon Cove Beach Resort/Jolly Beach Hotel, Antigua, W.I.
(809) 462–0256/(809) 462–0061

BARBADOS

PETER HUGHES UNDERWATER BARBADOS
Southwind Hotel, St. Lawrence Gap, Barbados, W.I.
(809) 428–3504

WILLIE'S WATER SPORTS
Heywoods Resort, Barbados, W.I.
(809) 422–4900, ext. 2831

DIVE SHOP LTD.
Holiday Inn, Aquatic Gap, Barbados, W.I.
(809) 426–9947

JOLLY ROGER WATERSPORTS
Sandy Beach, Worthing, Barbados, W.I.
(809) 428–9033

DIVE BOAT SAFARI
Hilton Hotel, Needhams Point, Barbados, W.I.
(809) 427–4350

BEQUIA

DIVE BEQUIA (NAUI, CMAS)
P.O. Box 16, Bequia, St. Vincent, W.I.
(809) 458–3425

BRITISH VIRGIN ISLANDS

VIRGIN GORDA

DIVE BVI LTD. (PADI)
P.O. Box 1040, Virgin Gorda Yacht Harbor, Virgin Gorda, BVI
(809) 495–5513

KILBRIDES UNDERWATER TOURS
P.O. Box 40, Saba Rock, Virgin Gorda, BVI
(809) 494–2746

ANEGADA

ANEGADA REEFS HOTEL DIVE SHOP
Anegada, BVI
(809) 776–8282

TORTOLA

UNDERWATER SAFARIS
P.O. Box 139, Road Town, Tortola, BVI
(800) 535–7289/(809) 494–3235

BLUE WATER DIVERS (PADI)
P.O. Box 437, Road Town, Tortola, BVI
(809) 494–2847

AQUATIC CENTRES
P.O. Box 108, Road Town, Tortola, BVI
(800) 345–6296/(809) 494–2858

LIVE-ABOARD DIVE BOATS

TROPIC BIRD (PADI)
The Anchorage, Estate Nazareth, St. Thomas, USVI 00802
(800) 524–2027
Stateside: Scuba Tours, Inc., 5 Patterson Ave., Little Falls, NJ 07424
(800) 526–1394/(201) 256–9115

LAMMER LAW–MISTY LAW
Trimarine Boat Co. Ltd., St. Thomas, USVI 00801
(800) 648–3393

DOMINICA

DIVE DOMINICA LTD. (NAUI/PADI)
Castle Comfort Guest House, P.O. Box 63, Roseau, Dominica, W.I.
(809) 445–2188

GRENADA

H.M.C. DIVING CENTRE
P.O. Box 168, St. George's, Grenada
(809) 440–2508/2883, (evenings) 440–3552

UNDERWATER DISCOVERY OF GRENADA (PADI)
P.O. Box 79, St. George's, Grenada, W.I.
Stateside: 2722 Rt. 37 E., Toms River, NJ 08753
(201) 270–9100

JAMAICA

DIVE JAMAICA
Sea World Resorts Ltd., Montego Bay (809) 953–2180
Negril Tree House, Negril (809) 957–4287
Janet Lee, Port Antonio (809) 993–3318
Garfield Diving Station, Ocho Rios (809) 974–2822

DISCOVERY BAY DIVING CO. LTD.
P.O. Box 814, Montego Bay 1, Jamaica, W.I.
(809) 952-1414

SCUBA JAMAICA
Half Moon Club, Montego Bay, Jamaica, W.I.
(809) 953–2211

TOJO WATER SPORTS
Trelawny Beach Hotel, Falmouth, Jamaica, W.I.
(809) 954–2450

NEGRIL SCUBA CENTER
Negril Beach Club, Negril, Jamaica, W.I.
(809) 957–4220

MARTINIQUE

CRESSMA
BP 754—97200 Fort-de-France, Martinique, F.W.I.
(011–596) 61–34–36/58–04–48

MARTINIQUE SCUBA CLUB
Pointe Simon, 97200 Fort-de-France, Martinique, F.W.I.

ST. BART'S

LA BULLE (PADI)
"Le Camp," St. Jean Beach, St. Barthelemy, F.W.I.

ST. BARTH'S SPORTS AND SCUBA DIVING
Gustavia, St. Barthelemy, F.W.I.
(011–596) 27–66–16

ST. LUCIA

SCUBA ST. LUCIA (PADI)
Anse Chastenet Beach Hotel, Soufrière, St. Lucia, W.I.
(809) 454–7355
The Moorings, Marigot Bay, St. Lucia, W.I.
Stateside: The Moorings USA, Suite 402, 1305 U.S. 19 South, Clearwater, FL 33546
(800) 535–7289/(813) 535–1446

DIVE ST. LUCIA
P.O. Box 412, Vigie, Castries, St. Lucia, W.I.
(809) 452–4127

TOBAGO

DIVE TOBAGO LTD.
P.O. Box 53, Scarborough, Tobago, W.I.
(809) 639–2266/2385/3695 (eves.)

U.S. VIRGIN ISLANDS

ST. JOHN

ST. JOHN WATERSPORTS (PADI)
P.O. Box 431, St. John, USVI 00830
(809) 776–6256

CRUZ BAY WATERSPORTS
P.O. Box 252, St. John, USVI 00830
(809) 776–6234

CINNAMON BAY WATERSPORTS CENTER (PADI)
P.O. Box 720, St. John, USVI 00830
(800) 223–7637/(809) 776–6330

ST. CROIX

CRUZAN DIVERS, INC. (NAUI)
12 Strand St., Frederiksted, St. Croix, USVI 00840
(809) 772–3701

SEA SHADOWS SCUBA
P.O. Box 505, Cane Bay, St. Croix, USVI 00820
(809) 778–3850

DIVE EXPERIENCE (PADI/NAUI)
P.O. Box 4254, Christiansted, St. Croix, USVI 00820
(809) 773–3307

SEASPORT INC.
Rainbow Beach, Frederiksted, St. Croix, USVI 00840
(809) 772–4056

UNDERWATER ST. CROIX
Green Cay Marina, St. Croix, USVI 00820
(809) 778–7350

V.I. DIVERS LTD.
Pan Am Pavilion, Christiansted, USVI 00820
(809) 773–6045

ST. THOMAS

ST. THOMAS DIVING CLUB
P.O. Box 7337, St. Thomas, USVI 00801
(809) 775–1800, ext. 185

UNDERWATER SAFARIS
P.O. Box 8469, St. Thomas, USVI 00801
(809) 774–1350

V.I. DIVING SCHOOLS
P.O. Box 9707, St. Thomas, USVI 00801
(809) 774–8687

CHRIS SAWYER DIVING CENTER
41–6–1 Estate Frydenhoj, St. Thomas, USVI 00801
(809) 775–7320

AQUANAUTICS WATERSPORTS (PADI/NAUI)
P.O. Box 4293, St. Thomas, USVI 00801
(809) 776–0382

AQUA ACTION, INC.
P.O. Box 12138, St. Thomas, USVI 00801
(809) 775–3275

SEA ADVENTURES
P.O. Box 9531, St. Thomas, USVI 00801
(809) 774–9652

CARIBBEAN DIVERS
Red Hook, St. Thomas, USVI 00802
(809) 775–6384

THE HEDONISTIC OPTION

Wining on the street of Port-of-Spain.

BOOM BOOM TIME—CARNIVAL IN TRINIDAD

Wine de boom boom. It's the motto of Carnival. The "wine" is a wonderfully lewd grind of gyrating hips that would shame Elvis. It's usually—but not always—done in duos with both participants *pressed* together in any number of lascivious ways. The slower and more exaggerated the better. *Boom boom* is local slang for one's rear end. And Carnival, in the words of a calypso hit, is boom-boom time. There are more pelvises pushed, shoved, and slammed in the last forty-eight hours of Carnival than in a million reruns of *Deep Throat.* Sex is in the air—you can feel it everywhere. This is hedonism at its finest.

Where does this bacchanalia happen? How soon can you get reservations? Carnival takes place in Port-of-Spain, Trinidad, a relatively large metro area wedged between the Gulf of Pariah and the hills of the Maraval Valley. The focal point of the celebration is the Queen's Park Savannah—an open expanse right in the middle of the city with most recommended hotels within easy walking distance. Carnival always falls in the dry season, although Port-of-Spain is still rather humid and very hot (you're only 10° above the equator). This is wilt weather. The Savannah is appropriately named—it looks like Africa, especially when the wind blows and huge dust clouds swirl (bring an array of bandannas to cover your nose and mouth—most locals do).

But Carnival is really a street scene. That's where most of the jumping takes place. "Jump-up" is the West Indian term for a party or good time and often you *are* literally jumping up and down. Most of the downtown area south of the Savannah is packed, particularly on Frederick St. and Independence Square. Music blares from the largest collection of PA systems in the Caribbean. Each road march has about fifty life-size speakers precariously balanced on a tractor-trailer and every corner seems to have a system suitable for a concert in New York's Central Park. These provide the amperage for the calypso. Perhaps it is the decibel level that makes one learn the songs so quickly.

Now Carnival is not for everyone. It's not Mardi Gras in New Orleans or Carnaval in Rio. The former is a real drunk and the latter more of a spectator event. Trinidad's Carnival is truly a people celebration. To enjoy it, you must participate, get down, lose your inhibitions, and join the boom-

boom spirit. Those that don't participate stand out, looking like misplaced tourists who took the wrong exit for Disneyworld. They stay on the fringes, avoiding the hot and steamy downtown streets—where the action is.

What does it mean to participate? It means throwing yourself into the sweaty crowd, giving in to the calypso beat, and having a good sense of humor. Above all Carnival is meant to be fun. In fourteenth-century France, the celebration was a public orgy. While I never saw anybody doing it in the street, it's likely that any female companions—particularly if they are sexy and white (a novelty on the streets)—*will* get wined a lot. So women, be forewarned that you will be treated as sex objects. Of course, you can turn the tables and surprise the winers. But please don't take offence—it's really harmless play and you won't be "molested." However, don't march through the streets in skimpy regalia that accentuates your assets—you're asking for it. Undoubtedly you'll hear lots of "psssssts" and lip-smacking. These are meant as compliments and the appropriate response is a good-natured one. Like it or not, that's the way it is.

The people of T & T make Carnival the celebration that it is. There are no brawls or drunken fights—people don't get "ugly" drunk, just silly and happy. You won't see this in Times Square on New Year's Eve. Why is everyone so up?

It is the music. Calypso has a contagious rhythm that makes the body move almost involuntarily. The lyrics are pretty much incomprehensible to the inhabitants of middle latitudes. But the constant repetition will make at least the refrains familiar. By the last three days, you should have a repertoire of about ten songs you just can't live without. Several of the smaller record shops sell mix tapes of your favorite calypsos—for about $20 TT (or about $6 U.S.). Just ask at the counter. It also helps to buy one of the lyric books sold at record stores or from vendors on the Savannah.

Sharing the music scene is steel-band music—or "pan," as it is called in the West Indies. Both calypso and pan were born in Trinidad and both have avid fans. Pan in particular has become a high art form. Purists can tell if just one of almost a hundred drums is out of sync. What's really amazing is that most pan musicians can't read music; they learn each song in pattern segments. For the Panorama competition (the main pan event of Carnival), new songs are often rehearsed on paper patterns so that no other band will hear the practice sessions and lift the tune. Even the band members won't have heard the song until it is played in the competition. It's a tough business.

Carnival actually begins right after New Year's although preparations start immediately after the previous Carnival. It's a local joke that if Trinidadians put as much effort into work as they do into preparing for Car-

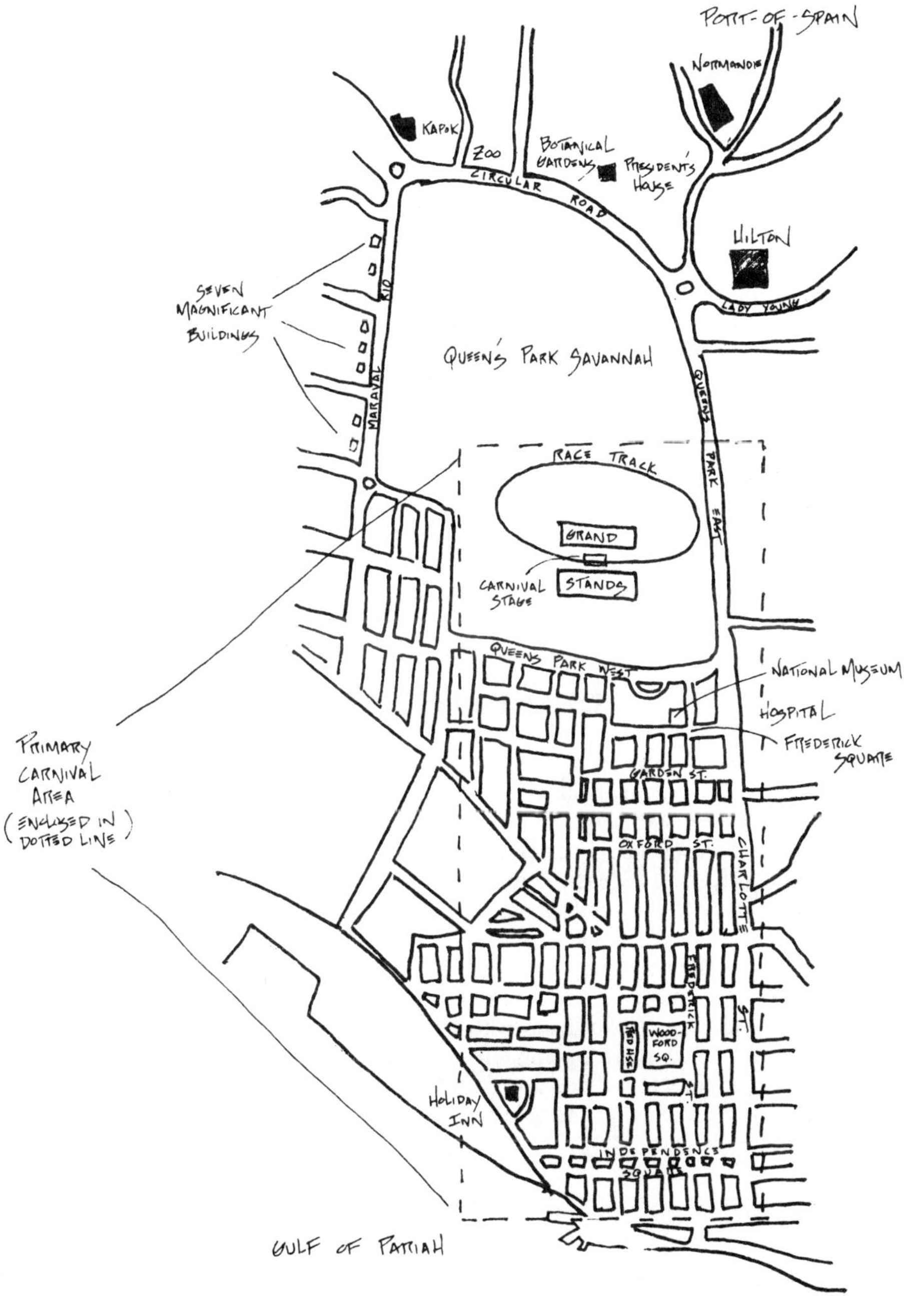
PORT-OF-SPAIN
NORMANDIE
KAPOK
ZOO
BOTANICAL GARDENS
PRESIDENT'S HOUSE
CIRCULAR ROAD
HILTON
LADY YOUNG
SEVEN MAGNIFICANT BUILDINGS
MARAVAL RD
QUEEN'S PARK SAVANNAH
QUEENS PARK EAST
RACE TRACK
GRAND STANDS
CARNIVAL STAGE
QUEENS PARK WEST
NATIONAL MUSEUM
HOSPITAL
FREDERICK SQUARE
GARDEN ST.
OXFORD ST.
CHARLOTTE ST.
FREDERICK ST.
RED HSE
WOODFORD SQ.
HOLIDAY INN
INDEPENDENCE SQUARE
PRIMARY CARNIVAL AREA (ENCLOSED IN DOTTED LINE)
GULF OF PARIAH

nival, they'd be a major power. The fact is that Carnival is big business, employing tens of thousands in such cottage industries as costume making. And, of course, there are thousands more in calypso and pan entourages. While the last three days are the climax, there are scores of "fetes" from New Year's on. Each road march or "mas" camp (for masquerade) has several and the rounds of eliminations for "Calypso Monarch" and "Pan King" take weeks throughout Port-of-Spain and Trinidad.

If you only have a week, the best way to do Carnival is to fly in on Friday night or Saturday before Ash Wednesday, stay in Port-of-Spain until Wednesday, and then take the Airbridge to Tobago to recuperate for a few days and fly out the following Saturday or Sunday. This allows you to see the best of both islands. While the week before Dimanche Gras (the start of the major festivities on Sunday night) is packed with activities, its primary attraction is the music eliminations. Otherwise, unless you are in one of the mas camps, you won't be plugged into all the fetes going on about town. Thus, arriving on Saturday will place you right in peak Carnival time. You'll be able to see the Panorama finals, join some of the big fetes around the Savannah (you'll hear them, everyone is welcome, some have small covers if they're inside a tent), and sleep in on Sunday—a major requirement for survival during the next three days.

So put on your dancing shoes, it's time to *j-u-m-p*.

DIMANCHE GRAS

This is the big wind-up. Eat a good dinner. It will probably be the last relaxed, balanced meal you will have until Wednesday. Then head toward the Savannah to catch the finalists for the Calypso Monarch. This event can look like a set for a Cecil B. DeMille epic. People are *literally* hanging from the rafters. There is a continuous roar from the crowd and the ever-present dust cloud shimmering in the spotlights casts a surreal edge to the whole scene. Don't miss it. It is an unforgettable experience to be wedged among thousands chanting "burn he" or "burn she" when the name of some Third World oppressor is mentioned in a song. Once the Monarch is crowned, it's best to head down to Frederick St. for the beginning of a twenty-four-hour nonstop jump. Around three A.M. you may want to return to your hotel to freshen up. Then listen for the nearest road march—its distance detected by the volume of the calypso—and join in the band. *J'ouvert* has begun.

J'OUVERT (PRONOUNCED JOO-VAY)

Meaning daybreak en *français,* J'ouvert (Jour Ouvert) is my favorite part of Carnival. It is the most free-spirited and silly day of Carnival. It begins with the road march bands assembling at bars and other locations throughout Port-of-Spain. At four A.M., they begin a slow procession through the neighborhoods and toward the Savannah. Bands can number anywhere from 100 to 5000 people. For J'ouvert they usually have a theme, often different from the next day's, which can be outrageous. One that comes to mind is the Zulu Warriors. Members of this troop cast spells on spectators' private parts. One of the female warriors even had a retractable penis—and boy, was she having fun with that!

Once you hear the march, grab a Carib—the beer of choice—and start "chipping" with them. Chipping can best be described as a pouty walk where you slide the balls of your feet ahead in small steps to the beat of the music. Dawn will break with a twist. Usually you would be heading home after a night of partying. Here, the fun is just beginning.

After chipping with the march for a while, step out and head for downtown. As the road marches approach the central streets, it becomes more fun to party-hop, or party-jump. Allow yourself to wander and explore the streets to see what might turn up. With a crowd on virtually every corner, there is no shortage of possibilities. Pickup trucks piled high with fresh coconuts provide refreshment as well as a man wielding a huge and intimidating machete. He'll adroitly split one open for you. The milk is warm but very tasty and nourishing. A piece of the shell is used to scoop out the meat. There are also vendors selling peeled oranges if you don't want coconut juice dripping down your chin. And, of course, you can always have another beer, rum punch, or soft drink, which are on sale about every hundred feet.

As you wander, you'll notice lots of bodies smeared with mud or pitch (a Trinidadian natural resource). Beware of a group of Brits called the Muddies who look and act like extras from a Monty Python epic. Slogging along with a bathtub of mud on wheels, they scout out white T-shirts (as they did mine), surround you, and begin smearing. At that point there's not much you can do. The mud does keep you cool and it *is* a look. Just don't wear your favorite clothes. The stains still haven't come out of mine—my personal souvenir.

Around noon you'll begin to fade. The combination of heat, jumping, and a walking hangover will have taken its toll. Time to take refuge in your hotel pool. The swim will feel marvelous and lunch may quell your throbbing temples. You might want to sneak in a quick nap but plan to be back on the streets by three P.M. as many road marches will now be in partial costume. Jump until about seven P.M. and retire for a simple repast.

Above: On board the P.A. truck at the grandstand. Below: Minshall's Carnival King '87.

Chances are you'll crash around ten. But for those with more energy to burn, the party goes on all night.

CARNIVAL TUESDAY

Rise and shine at around eight A.M. as the grand finale is ahead and you shouldn't miss any of it. Eat a good breakfast and once more head downtown. The road marches are in full regalia and seemingly there's one on every street. Bring your camera for today everyone who's not a tourist is in costume. I would strongly suggest a camcorder as the music is so much a part of what you are seeing. The mas camps will be winding their way swiftly through the streets to get in good position to cross the stage for the final judging (judges are posted throughout the city). The grandstand, for which you will need tickets, is a good place to watch Tuesday's parade—especially if it's your first time. It's a long show in hot, dusty conditions. Sitting down in the shade will help you stand the heat. Keep an eye out for the mas camps of Peter Minshall, Stephen Le Heung, and Edmond Hart—they are the best. Mr. Minshall, the enfant terrible of Carnival bandleaders, is the most creative and visionary. His mas camps are tight, well conceived, and well organized. The full impact from watching Minshall's road march comes not from the sight of a single costume but from seeing all 5000 en masse.

If you take a break and peer down the Savannah, you'll see an endless sea of bands. The show goes on for hours. If you get itchy, take a walk past the bands, still jumping, chipping, and having fun.

By six P.M., you'll most likely be "mas'd out." Head back to the hotel, have a swim, grab a bite to eat (maybe some pelau), and be back out on the streets by nine P.M. for "Las Lap"—the final hours of partying before the ax falls at midnight on Ash Wednesday. There's a sort of sentimental air about Las Lap. It's almost like graduation—everyone is trying to make the most of their last few hours together. In reality, Lent doesn't stop Trinidadians from partying as it used to. There are several big parties the following weekend (they say it's for the tourists but we're no fools). Lent *does* mark Carnival's symbolic end, which is what makes Carnival so much fun and so intense.

The music will be going strong and then suddenly it will stop at twelve A.M. sharp—right in the middle of a song. The dancing and jumping will cease and people will momentarily mill around, then gradually disperse. You'll walk home incredulous, planning Carnival for next year, not wanting the fun to end. Now is a good time to sit by the pool, mellow out with some cold Caribs (stored in a cooler in your room), and recap this truly wonderful experience.

PORT-OF-SPAIN: KEY FACTS

LOCATION	10°N by 61°W
	8 miles east of Venezuela
	250 miles southeast of New York
SIZE	1864 square miles
	50 miles long by 37 miles wide
HIGHEST POINT	Cerro del Aripo (3087 feet)
POPULATION	1,200,000
LANGUAGE	English
TIME	Atlantic Standard Time year round
ELECTRICITY	AC/DC, ask
CURRENCY	The TT dollar ($3.6 TT = $1.00 U.S.)
DRIVING	On the left; valid driver's license okay
DOCUMENTS	Valid passport and ongoing ticket
BEER TO DRINK	Carib
RUM TO DRINK	Vat 19

GETTING THERE

Most of the major U.S. airlines fly nonstop from many cities in the States, including American, Pan Am, and Eastern. BWIA and Air Canada also have several nonstops from the U.S. and Canada. *You must have a valid passport and an ongoing ticket for entry.* All flights land at Piarco International Airport, which is about a forty-five-minute cab ride to downtown Port-of-Spain (about $60 TT/$17 U.S.). There is a bank at the airport that is open late. Be sure to keep your bank receipt because you'll need it to change your TTs back into U.S. dollars (you can't change TTs outside of Trinidad and Tobago).

STAYING THERE

Here are a few hotels that work well with Carnival. Nothing quaint or cozy—these are city accommodations. Keep in mind that the rates increase dramatically during Carnival (up to 50% in some cases). The hotels listed are all within walking distance of the Savannah and downtown.

HILTON INTERNATIONAL TRINIDAD (809) 624–3211
Lady Young Rd., Port-of-Spain, Trinidad

Yes, it *is* a Hilton, replete with J. C. Penney–designer decor. However, it's close and has essential services and a nice pool. You know what to expect, and after a few days of jump-up, even the Hilton seems like an oasis. All rooms have balconies and face the Savannah—a plus when you want to join a road march on J'ouvert. Two disadvantages: no room service during Carnival and a hill that feels like Everest when you're tired. Rates are VERY PRICEY to WICKED PRICEY for single and double rooms during Carnival.

HOTEL NORMANDIE (809) 624–1181
10 Nook Avenue, St. Ann's, Port-of-Spain, Trinidad

A smaller, more stylish alternative to the Hilton and just as close. It looks like it belongs in Santa Fe. An artsy pool and courtyard are the focal points of the hotel. There is also a terrific nouvelle West Indian restaurant (everything goes nouvelle eventually) called La Fantasie, but don't go there during the three major Carnival days—service will take forever. Four galleries featuring local artists round out the complex. And it's half the price of the Hilton. Rates are PRICEY to VERY PRICEY for singles and doubles during Carnival.

QUEEN'S PARK HOTEL (809) 625–1061
P.O. Box 602, Port-of-Spain, Trinidad

Once the chi-chi place to stay, its style is now more faded elegance bordering on shabbiness. The rooms have balconies and the hotel is right on the Savannah. Rates are NOT SO CHEAP during Carnival.

KAPOK HOTEL (809) 622–6441
16–18 Cotton Hill, St. Clair, Port-of-Spain, Trinidad

Near the Savannah in a nice residential area. It has seventy-one rooms with views, a pool, and an excellent restaurant called Café Savannah. Rates are NOT SO CHEAP to PRICEY for singles and doubles during Carnival.

HOLIDAY INN (809) 625–3361
Wrightston Rd., Port-of-Spain, Trinidad

It's near the party and has 235 rooms and a pool. You also know what to expect here. Rates are PRICEY for singles and doubles during Carnival.

EATING THERE

Going out to eat at a restaurant during Carnival is a bad idea because no one wants to work. Thus, the restaurants will be understaffed with service by the next century. So why bother? Your best bet is to eat on the street.

Are you dreaming about Carnival but it's the middle of July? Don't worry, you can create your own festivity with this recipe.

RUM AND REGGAE PUNCH

Ingredients **(serves one)**
2–3 oz. good dark rum (the stronger, the better)
2 oz. of sugar water*
1 lime
4 oz. water
bitters
fresh grated nutmeg
ice

Directions
Squeeze the lime and add the juice to the rum and sugar water. Shake the bitters into the glass four times. Add the rocks, then sprinkle with fresh grated nutmeg (it must be fresh!). Yum!

***To make sugar water, dissolve 1 lb. sugar in 2 cups of water. Keep handy for quick and easy rum punches.**

Don't be scared—it's good stuff and it's cheap. Here are some of the most popular selections:

PELAU: CHICKEN OR BEEF

This is a national dish of T & T, composed mainly of rice with pigeon peas or black beans. There are chicken or beek chunks mixed in, too. It's tasty, nutritious, and not too spicy for tender tummies.

ROTI: CHICKEN OR BEEF

This is the Caribbean version of a burrito minus the rice and beans. Instead, you get curried potatoes and chunks of meat. If you get chicken, make sure you ask for boneless or you'll be biting into the more esoteric parts like the neck or parson's nose. A safer bet is beef.

BUSS UP SHOT

The mock-pasta dish of T & T. It tastes like shredded flour tortillas with meat, curry, and spices. The name alone is compelling enough.

OTHER ATTRACTIONS OF PORT-OF-SPAIN

MARACAS BEACH

Where everyone goes. It's a short drive over a very scenic North Coast Road and good for a swim and general oooh-cruise. Las Cuevas, about 8 kilometers to the west, is a less crowded alternative.

TOBAGO (See "The Privacy Option," page 10–18)

The best place I can think of to be on Ash Wednesday.

ALL YOUR BRAIN AND BODY NEEDS—NEGRIL, JAMAICA

There is a resort in Negril called Hedonism II—an "all-inclusive" hotel that has usurped Club Med's reputation as the premier hot spot in the Caribbean. The tales emanating from here are mind-boggling, especially in this time of sexual paranoia—when no one is supposed to want to have sex, let alone seek it out. Stories abound of people going at it in public. And not

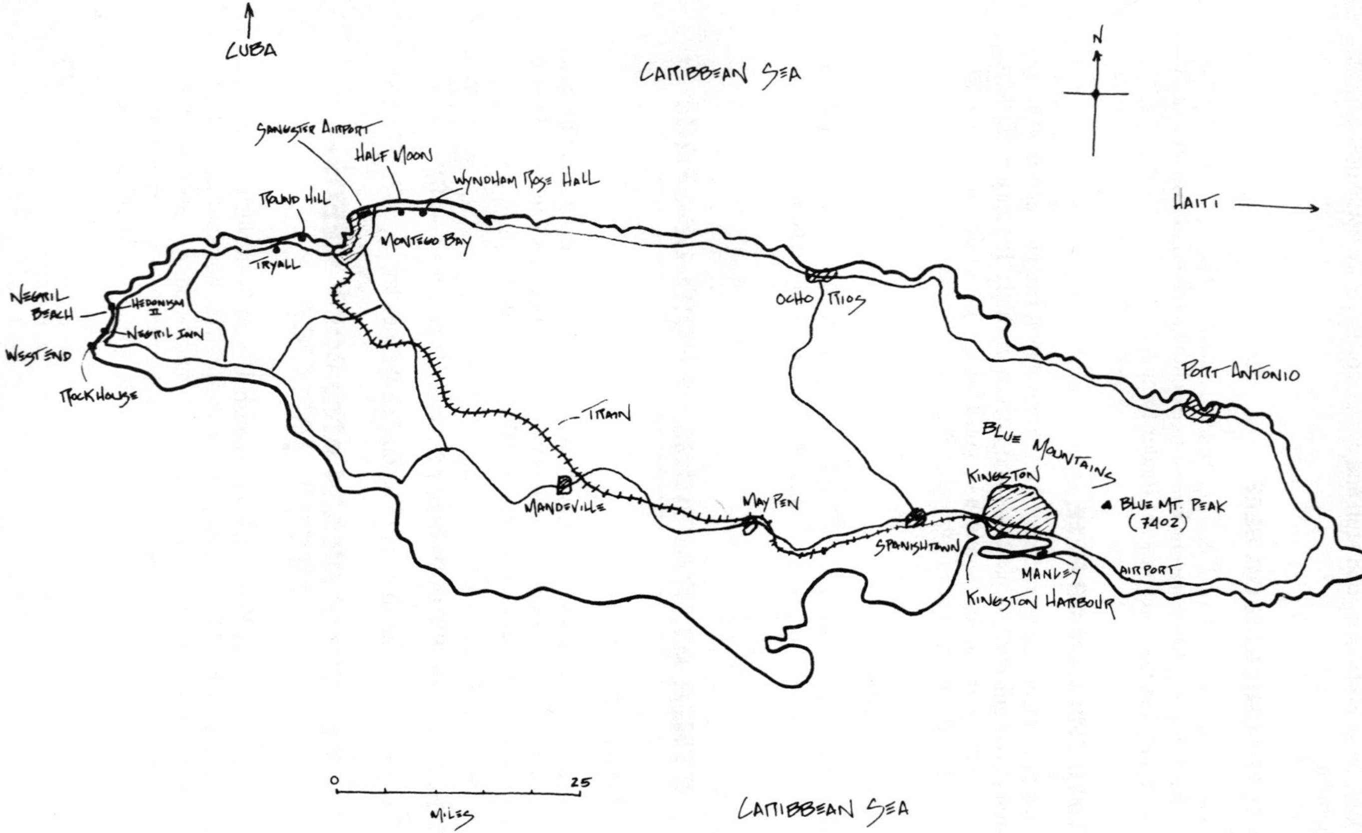
Cuba
Caribbean Sea
N
Haiti
Sangster Airport
Half Moon
Wyndham Rose Hall
Round Hill
Montego Bay
Tryall
Negril Beach
Hedonism II
Negril Inn
West End
Rockhouse
Ocho Rios
Port Antonio
Train
Blue Mountains
Kingston
Blue Mt. Peak (7402)
Mandeville
May Pen
Spanishtown
Manley
Airport
Kingston Harbour
0
25
Miles
Caribbean Sea

JAMAICA

only in the usual places like hot tubs, but in the middle of the dining pavilion—while dinner is being served! This is adult summer camp at its raunchiest.

There is also a place in Negril called Miss Brown's where you can get "magic" mushroom tea and "special" cake (not unlike the brownies we used to make in college), as well as more down-to-earth fare. A visit here will definitely put a smile on your face. Located about a half-mile from the roundabout that separates the Beach from the West End, it's a typical rum shop, small and somewhat rundown, with more than just rum on the menu. It is run by warm and modest country folk who are most comfortable with inquisitive tourists who seek out their store. So it's somewhat surprising when Ms. Brown hands out attractive business cards describing her shop as "World Famous" (the logo is, of course, mushrooms).

Sex and drugs—all that's missing is rock 'n roll. As Ian Dury (of the Blockheads) once said, "It's all me brain and body needs." If you don't mind replacing rock 'n roll with reggae, you should be very happy in Negril, the land of anything goes. Now don't get me wrong—Negril is not one huge bachanalia (unless you stay at Hedonism II). It's just an extremely mellow place where rules and regulations seem to evaporate in the tropical heat. The quintessence of laid-back, the ambience here is not some developer's contrivance but its own natural karma. I've never experienced anything quite like it. This is where Jamaicans go to relax, and they're already a helluva lot more relaxed than we are. So if you need to cool out at your own pace (without feeling programmed), this is the place to do it. Or if you are a big believer in sunbathing in the buff, it's no problem here.

There are actually two parts to Negril, the Beach and the West End. The Beach is a seven-mile arc of sand, calm turquoise water, and palm trees. It is developed, but in Negril fashion. There are no high-rise hotels, condos, or mammoth resorts (except Hedonism II, which is at the northern end of the beach). One of the few rules in Negril (that is followed) is a strict building code that dictates no building can rise higher that the trees. The Beach itself is very public, making Negril one of the few tourist destinations in Jamaica where tourists and Jamaicans can mingle freely without security gates, guards, and the heightened racial consciousness that accompanies such barriers. The Beach is also a moving bazaar, with all kinds of goods and services (including those of bodily pleasure) brought to your beach towel or chaise for scrutiny. You will never really want for anything. Fresh fruit, sodas, beer, nuts, ganja—all the refreshments that make for a great beach day—are available cheaply with a simple wave of the hand. If you're already taken care of, then a pleasant "no thank you" will keep the traffic moving. Despite all this human commotion, the beach's beauty is mostly intact. And the sand extends way out, creating a natural swimming pool of very clear water. The shoreline is shallow, which allows you to go far out before you're over your head.

The West End is a rocky peninsula that juts out from the southern end of the Beach. It is the funkier, "hippyish" section of town. Here you'll find lots of Rasta/vegetarian restaurants, bars and rum shops as well as local arts and crafts and the more *Whole Earth Catalog* types of lodgings, such as Tensing Pen and Rockhouse. Rick's Café, located well down the West End Road, is very popular for sunset cocktails and is probably the biggest attraction in Negril. It is also where local boys dive off the cliffs to the clicks of scores of camera shutters.

JAMAICA: KEY FACTS

LOCATION	18°N by 77°W 90 miles south of Cuba 1450 miles south of New York
SIZE	4411 square miles 144 miles long by 52 miles wide
HIGHEST POINT	Blue Mountain Peak (7402 ft.)
POPULATION	2,180,000
LANGUAGE	English
TIME	Eastern Standard Time all year
ELECTRICITY	110 or 220—check before plugging in
CURRENCY	JA dollar (about $5.30 JA = $1.00 U.S.)
DRIVING	On the left; valid driver's license okay
BEER TO DRINK	Red Stripe
RUM TO DRINK	Wray & Nephew Overproof

GETTING THERE

Jamaica is a big island, especially compared to the smaller ones of the Lesser Antilles. There are two major international airports, one in Kingston and the other in Montego Bay. If you fly into Kingston, it's a four-hour drive to Negril, but from Montego Bay (Mo Bay), it is less than two.

Several carriers fly into Mo Bay nonstop from the States and Canada. Probably the most frequent and inexpensive airline is Air Jamaica, which flies 747s, Airbus 300s, and 727s nonstop from New York (JFK), Philadelphia, Baltimore/Washington, Miami, Atlanta, Tampa, Los Angeles, and Toronto. American, Eastern, and Air Canada also fly nonstop to Mo Bay from several continental locations.

When you book your flight and accommodations, try to get airport transfers included in the package as cab fare to Negril will run you over $50 U.S. Getting to Negril from Montego Bay has to be one of the most beautiful drives you will ever make. You'll see an ever-changing landscape of fishing villages, old sugar mill ruins, mountains, bays, rivers, plains, and people. Even if you are tired from your flight, do try to stay awake for this and have your camera ready.

STAYING THERE

In Negril there are more options for lodging, from rustic to fairly deluxe, than in practically any other part of Jamaica. You can choose according to your style and budget, though the "granola"-type accommodations seem to be a Negril specialty.

There are two offerings here in the "all-inclusive" category—the Negril Inn and Hedonism II. The all-inclusives abound on Jamaica. These are resorts where everything—room, meals, drinks, tips, and all kinds of activities—are included in one price. Generally, I would recommend against staying at one. The exceptions would be the Negril Inn (see below) and Boscobel Beach (east of Ochos Rios and tailored for families with small children). The rest seem mired in mediocrity. They are really just adult summer camps with double rooms instead of bunkhouses and aerobics and crab races replacing arts and crafts. The all-inclusives are great for people for whom luxury is a fibreglass hot tub, an open bar, or "ethnic night" in the dining room.

If you are traveling alone to an all-inclusive, there's a good chance you will have to share a room with someone of the same sex. Just think of how much fun that would be, being stuck in close quarters with some geek on *your* vacation. So be advised—make sure you can get your own room, or look elsewhere.

Here's the scoop on accommodations in Negril:

THE NEGRIL INN (809) 954–4209
Negril Beach, Negril, Jamaica, W.I.

Of all the all-inclusives, the Negril Inn (just opened) is among the best. Unlike the others, it's small—only forty-six rooms—so it doesn't look like a convention center. Its design is simple, harmonious, and attractive. There is a full range of activities and facilities. But the schedule isn't structured, so you don't feel like you *have* to go to the welcoming disco party or participate in the scavenger hunt. All meals are included and at this point the kitchen shows potential. Once the place gets into full gear, the menu and presentation should get better, especially if they limit the buffets to one a day (I hate buffets!). Other pluses are a very friendly staff and a location right on the beach.

The rooms are comfortable, and while not designer decorated, the furnishings are new and clean. Each of the rooms has a balcony or a terrace. I'd recommend the "superior" rooms as they have high-vaulted ceilings. Keep in mind that due to building codes, the rooms have tree and garden views rather than ocean views.

The cost of a week here will run about $1000 per person in high season, exclusive of airfare. Three-day packages are also available.

HEDONISM II (809) 957–4201
P.O. Box 25, Negril, Jamaica, W.I.
Stateside: (800) 858–8009/NY (516) 868–6924

The name of this resort couldn't be more appropriate, though I'm not too clear on what the "II" means (there was never a Hedonism I). This place was founded on the pleasure principle and has built its reputation on sophomoric play. Personally, you'd have to pay me to stay here. This is not because I disapprove of its philosophy. It fills a valid need for many people who are frustrated by the current social scene and just want to let loose. I simply don't find the clientele terribly sophisticated or attractive. Of course, that might have been the particular group that was there when I visited. And who needs culture when it comes to bodily pleasures anyway? The management tries to sell Hedonism II with the line "Pleasure comes in many forms: the mind, the body, the spirit, and the soul." Judging from what I witnessed here, I'd say the overwhelming focus was a spirited and mindful effort to enhance the pleasures of the body to the point of selling one's soul.

The buildings and grounds are not very exciting. Frankly, I thought the blocks of rooms looked a lot like a suburban medical center. There is a relatively small free-form pool that adjoins the main bar and entertainment/dining amphitheater. The bartenders there are kept very busy. At the other end of the pool is the disco roof. The throbbing beat of the music penetrates the poolside air. The disco bar has windows that look into the pool, much the same as you would find in a public aquarium. You'll see lots of dangling feet, legs, and torsos—the effect is quite provocative. There are stories of more explicit happenings—a true exhibitionist/voyeur's dream. Down the slope from the disco is the beach, which is nice once you get away from the main staging area.

The management does pull in some superb entertainment, especially on Saturday nights. The resident band, Roots Explosion, is excellent. The staff, in the mode of camp counselors, is very friendly and very "up."

Prices at Hedonism II will run you about $1000 per week per person in high season, exclusive of airfare. Four-day/three-night packages are also available.

ROCKHOUSE (no local phone)
Stateside: (312) 699–1726/296–1894
P.O. Box 78, Park Ridge, IL 60068

On the flip side of Hedonism II is Rockhouse, a series of thatched-roofed rondavels on a rocky peninsula on the West End. This is where I would stay when in Negril. The octagonally shaped villas look like huts out of *South Pacific,* especially as you approach from the West End Road. On closer inspection, they're not quite as primitive as they might seem. There are sliding glass doors that face the water, and real furniture inside, including a sleeping loft in many. There is a hot plate and fridge—groceries are available at the market next to the roundabout. There are kerosene lamps if you want to forgo electricity and add to the primitive ambience. The showers are outdoors.

Perhaps the best reason to stay here is the swimming. You can dive right off the rocks into the crystal-clear water. The water has carved out various coves and caves where man-made ladders provide several exits. In addition, the snorkeling is very good and the access easy for scuba divers. There is no beach here, but if you're a good swimmer, this is heaven.

And the best news is that rates are very reasonable, in the CHEAP category for studios and NOT SO CHEAP for villas (EP).

TENSING PEN (no phone)
West End, Negril, Jamaica, W.I.

This is a more primitive version of Rockhouse, a true "peace, love, tie-die, no hassles, granola" establishment. There are seven well-kept thatched huts, lovely grounds for strolling, and a communal kitchen if you want to cook your own meals. If you don't, it's right next to Rick's Café and there's a veggie restaurant across the street. There is cliff-and-cove swimming à la Rockhouse.

Rates are CHEAP for singles and doubles (EP).

SUNDOWNER HOTEL (809) 957–4225
P.O. Box 5, Negril, Jamaica, W.I.

If all you really want is a hotel that's simple, comfortable, and on the beach, then this is a good choice. The Sundowner was the first hotel in Negril, and its easygoing ambience hasn't changed since day one. It looks like a motel, but that's part of its casual appeal.

Rates are PRICEY for singles and doubles (EP).

DON'T MISS

PETE'S RESTAURANT ON THE BEACH (no phone)

Located close to the Negril Beach Club, Pete's is the ultimate in eating on the beach. There are picnic tables set up about 20 feet from the water and Pete, the chef, will grill up some mean red snapper, lobster, or chicken for you. The price is right ($$) and the dance-hall music (a sort of reggae-rap) on the PA will keep your feet tapping in the sand. For dessert, there are all kinds of "special" cakes to keep you happy well into the night.

BOOBY CAY

This is a tiny islet off Bloody Bay, adjacent to Hedonism II. Originally named after the local bird, the tide of nudies from the resort have given the name a new meaning. This was the location for the film *20,000 Leagues Under the Sea.*

KAISER'S CAFE (no phone)

Located on the West End Road, Kaiser's offers the best reggae in town.

THE CRUISING OPTION

R&R

To some people, sailing is torture. Visions of ice-cold water flying over the bow into your face, or that salt-caked skin sensation without a hot water shower antidote, or the queasy feeling that rises when your vertigo gets Osterized from the constant motion, and that insipid dampness that permeates everything, especially your towels and sheets—who needs it! Fortunately, these images should keep the crowds on the beach and off the high seas because for many, sailing is sheer bliss. The art of moving very slowly but expensively is for some the ultimate therapy. It causes you to focus on getting from point A to point B. And all the variables that constantly surface—like wind, seas, breakdowns, mutinies, and so on—keep your thoughts on sailing, allowing all other disturbing thoughts and anxieties to float away in your wake. It's no wonder that so many high-stressed movers and shakers have sailboats.

The Caribbean Sea, and more specifically the Virgin Islands, offer some of the best sailing waters in the world. They rival the Mediterranean and the South Pacific for steady winds and warm, clear water, providing superb opportunities for swimming and snorkeling as well as eyeball navigation for those unfamiliar with the waters.

WHAT COLOR IS YOUR SPINNAKER?

Don't let the idea of a sailboat for a week lead to angst, because you *can* do it. For sure, sailing is certainly more rigorous than cruising on an ocean liner. But there are all kinds of options open to you depending on your experience and motivation. A word of caution here—pay careful attention to the personalities being assembled. A boat provides little refuge from others.

THE CREWED BOAT

If you just enjoy lying on the deck and having someone *else* do the work, or if your sailing experience was a Sunfish at camp, then a crewed boat is for you. In this situation, the degree of effort, from hoisting the sail to hoisting a drink, is up to you.

So you want the easy way out? No problem. There are two major considerations: where and how much. Let's talk about the latter first. Costs can run you on average for four adults from $4500 to $10,000 per week during the winter season. Of course, the "mega" boats are higher, such as the *Magic Lady*—a 105-foot Alden cutter—yours to love for the base price of $16,000 a week. Once you've decided your budget, the choice becomes simpler. With over 300 boats to choose from, here are some carefully considered suggestions (prices quoted are for the number of people the boat sleeps and for the winter season):

CREWED CHARTER BOATS

- *Bambi*—The most wonderful Swedish couple, 37 ft./2 crew/sleeps 4/$2950
- *Emily Morgan*—A very comfortable performance boat/57 ft./2 crew/sleeps 4/$5000
- *Symfoni*—Built for a Swedish king in 1937, 60 ft./2 crew/sleeps 4/$4750
- *Saga*—Ocean ketch, long-time friendly crew, 62 ft./3 crew/sleeps 6/$6000
- *Margin Call*—Elegant Ted Hood Custom, 75 ft./2 crew/sleeps 6/$9500
- *Sheerwill*—A Swan, the Ferrari of sailboats, 65 ft./3 crew/sleeps 6/$7000
- *Southern Cruz*—The *Architectural Digest* of boats, 68 ft./2 crew/sleeps 6/$7000
- *Rhapsody*—A custom ketch with a parrot mascot, 72 ft./3 crew/sleeps 8/$9800
- *Rangga*—A French-built schooner—lots of teak, 73 ft./4 crew/sleeps 10/$10,500
- *Nirvana*—The crew must be able to climb the main halyard hand over hand, 83 ft./sleeps 6/$15,000
- *Whitehawk*—The most beautiful sailboat ever built, 105 ft./5 crew/sleeps 6/$16,000

Generally, these boats are not limited to one region and will consider guest preferences when scheduling their itineraries. Keep in mind that the laziest time will be in the Virgins and the most invigorating in the Grenadines.

How does one get set up with his dreamboat? As with just about everything else in life, you call a broker. And we all know how we feel about brokers—they're pretty far down the list. Where there's money to be made, there's a broker. However, there are some that are very good and very reliable, including:

CREWED CHARTER BROKERS

- SWIFT YACHT CHARTERS, 38 North St., Hingham, MA 02043, (617) 749–8340.
- AVERY'S BOATHOUSE, P.O. Box 3693, St. Thomas, USVI, 00801 (809) 776–0113
- NICHOLSON YACHT CHARTERS, 9 Chauncy St., No. 50, Cambridge, MA 02138, (617) 661–8174
- VIRGIN ISLAND WATER SAFARIS, Long Bay Rd., St. Thomas, USVI 00801, (800) 524–7676

Your broker will be able to send you brochures on the boat of your choice as well as others that are in the same ballpark. They will also help you make captain contact. Since you will be spending a week with him and his crew in very close quarters, this is a crucial step to follow through before laying out cash. Don't be shy to ask pertinent questions like "Do you mind more than two unmarried people sleeping together?" or "Is it okay to sunbathe topless or au natural?" Bad chemistry between captain and guests can ruin your vacation. Using our recommendations later in the chapter, hash out an itinerary with the captain before you embark. Because he is more familiar with the waters and because he is the captain, be flexible and defer to his judgment. What might be a serene little harbor one day will look like Coney Island the next due to the migratory habits of bareboaters. The captain will know these things.

THE BAREBOAT

While the bareboat doesn't have all the amenities of the crewed yacht, it still has some significant advantages. The privacy (among friends) is hard to beat, the freedom to go wherever your charter agreement permits will allow you the spontaneity that makes vacations great, and it's a helluva lot cheaper. You'll have to work harder, but you will get off on the accomplishment, and deservedly so. However, there must be at least one person on board who has a thorough understanding of, and experience in, big-boat sailing. He or she should be somewhat mechanical and very patient with those who don't comprehend the arcane language of sailing nomenclature. You will have to pass a proficiency test before you set sail—and failure could be very embarrassing to all involved (not to mention inconvenient). It is also a good idea to have a first mate who has been sailing before and can absorb unfamiliar maneuvers and territory very quickly. The rest can learn through osmosis.

Chartering a bareboat is different from chartering a crewed boat in that more emphasis should be placed on the composition of the crew and the size of the boat. With no objective authority figure like a professional captain, some friends become unnerved when a peer commands them to do something. When you're sailing, there often is not enough time to follow Miss Manner's rules of asking nicely. So use extra care in the crew selection—these are people you will be intimate with for at least a week. Directly related to the success of this fragile coexistence is the size of the boat. Since most charter operations have a wide range of boats available, consider the amount of privacy you'll need (from your friends) and don't be cheap here—the additional space is worth it. I recommend a center-cockpit boat, generally 35 feet or longer, as it creates two distinct staterooms fore and aft—each with its own head (bathroom). There's nothing worse than listening to a couple go at it all night long (when you're not able to) because all that separates you from them is a wafer-thin, louvered door. There is a general rule of thumb here: under 30 feet—one couple, 30 to 40 feet—two couples, over 40 feet—larger groups.

Once you've sized up your crew and boat, you're ready to contact one of the charter operations recommended below. Due to the intense competition among bareboat charter companies, especially in the Virgins, most boats are comparably equipped. Many boats used are designed for the charter business, and have options available for more money, such as a sail board or an inflatable dinghy (recommended for its stability and comfort) with an outboard on it.

BAREBOAT CHARTER COMPANIES (THE VIRGINS)

- SWIFT YACHT CHARTERS, 38 North St., Hingham, MA 02043, (617) 749–8340
- CARIBBEAN SAILING YACHTS (Tortola), Box 491, Tenafly, NJ 07670, (800) 631–1593
- CARIBBEAN YACHT CHARTERS (St. Thomas), P.O. Box 583, Marblehead, MA 01945, (800) 225–2520

- HINCKLEY CHARTERS CARIBBEAN (St. John), P.O. Box 70, St. John, USVI, (809) 776–6256
- STEVENS YACHTS (Tortola), 252 East Ave., E. Norwalk, CT 06855, (800) 638–7044
- THE MOORINGS (Tortola), 1305 U.S. 19S, Clearwater, FL 33546, (800) 535–7289

Call or write for brochures and then compare the pros and cons of the specific designs and features of the boats available and weigh them with the cost. Also check out packages offered: some include a hefty discount on airfare, provide ground transportation to the dock, strap a windsurfer on the deck, and have options for fully or partially provisioned (food and booze) boats. If you like eating ashore, then the latter is recommended. Costs for a 35-foot boat for a week run anywhere from $1600 to $3200 (the latter includes round-trip airfare from New York). Plan on $15 to $20 per day per person for full provisioning. If you're unsure about your sailing expertise, an additional $75 per day will give you the services (sailing related only) of a professional skipper.

SAILING THE VIRGINS

The Virgin Islands are the islands best suited for the sail-charters. Split in half into territories controlled by both the U.S. and British governments, the area's well-protected waters, abundance of sheltered harbors, and short distances between islands will show off sailing's best side. You will also find a surprising number of seasoned sailors who relish the relative calm of the waters and the immense variety of sailboat options available to them. Unfortunately, the near-perfect conditions contribute to a less than perfect overpopularity—translating into crowded anchorages. Virgins they *once* were, but alas, the past twenty years have taken their toll on the old girls.

But for even well-versed old salts, these islands are among the favorite sailing waters in the world. This sheltered sea of 35 miles by 10 (the Sir Francis Drake Channel), is still magnificent despite the *explosion* of cruising boats here. Charters begin in either St. Thomas or Tortola, the major gateways, both within easy distance of the choice spots to visit.

If you are starting out from St. Thomas, the name of the game is to get out as fast as you can. St. Thomas, especially the main port of Charlotte Amalie, is overcrowded with cruise-ship tourists on a bargain shopping frenzy. The roads around town resemble L.A. at rush hour—all day

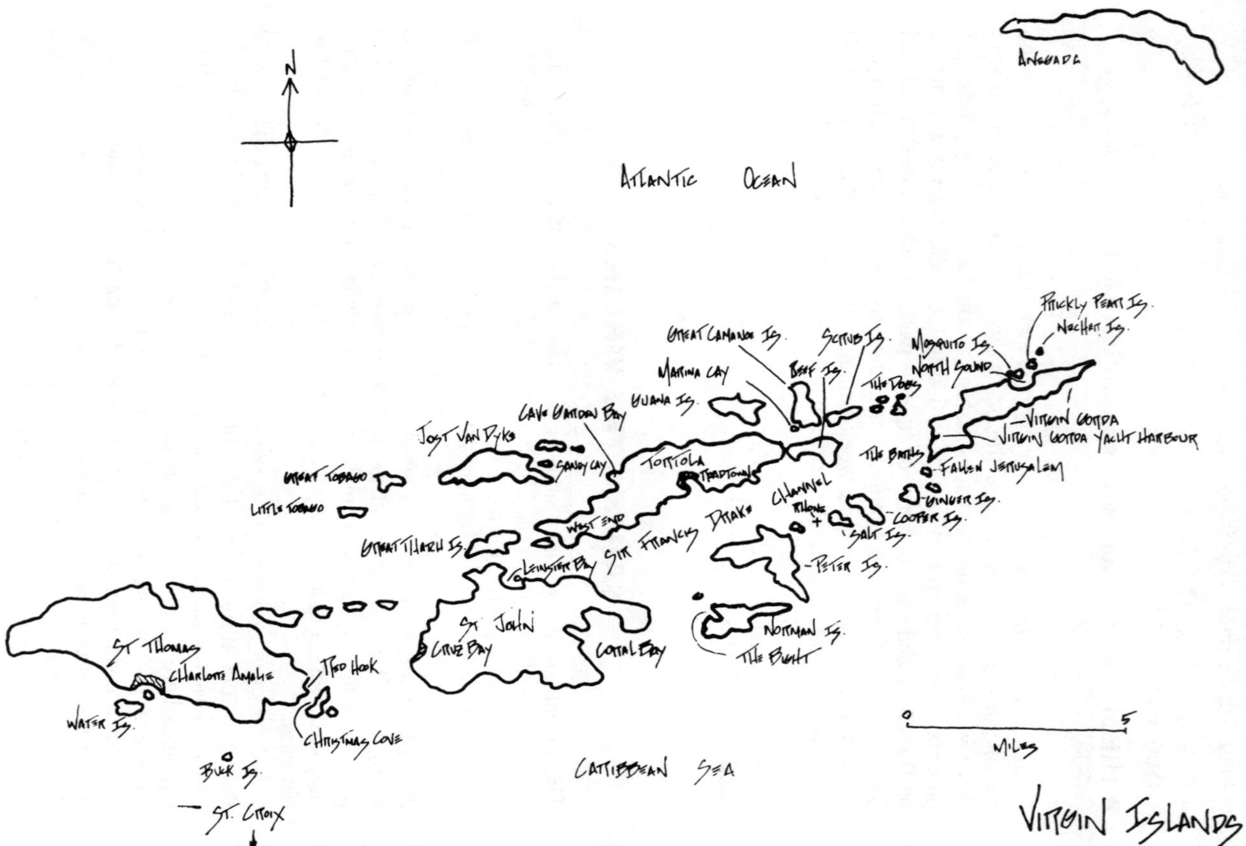
N
Anegada
Atlantic Ocean
Prickly Pear Is.
Necker Is.
Great Camanoe Is.
Scrub Is.
Mosquito Is.
North Sound
Marina Cay
Beef Is.
The Dogs
Guana Is.
Virgin Gorda
Virgin Gorda Yacht Harbour
Cane Garden Bay
Jost Van Dyke
Tortola
The Baths
Fallen Jerusalem
Sandy Cay
Roadtown
Great Tobago
Channel
Ginger Is.
Little Tobago
West End
Sir Francis Drake
Rhone
Cooper Is.
Salt Is.
Great Thatch Is.
Leinster Bay
Peter Is.
St John
Norman Is.
St Thomas
Cruz Bay
Coral Bay
The Bight
Charlotte Amalie
Red Hook
Water Is.
Christmas Cove
0
5
Miles
Buck Is.
Caribbean Sea
St. Croix
Virgin Islands

long—we're talking major bumper-to-bumper traffic. The harbor is polluted and is jammed with boats of all sizes. Now St. Thomas does have some redeeming qualities. It's just that compared to where you will be going, why bother? If you must stay, be sure to lock your boat—*really*—and take the Oldport Launch (thus avoiding traffic and the sometimes nasty cab drivers). It costs $2 and monitors Channel 9 on your boat's VHF radio. At night it's a pleasant trip to Frenchtown, where you'll find Famous—renowned for its delicious stir-fry and Creole dishes at affordable prices. You'll be able to get out of there for about $20 a head, which in the Caribbean is rare for a good meal.

Most people set sail the first day for St. John, one of the most beautiful islands in the Caribbean, with its bounty of beautiful harbors. If you're running out of daylight, head for Christmas Cove on St. James Island (just opposite Cowpet Bay on St. Thomas). Anchor on either side of Fish Cay for the calmest water and get out your snorkel gear. There's a great reef on the north side of the cay.

If you're starting out from the main port on Tortola, stop at Road Town (also known as Hot Town because the mountains block the cooling breezes); there are some places worth checking out before you leave. Right in the town is the Pusser's Rum Shop. This savory name is the "official Drink of the British Royal Navy." Some people think it tastes like it sounds although I think it's worth a shot. The shop has some great souvenirs with the Pusser's name on them, including mugs, hats, and a wristwatch that spells out Pusser's Rum in code flags. Nearby is the Caribbean Marketplace, which sells some terrific spices in tasteful mahogany that make great gifts for friends back home.

CRUISING GUIDE TO RESTAURANTS

RESTAURANT	CUISINE	COMMENTS
FAMOUS/St. Thomas	Stir-fry/Creole	Good, healthy food/funky decor
MEADA/St. John	West Indian	Very Jimmy Buffet
STANLEY'S/Tortola	BBQ/Fish	The lobster + T-shirt = tops
HARRIS'/Jost	BBQ (Mon./Thurs.)	On the beach w/Peace & Love
CARIBE CASSEROLE/Tortola	West Indian	Tortola's Famous
SKY WORLD/Tortola	Continental	Sour Sop daiquiri & the view
BITTER END Y.C./V. Gorda*	Continental	Overrated but good lobster
DRAKE'S/V. Gorda*	Continental	Very romantic/food's okay
MARINA CAY/Marina Cay	Continental/BBQ	Like a VFW Banquet
PETER ISLAND Y.C.*/ Peter Island	Continental	Dressy and expensive/great buffet
COOPER ISLAND Y.C./ Cooper Island	West Indian	Small but popular

*Make reservations as far in advance as possible.

For an incredible view overlooking Road Town and the Channel, take the free shuttle for a hair-raising ride up the mountain to the Cloud Room. Have a drink and go for dinner at Carib Casserole in Road Town, or continue on to Sky World for cocktails at sunset—the best spot in the Virgins for viewing. (Observant passengers will notice a beautiful fungus growing in the cow patties along the roadside.) Once arrived, sop up a Sour Sop Daiquiri, a Sky World specialty. Sour Sop is a local fruit that resembles a cross between a mango and a pineapple.

Once you've left the hustle-bustle of the major home ports, plan to sail as much to windward (east in this instance) as possible during the first days out. This will allow for leisurely exploration of the islands worth seeing, with the winds in your favor. Start with North Sound, Virgin Gorda, and work your way west through the southern string of islands and the fringes of Tortola and Jost Van Dyke. If you're ambitious, St. Croix is about 40 open-water miles south.

It is important that customs be dealt with in a timely manner, which in the BVIs means it will take forever to wait in line and fill out forms. (All they really want is your $4 pleasure-boating tax. So why not just have a cash register at the dock?) All you need is proof of citizenship, which in simplest terms means your passport. To minimize this inconvenience, stay in one territory until you leave it for good.

One of the nicest features of Virgin Gorda is Gorda Sound (called North Sound by locals), a splendidly protected bay near the northeast end of the island. The mountains to the south are a national park, which accounts for

A day in the life of the Sir Francis Drake Channel.

their pristine state. When you enter the Sound, there is a massive reef to the right that boats are *always* hitting. There are markers so just be prudent and leave plenty of room to starboard (the right). That reef, called Colquhoun Reef, offers some super snorkeling when sea conditions are calm. Most people head for a mooring ball at the Bitter End Yacht Club. It really isn't a yacht club in the proper sense but a nice resort with a marina and launch service. I prefer a mooring near Biras Creek, a very pretty inlet with a fabulous hotel/resort sitting on a promontory overlooking the Atlantic on one side and the Sound on the other. I'd stay here for some discreet rendezvous. There are actually three resorts in the area that comprise the "Bitter End": Biras Creek, the Tradewinds, and the Bitter End Yacht Club. If you can, take a hike out to the real Bitter End along the trail and be sure to *bring your camera.* It's a healthy hike so wear the appropriate footwear. There's also a good reef off Prickly Pear Island for snorkeling. On land, the Quarterdeck Bar has some high-octane cocktails and a very "You watch me, I'll watch you" crowd. The Dining Room is a standard stop, the most popular on Virgin Gorda. The Caribbean lobster is good here though, and it's only $9 more than the $24 prix fixe for dinner so you might as well have it, especially if you're splitting the bill. There are two free movies shown in the Sand Palace outdoor pavillion. Popcorn is served. In front of the Main Pavillion, there is a shark pen with a startlingly low fence around it (someone is eventually going to fall in or get thrown in) with real-enough-looking sharks lurking in the water. If you see a very absurdly shaped object being powered by an outboard—that's *Flipper.* The craft is supposed to resemble a dolphin (the builder was probably tripping at the time) and is also a glass-bottom boat. It's run by a character who would be at home in *Ripley's Believe It or Not.* It would be very Fellini-esque to spend the $15 for a ride—but only do it in an altered state of consciousness.

Across the Sound is Mosquito Island, a privately owned 125-acre resort called Drake's Anchorage. Moor here to avoid the Bitter End hubbub. The island is really worth exploring as it has trails all over its hilly terrain. Wear sneakers and hike to the eastern end, just beyond the last cottages of the hotel. There are underwater caves on Rocky Beach for snorkeling. Over to the west is Honeymoon Beach, a cozy cove that is just right for two people. On the other end of the island is Long Beach, which touts one of the best snorkel/dive spots in the Virgins. Jean-Michel Cousteau brings his students here. The Drake's Anchorage resort is very low-key, with weathered cottages, a solid restaurant, and a dining room that looks like it was built for the set of *South Pacific.*

When leaving North Sound, get out the binoculars and check out the palace of the founder of Virgin Atlantic. It is also the occasional home of that Kharma Chameleon, Boy George.

SO YOU WANT TO BE A ROCK 'N' ROLL SAILOR

There's a reprise from a song that Neil Young's buddies wrote that goes:

> **Wooden ships on the water very free**
> **Easy you know its the way it's supposed to be**
> **Silver people on the shoreline let us be**
> **Talkin' 'bout very free, and easy.**

Little did Neil know then that those words would present him with a double entendre later in life when he bought the *W. N. Ragland,* a very distinct wooden ship in its own right. And *you* can charter it. Needless to say, this is a must for all Neil Young fans. There are lots of Neilism's on the *Ragland* and if you follow his music, there are several allusions to her in his later songs.

The boat, a schooner rig carrying a yardarm, was built in 1913 as a cargo boat (a "tramp freighter" in merchant marine lingo). Named after Neil Young's grandfather, William Nathan Ragland, she's 100 feet long and is classified as a Baltic Trader. Neil renovated the boat after he bought her in 1976. His personal touch is evident as soon as you step inside the wheelhouse—there's a pullout electric keyboard ready to play "After the Goldrush" while enjoying a cocktail.

Down below, the entire interior was gutted and replaced with unique woods and furnishings. It's exactly how you would imagine Neil Young's boat would look—like a rustic old lodge from a town in North Ontario. The charm it exudes is wonderful. And there are lots of interesting things to appreciate. The huge redwood burl dining table is from Neil's ranch. The flooring is from the old Broward Hotel in Fort Lauderdale. The staves on the inner hull are from the ballroom of the Astoria in Windsor, Ontario. But the *pièce de résistance* is the owner's stateroom. I've never seen anything like it. It's huge, with the focal point a funky player piano hiding another electric keyboard, all framed by gigantic, antique elephant tusks. This boat, and especially this room, has romance written all over it.

The *W. N. Ragland* comes with all sorts of amenities, like A/C, VCR, and a Boston Whaler for waterskiing. It also comes with a very friendly and mellow crew of four, headed by Capt. Joe Trailer. Joe's been with the boat for years and can tell you lots of entertaining stories of various rock types who have been aboard. As charter boats go, especially in this league, the *Ragland* is very reasonably priced. Costs for a week range anywhere from $6500 for two to $9500 for six, all inclusive.

For more info, write: W. N. Ragland, P.O. Box 9997, St. Thomas, USVI 00801

DROPPING OUT TO DROP ANCHOR

Are you fed up with the corporate yuppie scene, a disillusioned child of the sixties who has lost interest in the next trend in cuisine? Try crewing on a charter boat. There are a lot of drop-outs floating around the American Paradise and many ex-execs doing everything from cooking to deckhand to captain. It is hard work—there is little time for private life, especially during high season, and virtually no chance for extended quality time. The pay is low, on average about $1000/a month and room and board.

So why bother? Leaving behind competitive pressures and phone bills is a major reason. It's therapeutic—manual labor in a very pleasant environment. It is also a good way to save money, something that current metro rents and mortgages don't allow. With no time or department store to spend your money in, it's easy to save.

Rebecca is one of these refugees. She left a lucrative ad sales job and Garden District condo in New Orleans to work aboard *Rangga,* a gorgeous 73-foot French-built schooner. She is the cook, meal planner, and provisioner. It's tough planning and stocking a boat with seven days' worth of food and drink for three meals a day—all within twenty-four hours. But despite the long hours and the loss of privacy, she enjoys the independence and the low-pressure environment of her position.

Rebecca has been on *Rangga* for nine months and plans to continue through the peak charter season. Then she will go up north to study holistic healing and massage at an institute in the Berkshires. Ah, the spirit of the sixties lives!

The Virgin Gorda Yacht Harbor, in Spanish Town on the southern end of Virgin Gorda, is a good port to call on if you want to disembark at will. It's a cramped but well-run and clean marina managed by Rockresorts (Little Dix Bay is around the corner). The Bath & Turtle is a good bar to hang out in and sip a cold beer. On Wednesday nights it holds a "jump-up" party. Dinner at Chez Michelle down the road is quite good and there are a few interesting shops to throw money around in, including a tiny record store if you're tired of your tapes.

Early the next morning, stop in for lunch at the Baths just south of Spanish Town. This stretch of gigantic boulders creates hundreds of caves and caverns with cool, clear saltwater pools in many. Because "it's special," an armada of boats descends to its shore and it gets very crowded here, particularly in the afternoon, so come early (seven to ten A.M. is ideal). The snorkeling is fantastic in calm water. Unfortunately, the surge (swells) prevents comfortable overnight anchoring. For privacy, take the walking trails to the Atlantic side of the point.

After the Baths, there's a fork in the road. You can head over to Marina Cay with a well-protected but not overly scenic anchorage. Or you can stop for another swim and explore Fallen Jerusalem—a rarely visited jumble of rocks named because it reminded someone of Jerusalem after one of its bad days. There's a small, private beach and lots of rocks to scramble over and under. Continuing on, you can really only sail by Ginger Island and wave, there is no suitable anchorage. Cooper Island doesn't offer much improvement, except for good dining at the Cooper Island Yacht Club. The next island west, Salt Island, has a protected spot on the south to throw out the hook. On the island there is an old black woman who sits on the beach and will barter bags of sea salt for anything you might have; a bottle of rum or, of course, cold hard cash. On the west side of the island is the site of the wreck of the R.M.S. *Rhone,* lost in the Hurricane of 1876 when she was loading cargo. The wreck is best suited for scuba divers as it's down between 30 and 85 feet. But when there are divers, the air bubbles create shimmering columns that are actually more interesting to look at from the surface than the wreck itself. The story of its demise is worth mentioning. Apparently, the captain knew the weather was going to turn real bad, so he threw out both anchors and rode out the first half of the tempest running the engines at full throttle and sheltered from the sea by the island. During the eye of the hurricane, when the sun came out and it was dead calm, he tried to hightail it for the open water because he knew the new wind direction would blow him right against the rocks. Of all times for the anchor to get snagged! The wind and seas roared in, pushed the *Rhone* up on the reef, demolished the boat, and took 125 lives. One last piece of lore, this is the wreck that Jackie Bisset swam around in *that* T-shirt in the film *The Deep.*

Next down the chain is Peter Island—home of the Peter Island Yacht Club (like the Bitter End, another pretender). This private little island is one of the Caribbean's most expensive resorts, so definitely go ashore to see if you think it's worth it. The buffet is good—expensive ($35) for a buffet, but good.

From Peter Island, head directly west for the Bight off Norman Island. This is one of the finest protected harbors in the Virgins, and one of the prettiest, too. There are no man-made structures on the island, but there are wild cattle of which you should steer clear. There are some caves around the western entrance, reputed to have held major treasure troves and provided Robert Louis Stevenson with the inspiration to write *Treasure Island.* I don't know about that, but you *can* pilot your dinghy right inside one of the caves—now that's inspiration. When you've had enough, go for a snorkel around the reef off the center shore in the Bight. Then hit the floating bar, the William Thornton, for a "Nelson's Blood" (grapefruit juice, orange juice, cranberry juice, and rum). The bar, a former Baltic Trader, serves burgers and similar fare. Around nine P.M., the "locals" (crew from the charter boats) flock to the bar, which makes it interesting. The Thornton stays open until the "lights go out."

CRUISING GUIDE TO SNORKEL SPOTS

LOCATION	COMMENTS
CHRISTMAS COVE, St. James I.	on the north side of Fish Cay
TRUNK BAY, St. John	a marked underwater trail
LEINSTER BAY, St. John	reef surrounding Waterlemon Cay
LONG BAY, Mosquito Island	Cousteau's students go here
WHITE BAY, Jost Van Dyke	excellent Elkhorn coral
SANDY CAY, Sandy Cay	nudie snorkeling
BREWER'S BAY, Tortola	several reefs in harbor
SEAL DOGS, Seal Dogs	sea turtles
ANEGADA, Anegada	the island is a huge reef/lobster
THE BATHS, Virgin Gorda	early in the A.M.

Now it's time for some sailing as you head across the Sir Francis Drake and around the West End of Tortola to Jost Van Dyke (named after some semilegend of a Dutch pirate, although I think it must mean "cheers" in Dutch). Jost is rather an unusual place. There can't be more than a hundred people living on the island, yet there are six bars. Obviously, such a situation demands a fitting response, that is, time to do some serious drinking. Keep those islanders in business, that kind of thing.

Great Harbor is the home of Foxy's; it would be called a dive anywhere else but it's a sailor's mecca in the Virgins. There's really nothing to it—it's like something you'd expect to see deep in Appalachia. Be careful not to step on the chickens. The bartenders are real nice guys, and Foxy Caldwell will occasionally play some tunes on his guitar. There are three well-worn hammocks on which to lounge and sway. But the real attraction is the crowd and the Painkiller Punch sold in plastic milk cartons for three bucks a pop (no wonder there are six bars). Next to Foxy's is Happy Larry's, another dive, but with pool tables. And down past the church is Rudy's, which is actually quite nice. Here you'll find jump-up to the reggae beat until two A.M., if you haven't already passed out.

Over at Little Harbor, a healthy and very beautiful couple of miles up and down the high road, is Sidney's Peace and Love Bar, where you're on the honor system to make your own drinks and write down how many you've had. Sidney apparently collects business cards; the walls are covered with them. Next door is Harris' Place, a cute little place with gusto-guzzling ice-cold beers and an excellent picnic-table-BBQ on Monday and Thursday nights. And across the harbor is Abe's, more of the same with a tiny marina. Before leaving Jost, White Bay to the west offers a quiet, secluded spot with a beautiful beach to help ease you out of your hangover. The same goes for Sandy Cay, a small, deserted island with trails, a marvelous beach with volleyball net, and plenty of privacy for nude sunbathing.

Just to the east of Sandy Cay is Cane Garden Bay on Tortola, with its gorgeous palmed beach, the old Caldwell Distillery where you can imbibe a wicked rum (if they feel like opening), and Stanley Hodge's Welcome Bar & Restaurant—one of the best bars in the Caribbean. At Stanley's, you can pig out on the lobster, get bombed on the one-two punch, and dance barefoot on the beach to the steel band. Before you leave, make sure you buy a T-shirt with its trademark tyre on a rope.

The last big island on the agenda is St. John, directly south of Jost. It remains one of the few unspoiled islands in the Caribbean, mostly due to its national park status. Don't forget to clear customs at Cruz Bay, the island's main port, and visit the National Park Visitors Center for current info on hikes and park excursions conducted by the rangers. Then head for Leinster Bay. It was so wonderful there the last time I visited that I stayed on an extra day just to hang out and snorkel off of Waterlemon Cay. The bay is rather idyllic, with an old plantation mill as the focal point. There's a road that runs right on the shore for walking and jogging. Further west is Francis Bay with a terrific vista of St. John, sunset over Pillsbury Sound, and the twinkling lights of St. Thomas. Be sure to anchor *at least* 200 yards off shore in Francis Cay as it does get buggy.

Off the beaten path and thus more private is the dryer southern coast of St. John. Coral Bay has plenty of room and several inlets to explore. Don't anchor too close—again, the bugs. Salt Pond Bay has a fun little buff beach and a 3-mile trail to Ram's Head, a huge rock promontory with valued sunset viewing potential.

Time permitting, the veteran sailors may consider making the 35-mile day sail to St. Croix to explore Christiansted, its only good harbor, rich in Dutch architecture, or Buck Island with its underwater national monument. But for most boats, it's time to head home.

THE VIRGIN ISLANDS: KEY FACTS

LOCATION	18°N by 64°W 1650 miles southeast of New York
SIZE	59 square miles
HIGHEST POINT	Mt. Sage, Tortola (1720 ft.)
POPULATION	12,000
LANGUAGE	English
TIME	Atlantic Standard Time (one hour ahead of EST, no Daylight Savings Time)
ELECTRICITY	110 volts (60 cycles)
CURRENCY	The U.S. dollar
DRIVING	On the left; local permit needed with valid driver's license

DOCUMENTS	Valid passport or proof of nationality and ongoing ticket or boat charter
BEER TO DRINK	John Courage
RUM TO DRINK	Cruzan

THE SAILING TROUSSEAU

While the emphasis on sailing is "less is more," there are a few items that the wise crew member should stow away in his or her duffle bag before leaving home. Generally, a bathing suit (at times optional) and a T-shirt are all you'll need. But there are a few other things you should think about packing. Periodically, sunny skies become mean, and ominous-looking clouds can drop a torrent of cool water on you after having just lotioned up. For these occasions, and for when the seas are sizable and the going gets wet and rough, the items below will be much appreciated.

- **FOUL-WEATHER JACKET—Even though the water temperature hovers around 80 degrees year round, the combination of cool rain, constant spray, and gusty winds can be bone-chilling. Foul-weather gear—the lighter the weight the better—keeps you dry, doubles as a windbreaker, and looks great in pictures. Some boats may provide this, so ask ahead of time.**
- **WATERPROOF SUNSCREEN—You'll be in and out of the water so much that this will save you a lot of effort. Don't use suntan oils—they get all over the boat, smudging and smearing everything in sight.**
- **TRANSDERM—This antiseasickness medicine is a miracle of modern science. Worn as a small circular Band-Aid behind your ear, it releases a drug through the skin that essentially dulls the nerve endings in the inner ear—the area that motion effects. It doesn't make you as drowsy as Dramamine and other oral medications and lasts for three days.**
- **TWO PAIRS OF BOAT SHOES—One invariably is wet so if you like dry feet bring an extra pair.**
- **MUSIC—Almost all of the crewed boats have decent sound systems but not a preferred selection of good party tapes. And some of the smaller bareboats don't even have a sound system. As dancing on the deck can be great fun, a Walkman or CD player with portable speakers will do the trick. Get ahold of the *Jaws* soundtrack and play it loud while others are having a late-night skinny dip.**
- **CAMCORDER—A video memory of your cruise will be treasured forever. The antics of a loved one struggling with the winch or helm will provide infinite pleasure.**
- **WATERPROOF TROPICAL REEF GUIDE—A laminated card or small book attached to your suit that allows you to know what those pretty fish are called.**

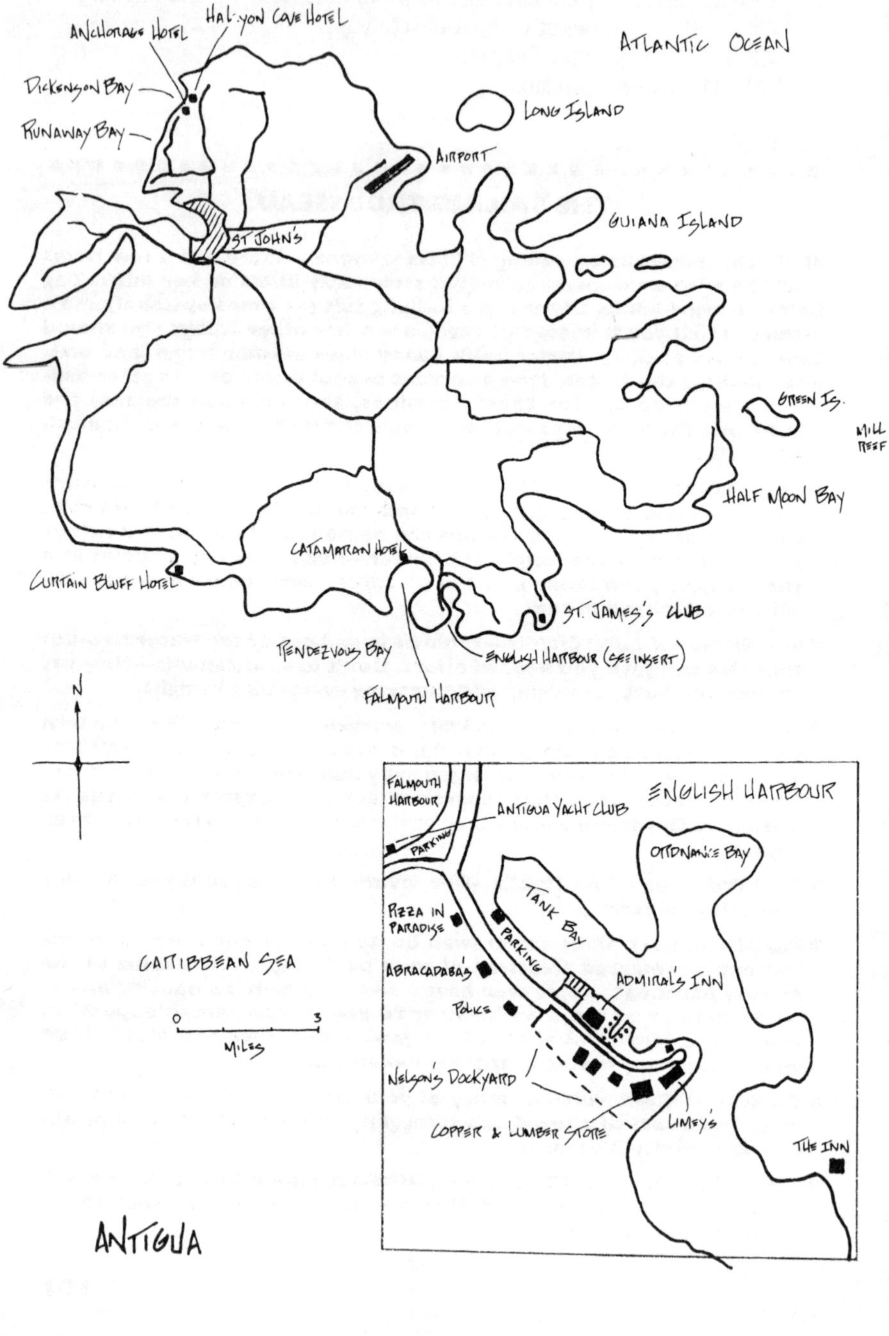
ATLANTIC OCEAN
ANCHORAGE HOTEL
HALCYON COVE HOTEL
DICKENSON BAY
RUNAWAY BAY
LONG ISLAND
AIRPORT
GUIANA ISLAND
ST JOHN'S
GREEN IS.
MILL REEF
HALF MOON BAY
CATAMARAN HOTEL
CURTAIN BLUFF HOTEL
ST. JAMES'S CLUB
RENDEZVOUS BAY
ENGLISH HARBOUR (SEE INSERT)
FALMOUTH HARBOUR
N
CARIBBEAN SEA
0
3
MILES
ENGLISH HARBOUR
FALMOUTH HARBOUR
ANTIGUA YACHT CLUB
PARKING
ORDNANCE BAY
TANK BAY
PIZZA IN PARADISE
PARKING
ABRACADABA'S
ADMIRAL'S INN
POLICE
NELSON'S DOCKYARD
LIMEY'S
COPPER & LUMBER STORE
THE INN
ANTIGUA

ANTIGUA SAILING WEEK

If there is one time in yachting where socializing is just as important as racing (if not even more so), it is Antigua Sailing Week (also known as Race Week). Having survived twenty years of festive inebriation, it's still going strong as the premier yachting event in the Caribbean. Always held during the last week of April, this ritual puts the final wrap on the winter season. Afterward, most boats head north to the States or east to the Med for the summer.

Race week also attracts a large crowd of nonracers. This is because of the range of activities that happen onshore. In fact, most people who participate in Race Week don't give a damn about the races and can't tell the difference between a shroud and a stay. What they want is to have a good time while rubbing elbows with the sailing set. On weekend nights, a good part of the younger Antiguan population will be there too as this is one of the major events on the island (the other being Carnival in August).

People get pretty smashed during this celebration. It's very orderly though, as what seems to be a policeman every 20 feet has a sobering effect. The presence of the police also reflects the potential unease that an event as white and wealthy as yachting might create on an island that is predominately black and very poor (the average per-capita income is below $1000). While I didn't find Antiguans hostile, they weren't particularly friendly either—particularly in St. John's, the capital. Since Sailing Week is a major tourist boost and allows the hotels to extend their winter rates until after the event (and three weeks longer than just about every other island), the Hotel Association and local government want to ensure that all goes smoothly—hence the cops. In the official programs, there is a plea to "please help us keep Antigua Sailing Week a happy, carefree, but controlled experience for the benefit of all."

Most of the activity during Sailing Week is focused on Nelson's Dockyard, a recently renovated historic complex of old Georgian brick buildings and warehouses that sits in the middle of English Harbour. Now a national park and a major tourist attraction (no ice cream shop yet, however), some of the buildings are stunning—especially the Admiral's Inn (see page 108).

In 1987, ninety-seven boats from twenty-five countries participated in Sailing Week. The boats are about equally split into racing and cruising categories. So you will know for future cocktail conversation, there are five days of races and three classes of racers and cruisers, Racing Class I, II, and III, and Cruising Class I, II, and III (the first—I—being the most advanced). The Racers are semipros, traveling around the seas on the race circuit. The Cruisers are more mellow—many of these boats are available for crewed charter any other week but this one. No Americans won their class in 1987—a good conversation ice breaker.

The main preevent to Sailing Week is the Guadeloupe Race, held a few days before the start. This is a 42-mile race from Des Hayes, Guadeloupe, to English Harbour. There are three classes of boats in this race: Multihulls, Racers, and Cruisers. The cocktail party hosted the night before by Les Amis de Voile de Point-à-Pitre is fabulous. Even more fun is the Rum Punch Party at 1400 hours in Nelson's Dockyard, followed by cocktails at six in the Antigua Yacht Club.

During Sailing Week nothing much really happens until Sunday and the end of the First Yacht Race. The race starts off of Falmouth Harbor and runs a course around the island from east to north to west. It is 33 miles long and finishes in Dickenson Bay on the northern part of Antigua.

This is where the real fun begins—many claim this is the best party of the week. The combination of a hundred-plus boats in the bay, a pretty beach, a large local turnout, and three big hotels (the Blue Waters Inn, the Anchorage Hotel, and the Halcyon Cove Hotel) create a very festive atmosphere. A traveling band of vendors sets up on the beach, offering chicken and chips, ice-cold beer, and an endless array of mediocre T-shirts. A good calypso band provides the pulsating beat for the huge crowd in front of the Anchorage Hotel. If you've ever wanted to dance barefoot on the beach, this is the ideal opportunity to do so. The action actually begins around noontime, as the non-mariners arrive at the beach for sun, fun, and to watch the boats come in—so plan to spend the day. You'll never be too far from the bar or a bathroom.

The Second Yacht Race is held the next day in the same area. It consists of a "Gold Cup" course similar to the 12 meters run during the America's Cup. The course is about 16 miles long for the Racing Classes and 10 miles long for the Cruising Classes. After the races, it's pretty much a rerun of the night before, but not quite as much fun or as crowded.

It's back to Nelson's Dockyard for the Third Yacht Race. The boats start around nine A.M. off Dickenson Bay and sail between 24 to 28 miles south, then east to the finish line at English Harbour. After the race, another party kicks off at 1800 hours on the waterfront in front of the Officer's Building. This is a major drinking event as the following day is Lay Day, that is, no races. A must-not-miss is Limey's Bar on the second floor overlooking the action. This is the place to rendezvous and talk about plans for the delivery north or the summer.

Lay Day is lots of fun for landlubbers, too. All the festivities are held at the Antigua Yacht Club, just down the road from Nelson's Dockyard, about a twelve-minute walk, on Falmouth Harbor. The action starts in the early afternoon with a rubber-raft race, tug-of-war, boardsailing races, a beer-drinking contest, and other "why-not" games. There is also a singlehanded yacht race for boats 45 feet and under and team racing in Lasers by country/territory, which can be real fun if you're a sailor.

There are two more days of racing after Lay Day. The Fourth Yacht

Race begins off Falmouth Harbour, beats east to Mill Reef, then runs west to Curtain Bluff, home of one of the most deluxe resorts—the Curtain Bluff Hotel—on the island. The course is 29 miles long for Racers and 17 miles for Cruisers. Once again, there is a party with a band in front of the hotel. For non-mariners, this is a wonderful beach on which to spend the afternoon drinking rum punches from the beach bar and greeting the arriving boats. The party starts around six and goes until your walking hangover says "enough already."

The final race, the Fifth Yacht Race, is an Ocean Triangle Course held off Falmouth Harbour and runs 24 miles for Racers and about 16 miles for the Cruising Classes. The "après" scene shifts back to Nelson's Dockyard for the last of the Race Day sailing parties. By now, you'll be feeling just a little weary and will probably want to venture over to one of the local bars outside of the Dockyard.

The most social of the local bars is undoubtedly Abracadabra's, located just across from the Dockyard parking lot. This is the place to go if you're trying to get picked up (if people still do that kind of thing in the paranoid eighties). The deck will be jammed with the sailing set—count on twenty minutes to get from end to end. Don't even think of trying to get through when the management shows video highlights of the day's races on the big screen. The crowd here is very attractive, generally bleached out and horny. In the garden, a reggae band sets up and gets to really jammin' later in the evening.

If you're hungry and don't want to spend a fortune eating out, head down the street from Abracadabra's toward Falmouth Harbor to Pizza in Paradise. Due to its relative cheapness—a combo pizza costs about $13 U.S.—the place is packed at dinner time. Later on, the kitchen closes and the bar turns into probably the hippest nightspot on Antigua. I knew that was the case when I heard "Peaches on Regalia" by Frank Zappa playing as I walked in; and it was followed by U2. My suspicions were confirmed when the DJ/bartender responded to my asking if he had "Innagadadavita" by nodding coolly and saying "the long version." The crowd here is very stylish, from hairdos to basic black outfits. It had a nice mix of Antiguans and Continentals and was just a fun place to hang out.

Probably the prettiest spot for having a drink or listening to music is the Admiral's Inn, located in the Dockyard. The grounds are beautiful, particularly the huge stone columns that line a narrow slipway and are the only remnants of the old boat house. The canopy created by some very old trees combined with the elegance of the inn make a quietly grand and stately sight. The bar inside is very comfortable and very nautical, with large French doors opening out onto the terrace and grounds. The live music here can be surprisingly good—one night I heard one of the best pan bands outside of Trinidad.

With the races over and the final standings posted, the atmosphere the next day becomes quite festive. Even while crews scurry around readying their boats for imminent departure, all seem to find time for a few pops here and there. Indeed, for many it's a liquid diet beginning with breakfast. So by the time things start happening, a lot of people are juiced up and ready to go. Not that there's really all that much going on, except for the greased-pole contest where local boys (the only ones daring enough) try to walk on a machine-greased wooden pole over the water. The goal is to touch a red flag before falling in. Winners get a bottle of rum and a pat on the back. It's amusing to watch for twenty minutes. Around three o'clock, the much-heralded Non-Mariner's Race takes place at the ramp in front of the Officer's Quarters. The requirements of the race are that the vessel be homemade, cost no more than $100 to build, and never have been in the water. The best part of the race is the start, when the contestants plunge into the water with their vessels. Their destination is the dock at the Admiral's Inn, where a crowd with cocktails awaits and cheers on the participants. Unfortunately, the race is over too soon and that's that. The milling around on the waterfront continues while a band kicks up to keep everyone going until the evening and Lord Nelson's Ball.

Lord Nelson's Ball is supposedly the culmination of the social events during Sailing Week, but in reality the first night at Dickenson's or the deck at Abracadabra's is much more fun. The ball is a throwback to the days when yachting was exclusively white and Anglo-Saxon. The crowd (when I attended) was almost entirely white, thanks to the jacket-tie dress code and the $25 U.S. admission fee. It just doesn't seem right in 1987, not that it ever was. I was embarrassed for the Governor-General who spoke at the ball to an audience that was hardly his constituency (they were not invited). That said, the ball is enjoyable for the alcohol flowing freely from the open bar. Also amusing is how women manage to stow away their best taffeta in their duffel bags and then throw them on for this formal occasion. Some of the men come up with black tie, although most are dressed in natty blue blazers and button-downs with wrinkled khakis or Lilly Pullitzers. The setting of the Admiral's Inn and grounds is very stunning and very colonial. When you've had enough, head over to Abracadabra's for reggae and a much more civilized environment.

ANTIGUA: KEY FACTS

LOCATION	17°N by 61°W
	40 miles north of Guadeloupe
	32 miles south of Barbuda
	1800 miles southeast of New York
SIZE	108 square miles
HIGHEST POINT	Babby Peak (1358 ft.)
POPULATION	75,000

LANGUAGE	English
TIME	Atlantic Standard Time (1 hour ahead of EST, same as EDT)
ELECTRICITY	110 or 220, depending on hotel
CURRENCY	The EC dollar ($2.64 EC = $1.00 U.S.)
DRIVING	On the left; need temporary permit—$30 EC/$11.36 U.S.
DOCUMENTS	Passport or proof of nationality w/photo; ongoing ticket
BEER TO DRINK	Red Stripe
RUM TO DRINK	Mt. Gay

GETTING THERE

Antigua is centrally located and is a major gateway to the Caribbean. Its airport, V. C. Bird International, can handle the jumbos and has daily nonstops from New York on American and from Miami on Eastern. Air Canada and BWIA fly nonstop from Toronto on weekends, and BWIA flies nonstop from New York, Washington, and Boston several times a week.

Within the Caribbean, LIAT has the most flights to V. C. Bird as Antigua is its hub and home base. From San Juan, you can also fly Eastern Metro Express, American Eagle, and BWIA.

STAYING THERE

Antigua is loaded with hotels, most of which are on one of the reputed 365 beaches (does the mud in St. John's Harbor count as a beach?). Like the other Leeward Islands, it's not cheap to stay here—especially at the large resorts. To make things easy for Race Week participants, only English Harbour's best digs are discussed. Some recommendations are also given for Dickenson Bay and Curtain Bluff. If you're really an enthusiast, you could arrange to be waterfront all week long by following the boats from one landfall to another.

ENGLISH HARBOUR AND VICINITY

If you like being at the hub, then I strongly suggest that you stay at Nelson's Dockyard at either the Admiral's Inn or the Copper and Lumber Store. Keep in mind that there will also be a lot of noise from bands and people.

ADMIRAL'S INN (809) 463–1027
P.O. Box 713, St. John's, Antigua, West Indies

The more private of the two and the home of Lord Nelson's Ball, this weathered-brick and white-shuttered Georgian building is set on the waterfront amid stately trees and old columns. There are fourteen twin-bedded rooms of various sizes and character depending on their location in this 200-year-old former engineer's quarters. The Admiral's Bar is festooned with tasteful nautical memorabilia and the terrace is a grand place to sip a rum punch while comparing the virtues of various winches.

Rates are NOT SO CHEAP for singles and PRICEY for doubles (EP). MAP is $34 additional per person.

COPPER AND LUMBER STORE HOTEL (809) 463–1058/1259
P.O. Box 184, St. John's, Antigua, West Indies

This is the elegant alternative if you want to stay at the Dockyard. The hotel was completely and beautifully renovated not many years back. It's in the middle of the action, fronting the main piazza on the bay where the bands play. Like the Admiral, it has a weathered brick and shuttered/louvered exterior with fourteen rooms and the same brick/wood decor throughout. It is the interior that makes the Copper and Lumber Store one of the classiest joints on Antigua. The restoration's attention to detail is evident in the woodwork, the hand-stenciled wallpaper, and the numerous and elegant antique furnishings. Even the bathrooms are special—the showers are paneled with mahogany. The best rooms are four suites that are "très deluxe." The other rooms are more "contemporary" but a lot cheaper. All the rooms have kitchenettes.

Rates are PRICEY to WICKED PRICEY for singles and doubles (EP).

THE INN AT ENGLISH HARBOUR (809) 463–1014
P.O. Box 187, St. John's, Antigua, West Indies

This inn is located across the bay from Nelson's Dockyard on Freeman's Bay. What it lacks in charm, character, and convenience it makes up with a beach, watersports, and a launch to and from the Dockyard. There are twenty-eight "modern" accommodations and an excellent bar/restaurant on the premises.

Rates are PRICEY to VERY PRICEY for singles and doubles (EP).

CATAMARAN HOTEL AND APARTMENTS (809) 463–1036/1503
P.O. Box 958, Falmouth, Antigua, West Indies
Stateside: (212) 535–9539; Canada: (416) 960–0710

This little pink delight sits right on the beach on Falmouth Harbor—it's especially delightful because it's relatively cheap and close to the Dockyard. There are thirteen rooms in various bungalows and cottages, including efficiency units. Don't expect much in the way of decor or furnishings. You stay here because of the price, beach, and location. There are rowboats and a Sunfish for use free of charge by guests (the poor man's Club Med) and a 31-foot Bertram. It's available for day charter and deep-sea fishing. A restaurant and bar are also on the premises.

Rates are CHEAP to NOT SO CHEAP for singles and NOT SO CHEAP for doubles (EP).

ST. JAMES'S CLUB (809) 463–1430/1113
P.O. Box 63, St. John's, Antigua, West Indies
Stateside: (800) 235–3505/(212) 308–3330
Canada: (800) 268–9051/(416) 598–2693

Affiliated with the St. James's Clubs in London, Paris, and L.A., this resort put the "p" in pretentious. With an "honorary committee" of Sirs and Ladies, the correct smattering of celebrities, and the appropriate amount of attitude, you'd think the Aga Khan built the place out of marble and gold. But in reality, it used to be a Holiday Inn! The main building is borderline tacky and the glass-walled pool is reminiscent of a chain hotel on Miami Beach. The villas, while interesting in design, are jammed together—hardly worth the $850-U.S.-and-up price during high season. There is an array of activities available, including the standard watersports and tennis. Some, like horseback riding, scuba, deep-sea fishing, and surf jetting, are offered for an additional charge (if you can believe it). After shelling out $850 you'd think they would throw in a masseur or masseuse. But here the motto should be "why pay less?" P.S.: Burt and Fay, the couple who run the scuba operation and Yacht Club boutique, are very nice.

Rates are OUTRAGEOUS for singles and doubles (MAP).

OTHER PLACES TO STAY ON ANTIGUA

DICKENSON BAY

■ HALYCON COVE BEACH RESORT & CASINO (809) 462–0256
P.O. Box 251, St. John's, Antigua, West Indies

Deluxe and expensive *but you can gamble*

■ THE ANCHORAGE (809) 462–0267
P.O. Box 147, St. John's, Antigua, West Indies

Where the boats are. Deluxe, expensive, and known for its service.

CURTAIN BLUFF

■ CURTAIN BLUFF (809) 463–1115
P.O. Box 288, St. John's, Antigua, West Indies

Some say this is the best hotel on the island and, while very expensive, it is cheaper than the St. James's. So if you're going to spend the money, stay here.

ST. JOHN'S

There are two cheap alternatives here worth mentioning even though it's very unlikely you'll want to stay in St. John's. The Spanish Main Inn, (809) 462–0660, and St. Mary's Court, (809) 462–4770, have loads of character and offer a different side of Antigua. While here, don't miss Brother B's and the Golden Peanut for good West Indian fare. At night, check out Tropix disco down at Redcliffe Quay.

THE DINGHY CRAWL

RODNEY BAY, ST. LUCIA

The joint was jumpin'. Already our table had been tossed out the window and a couple's unsuccessful attempt to execute a flip had smashed the stand-up menu in half. And it wasn't even ten o'clock. We hadn't even hit the other pubs—this one was just too interesting to leave.

It was just another Saturday night on the Dinghy Crawl—the wildest yachting nightlife scene in the Caribbean next to Antigua Race Week. But unlike Race Week it happens every weekend. It's called the Crawl because the festivities are reached by boat on a rather small bay—just about every bar has a dock. You need not have a boat, however, to join in the fun.

The action takes place at Rodney Bay on the northwestern corner of St. Lucia, where a new marina and Stevens Yachts have spawned a number of services, including no fewer than eight bars and clubs. Lining the perimeter of the bay are the A-Frame, Pat's Pub, Capone's, the Chart House, the Lime Inn, the Mortar & Pestle, the Eagle's Nest, and Splash (a disco in the St. Lucian Hotel). And then there's Gros Islet.

Gros Islet is a small town that borders Rodney Bay on the north. This is where the Dinghy Crawl weekend blow-out begins. Every Friday night, the town hosts what amounts to a minicarnival on the main street. You can't miss it, just head for the music.

An impressive PA system is set up in the middle of the town's major intersection, playing calypso mixed with reggae and disco. The street is lined with food and beer vendors. Smoke swirls around the crowd, making the scene look rather tribal. For $3 E.C. (about $1.14) you can buy BBQ chicken with pepper sauce or lambi (conch) on a skewer. Heineken, brewed on St. Lucia, is sold in buckets for $2.50 E.C. by children barely old enough to read. There are roadside carts selling rum punch and the western end of the street is an easy place to find ganja for $2 E.C. a stick.

There are three other notable fun bars. My favorite is Scott's Café, recognized by the Cockspur sign hanging in front. The two-story building has the look and air of a western saloon. The upstairs has a porch that provides a great vantage point to watch the action. Across the street is the Golden Apple and down the road near the beach is The Wall. It has its own calypso and jump space as well as a garden with tables to rest for a spell.

The best action, though, is on the street. The crowd is primarily black St. Lucians, who are friendly though the young males will try to hustle your money for almost any reason (except sex). There are some tourists—the bulk of whom are boat people. The town heats up around 10:30 P.M. and goes on until the wee hours.

Plan to sleep in on Saturday or catch some rays on pretty Reduit Beach (on the ocean side of Rodney Bay)—you'll need lots of strength for the second phase of the crawl. The commotion begins at sundown, when the boat people have finished their chores and are ready to party. They begin with a few stiff cocktails, then hop in their inflatables and roar off to the dock with the most dinghies tethered to it. Watching them dock is quite amusing. The name of the game is rubber-baby-bumper-boats, as the objective is to drive your dinghy as close to the dock as possible—splitting the flotilla up the middle to the sound of vinyl squeaks and rope groans.

Give your engine gas and let 'er rip. I've actually seen a boat plow through what appeared to be an impenetrable dinghy-lock and arrive at the dock without major damage. Getting back out is another ball game.

The current hot spot could be any of the bars on the bay. But at the moment it seems to be the A-Frame, where the owner's laissez-faire attitude is very popular among the charter crews who frequent or turn around at Rodney Bay. Here they can act out their fantasies, whether it be Fred and Ginger gliding across the crowded dance floor, or Hulk Hogan and André the Giant in Wrestlemania V. It was at the A-Frame that our table flew out the window (followed by my beer mug) and twirling couples wiped out several tables. The music is very eclectic, from the Andrews Sisters and Johann Strauss to Springsteen and calypso. The floor bounces so much you have to cover your glass with a coaster *while* holding it, to keep it from spilling. Good humor prevails, and the staff seems to get a big kick out of the patrons' antics. On Sunday morning, there's a run on aspirin and bromides at the marina drugstore, so make sure you've brought an adequate supply.

For the less fortunate not on boats (or more fortunate, depending on your point of view), there are several accommodations on the bay that are only a crawl from the action. All are of the cookie-cutter motel/hotel mode and are fairly expensive. The St. Lucian (formerly the Holiday Inn) has the standard big-hotel setup on Reduit Beach. It does have a good-sized pool with tall coconut trees and chaise longues for proper recuperation. There's also free tennis, waterskiing, sailing, and windsurfing available for guests of the hotel. Rooms are VERY PRICEY, over $150/night EP double. Down the road on the bay, not the beach, is the Harmony Apartel—the standard multilevel efficiency setup, great if you want to cook your own meals and have more space than a hotel. It has a small pool and free use of the sailboards. The Mortar & Pestle is on the premises. Prices are PRICEY.

If you're staying south in Castries, you can reach the Dinghy Crawl by taxi (about $25 E.C.) or bus, which is real cheap ($1 E.C.) and a lot more fun. The buses are actually minivans with names painted on the front. They leave for Gros Islet (be sure to ask) from Jeremy St. near the market in Castries and will stop for anyone who flags them down. It's remarkable how many people they can hold. Calypso or reggae resounds from the formidable stereo, creating a convivial atmosphere. All types ride the bus, from Rastas to old ladies with baskets on their heads. The bus I was on had a flat that was fixed within five minutes—uncharacteristic efficiency for the islands. The buses run until very late on weekends and leave from the eastern end of the main street in Gros Islets.

For more information on St. Lucia, see "The Outdoors Option," pages 166–178.

THE **CEREBRAL** OPTION

Bob Marley statue in Kingston.

RASTAMAN VIBRATIONS, YEAH (POSITIVE)

You're going to lively up yourself and
don't be no drag,
You're going to lively up yourself 'cause reggae is
another bag.
You lively up yourself and don't say no,
You're gonna lively up yourself 'cause I said so.

Thus spake Bob Marley. As the undisputed king of reggae, his 1974 song "Lively Up Yourself" was a call to action on behalf of Jamaica's biggest export—his music. At the peak of his career, his record sales accounted for about 10% of the country's gross national product. Even after his premature death in 1981 at the age of thirty-six, he is still considered the prime mover in popularizing reggae in North America and throughout the world.

Bob Marley is a national hero. His statue stands in the middle of a square across from the National Arena in Kingston, a tribute to his contribution not only to Jamaican music, but to his country's cultural identity. But as reggae music goes, he is certainly not the only Jamaican to leave his or her mark. Bunny Wailer, Judy Mowatt—former members of Marley's band, The Wailers and its female vocal back-up, the I-Threes respectively—are accomplished solo reggae musicians. The late Peter Tosh, also a former member of the Wailers, was renowned worldwide. So are Jimmy Cliff, Gregory Isaacs, Dennis Brown, Freddie "Toots" (of the Maytalls), Sister Carol Burning Spear, Carlene Davis, and the bands Third World, Black Uhuru, and Chalice. There are countless more. A visit to a Kingston record shop will reveal artists you've never even heard of, and a huge selection of 45s (from local talent and labels) that I haven't seen since the midsixties. Surprisingly, two of the most popular reggae bands today are British, UB40 and Steel Pulse, although many of these groups' band members trace their roots to Jamaica.

While reggae has a strong following in the States, Canada, and Britain, few reggae bands have had top-forty reggae hits. In 1969, Desmond Dekker reached number twelve on the *Billboard* chart with "The Israelites." Jimmy Cliff had a hit in 1970 with "Wonderful World, Beautiful People."

Probably the best showing was Bob Marley and the Wailers' 1976 album, "Rastaman Vibrations," which reached number eight on the *Billboard* album charts—unprecedented for both Marley and reggae musicians in general.

On the other hand, "mainstream" musicians have made it big with reggae. Paul Simon led the way when he wrote "Mother and Child Reunion" back in 1972 (as he did recently with "Graceland" and the music of native South Africa). About the same time, Johnny Nash took Bob Marley's song "Stir It Up," made it a hit, and followed shortly thereafter with the reggae-influenced "I Can See Clearly Now." Then came Eric Clapton's blockbuster version of "I Shot the Sheriff"—another Marley tune. After that, a number of groups jumped on the reggae bandwagon, from The Police with songs like "Roxanne" and "Walkin' on the Moon" and Blondie ("The Tide Is High"), to Kool and the Gang ("Let's Go Dancin' [Ooh, La La La]"), Club Nouveau ("Lean on Me"), to such all-time greats as the very talented Bonnie Raitt ("True Love Is Hard to Find") and Mick Jagger with Peter Tosh ("Don't Look Back").

REGGAE'S ROOTS

Reggae evolved from a variety of Jamaican musical styles. Its roots can be heard in the traditional Jamaican music called "mento." It had a slow beat and rather lewd lyrics—much like the Beguine of Martinique. Like the "wine" and calypso music, it was danced very intimately, with two people joined at the hips simulating intercourse.

The advent of rhythm-and-blues in the U.S., coupled with the spread of transistor radios, doomed mento. The powerful AM broadcasts out of Miami brought the R & B sound home to Jamaica. So did the growing popularity of "sound systems"—traveling DJs with PA systems and the hottest singles from the U.S. American music soon influenced Jamaica's own, resulting in a fast-paced synthesis called "ska."

While ska was not tremendously popular elsewhere, Millie Small's 1964 song, "My Boy Lollipop" was a worldwide hit. By the late sixties, ska gave way to yet another music called "rock steady." It was much slower, with a more evenly paced beat—reggae's forerunner. Rock steady delivered an increasingly more serious message than its lighthearted predecessor. The music soon expressed the movement for independence as well as the heightened sense of black pride brought on by the U.S. civil rights movement.

It was rock steady's growing lyrical consciousness that gave birth to the slower, more powerful reggae. Reggae became the vehicle of discontent, rooted in the shantytowns of West Kingston and Trenchtown. Bob Marley and the Wailers became the stewards of this new music, formulating the now-familiar guitar rhythms and timing. In 1970, Marley founded the Tuff Gong studios and by 1971, he and his band were on their way with the hit "Trenchtown Rock." At the time of his death in 1981, Marley had produced over twenty albums and had made reggae a dynamic force worldwide.

While reggae still reigns supreme on the Jamaican music scene, a new

JAMAICAN ART

There are few places in the Caribbean where the art scene is as dynamic or impressive as it is in Jamaica. This can readily be seen in Kingston, the capital and largest English-speaking city (pop. 700,000) south of the U.S. The average tourist may think that the crafts markets of Ocho Rios or Montego Bay, with their wood carvings and amateur paintings, encapsulate the Jamaican art scene. But this is hardly true.

For a true perspective on Jamaican art, you must visit the National Gallery on 12 Ocean Blvd., Block 3, Kingston Mall, Kingston, (809) 922–1563/8544/8540. Since 1982, the gallery has occupied two floors of a new building it has already outgrown. Its eighteen galleries house various collections of paintings, prints, and sculptures from different eras and artists of Jamaica. The gallery also has an international collection that focuses on Caribbean works.

Of particular interest at the gallery is the magnificent sculpture collection of Edna Manley, one of the primary forces in modern Jamaican art. Her work is truly moving, from the reflection on recent political violence called *Ghetto Mother* (1982) to such timeless pieces as *Negro Aroused* (1935), *The Beadseller* (1922), *The Diggers* (1936), and *Horse of the Morning* (1943).

There are other prominent artists whose works should not be missed. These include Mallica Reynolds (known as Kapo), Barrington Watson, Christopher Gonzalez, Karl Parboosingh, and Albert Huie. Kapo is probably Jamaica's most prolific primitive sculptor, with evocative pieces like *All Women Are Five Women* (1965). He is also a renowned painter. Barrington Watson's neorealist oil paintings of the human form are outstanding, including *Conversation* (1981) and *Mother and Child* (1968). Christopher Gonzalez' mahogany sculpture titled *Man Arisen* (1966) explodes with emotion. *Ras Smoke I* (1972), by Karl Parboosingh, and *The Constant Spring Road* (1964), by Albert Huie, both oils, are powerful documentations of the lives and times of the Jamaican people.

The gallery is open Monday through Saturday, ten A.M. to five P.M. If you're in the mood to buy or browse, check out the Contemporary Art Centre at One Liguanea Ave. in Kingston. It is run by Barrington Watson and presents not only his work but also the art of over thirty other artists in a comfortable and well-lit gallery. No art adventure in Kingston would be complete without seeing the monumental wall murals on the campus of the University of the West Indies. While there, pick up a catalog. Who knows, the Jamaican art experience may arouse new interests that demand further study.

offshoot called "dance hall" music is rapidly gaining popularity. It can best be described as a combination of reggae and rap—the steady reggae rhythm supports a monotone of nonstop rap. Yellowman and Tiger are just two musicians who have adopted this music.

THE BOB MARLEY MUSEUM (809) 927–9152
56 Hope Rd., Kingston, Jamaica, W.I.

This is a must stop for any reggae fan in Jamaica. Run by Rastas, it occupies the former Tuff Gong studios where most of Bob Marley and the Wailers' best music was recorded. It's located in a well-heeled neighborhood near Jamaica House (the official residence of the Prime Minister). When you pull up to the gate, you are greeted by a bearded and knit-capped Rastaman who announces that the only pictures allowed are of the Marley statue inside. After that, all cameras and recording devices must be checked at the gatehouse. A guide will then take you inside to view an hour-long video presentation that shows Bob Marley in concert, recording at the studio (which is where you are sitting), and out and about. The rest of the tour includes the grounds, notably murals, herb gardens, Marley's statue, a beehive, and a real, live ganja plant with the words "I Love You" written in white stones at its base.

Back inside the museum, which originally was an old Victorian house, there are two floors of memorabilia. They include two rooms of news clippings pasted to the walls, a replica of Bob's first record shop in Trenchtown called Wail 'n Soul Records, his bedroom preserved intact (it looks like a hippie den—with pillows on the floor and a large smoking pipe), as well as a wax statue à la Madame Tussaud that will eventually move to simulate him singing. When you finish the tour, you'll want to check out the Bob Marley Museum Souvenir Shop for T-shirts, beach towels, and all of his records available for about $5 U.S. each (beware of the pressing quality).

Admission is $10 J.A. (about $2 U.S.) for adults and hours are 9:30–5:00 on Mondays, Tuesdays, Thursdays, and Fridays. The museum is open from 12:30–6:00 on Wednesdays, Saturdays, and holidays and is closed on Sundays.

REGGAE SUNSPLASH

Now here is an event for hard-core reggae fans. Held in August every year in Montego Bay, this four-day festival always features the best talent in the field—a mini-Woodstock of reggae music. It has been going on for ten

Bob Marley Museum
in Kingston.

years and its popularity shows no sign of waning with the more than 150,000 people now attending the shows.

A concert and party at Cornwall Beach in Montego Bay kick off the festivities. The Bob Marley Centre is the scene of the next four concerts, which last from eight P.M. until dawn. This gives you the whole day to crash on the beach or float in the pool.

Over twenty bands perform, including such reggae megastars as Steel Pulse, Dennis Brown, Burning Spear, and Yellowman. Each year the roster changes, but you're almost assured of hearing the best and latest groups, as Sunsplash is reggae's premier event and a major showcase for new music. There are plenty of vendors so you should have no problem finding cold beers and hearty splifs.

While you can buy tickets for each concert for $7.50 U.S., your best bet is to purchase a package that includes airfare, lodging, concert admission, transfers, and so on. Sunburst Holidays, (800) 223–1277, is an outfit specializing in Sunsplash packages. The Jamaica Tourist Board will also be helpful. Or you can stay at Round Hill or Tryall and let them work out the details!

For more information on Jamaica, see "The Hedonistic Option," pages 77–84, and "The Golf Option," pages 143–146.

GRENADA PHOTO SAFARI

Grenada is an evocative country. Its tranquil natural assets of lush tropical vegetation, gushing rivers, scenic mountains and coast contrast startlingly with Grenada's recent political upheaval. The American military invasion combined with the island's traumatic postrevolutionary experience has made Grenadians leery of foreigners and foreign influence. The feeling one gets as an aware tourist—particularly an aware American tourist—is that in the Grenadians' eyes, you are suspect.

Much has been written by American journalists about Grenada then and now and its love affair with the U.S. In the February 1987 issue of *Esquire* one writer went so far as to refer to the invasion as the "Rescue." You won't find anyone in Grenada calling it that. They term it the "Intervention." And all that pro-American graffiti you may have heard about is on the side wall of one highly visible shop on the fringes of St. George's (probably paid for by some conservative American organization). This is not to say that Grenada is an unfriendly or hostile country. People are friendly, particularly in the north. But they won't lay palm fronds in your path because you're a Yankee.

At present, Grenada is a great place to visit if you want to hike and

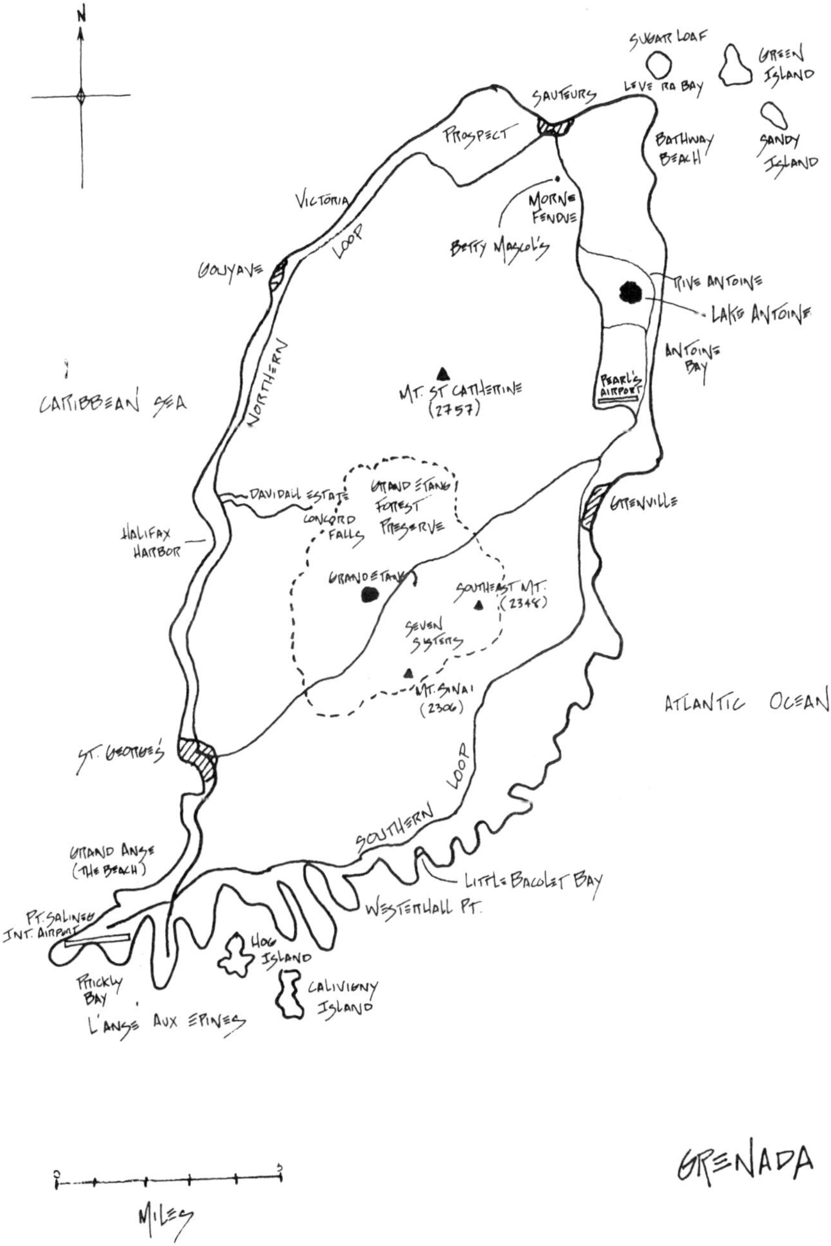
N
SUGAR LOAF
GREEN ISLAND
LEVERA BAY
SAUTEURS
PROSPECT
BATHWAY BEACH
SANDY ISLAND
VICTORIA
MORNE FENDUE
BETTY MASCOL'S
LOOP
GOUYAVE
RIVE ANTOINE
LAKE ANTOINE
ANTOINE BAY
NORTHERN
MT. ST CATHERINE (2757)
PEARL'S AIRPORT
CARIBBEAN SEA
DAVIDALL ESTATE
GRAND ETANG FOREST PRESERVE
GRENVILLE
CONCORD FALLS
HALIFAX HARBOR
GRAND ETANG
SOUTHEAST MT. (2348)
SEVEN SISTERS
MT. SINAI (2306)
ATLANTIC OCEAN
ST. GEORGE'S
LOOP
SOUTHERN
GRAND ANSE (THE BEACH)
LITTLE BACOLET BAY
WESTERHALL PT.
PT. SALINES INT. AIRPORT
HOG ISLAND
CALIVIGNY ISLAND
PRICKLY BAY
L'ANSE AUX EPINES
MILES

GRENADA

immerse yourself in its people and past. Outside the primary tourist areas of Grand Anse, L' Anse Aux Epines, and St. George's—all on the southwest corner of the island—you begin to experience the real Grenada. Vivid images come to mind of women washing clothes in a river, potholed roads, spice stations, rich hues of green, and the ever-watchful eyes of the people.

Grenada's physical beauty makes it a natural for the camera. But getting to your subject matter can prove difficult. I wouldn't recommend renting a car to explore the north of the island unless you hire a guide. The roads are bad and there are no directional signs. For those who know the territory (and with a sense of adventure), there is the bus—an experience in itself. This is a fine way to get to know Grenadians. The buses, really minivans, play calypso music and squeeze in as many people as possible as they zip around the island.

If that isn't what you had in mind, a great way to see the island is with Dennis Henry. His company, Henry Tours (phone 5313), will take you for an all-day tour leaving at nine A.M. from your hotel or guest house and will return you there at around five P.M. for $53 EC (about $20 U.S.). Dennis, who goes by at least five names, will design a photo safari that will let you put the best of Grenada on film. The tour features frequent stops for photo opportunities as well as a tasty lunch (you pay) at Betty Mascol's Plantation House. The vehicle is an air-conditioned, comfortable van with good visibility and height to let you take in as much as you can. Dennis is also an avid hiker and conducts mountain walking tours (see pages 165–166).

CAMERA ETIQUETTE

Many people get irritated when you snap a picture of them without permission (just look at Sean Penn). To show courtesy and to avoid unpleasantness, it is wise to ask before clicking the shutter. Sometimes a friendly gesture and a smile will do the trick. With group shots, use your judgment. A group of women washing clothes in a river may not mind as much as a group of Rastas who may end up taking the film—and your camera—from you.

PHOTO SAFARI #1—ST. GEORGE'S

St. George's is best seen on foot. The town, built on steep hills around a small harbor, has many stair accesses and roads too narrow for cars. It's easy to get to St. George's from your hotel as you are never more than 5 miles away by taxi, minibus, or thumb.

Plan on doing the walk in the morning as it gets too hot by lunchtime. (Also, the bright light bleaches the color and life out of your subjects until about three P.M.) The best place to start is at the Carenage. You'll find a Cable & Wireless office for overseas calls, a LIAT office to reconfirm your return flight, and the tourist board to buy a good map—all in a row. Across the street to the right, the mailboats *Alexia II* and *Adelaide* depart Wednesdays and Saturdays for Carriacou. These wooden boats with sails, mast, and so on may not inspire much confidence either as a form of public transit or especially as a pleasure craft. But it's possible to secure passage on one—which is, in fact, a great experience.

Moving along, you'll pass the Nutmeg—a good spot for lunch later on and a rum punch now. If you need the Post Office, it's further down the Carenage past Rudolph's restaurant. Otherwise, turn right on Young St. (Rudolph's will be on the corner). Walking up Young St., you'll pass the National Museum on the left. Admission is $1 EC (about $.38 U.S.) and will take you about fifteen minutes to scour. Far more interesting is the Rasta in front, selling all kinds of stuff including prerecorded calypso and reggae tapes.

At Church Street, take a right and follow it all the way past several good examples of both English- and French-influenced island architecture—including the Anglican church and the cathedral that dominates the top of the hill. Then cruise down the Market Hill to Market Square where tables are set up and anyone can come in and sell their wares. Be friendly and open here as you may be the only nonlocals in sight. This is a good place to strike up a conversation, especially in one of the surrounding rum shops.

When you're ready to move on, head up Halifax Street to the Yellow Poui art gallery. This is a legitimate gallery, not a tourist joint. There are several Grenadian and West Indian artists on display. Prices are too high but it's worth a look.

You're in the home stretch now. Take a left on Church St., right on Simmons, and down the steps to Scott St. and the Carenage. That should put you right at the Nutmeg for lunch and a much-needed rum punch.

PHOTO SAFARI #2—NORTHERN GRENADA

For this expedition, you need a guide. The roads aren't marked and are in bad shape—your AAA card won't work here. The guide will show you places you could never find on your own.

This is an all-day affair. Your guide (I'd recommend Dennis Henry; phone 5313) will pick you up at your hotel and whisk you through St. George's to the western road. As soon as you leave St. George's you'll know you're entering the real Grenada.

■ LAUNDRY

Never did laundry look so photogenic. Several times along the west coast you will encounter women doing laundry in the rivers. The light is muted from the green canopy and the subjects are almost always interesting from any angle.

- CONCORD FALLS
A one-lane road snakes up the hill past countless nutmeg trees to the falls. Get out of the car and walk up to the Fontainbleu falls (which takes about thirty minutes)—it's much prettier. There are heavy lush greens with peaked hills as background.

- RUM SHOPS
One thing that becomes clear as you drive around Grenada—and most other West Indian islands—is that just about every house has a liquor license. These shops sell sundries as well as drinks, so you can have a rum punch while looking at the eggs. Now that's progress.

- DAVIDALL ESTATE
This is a spice-processing station near Concord. Outside, there are several drying racks on rollers. Should it rain, they are swiftly pushed into the workhouse and rolled out when the sun shines again. Inside, women separate the mace from the nutmeg seed as well as prepare cocoa beans, cinnamon, and bay leaves. The faces of the workers alone are worth the trip.

- GOUYAVE (pronounced guave)
Here is a large nutmeg-processing station (the next step after Davidall). Gouyave is notorious for its looney citizens who seem to burn the midnight oil more here than anywhere else on the island. There is a sizable fishing community whose odd hours may add to the general wackiness.

- WOMEN WITH THINGS BALANCED ON THEIR HEADS
You won't see this on the streets of New York. These women have strong necks. It's astonishing what they can balance. Brownie points if you can snap a woman carrying a case of Coke or Carib on her head.

- PROSPECT
If the bridge is still out, or just for the fun of it, take the road through this area. It's real Grenadian back country with fine examples of rural dwellings.

- SAUTEURS
Past Prospect, the road will suddenly end on a beach with a commanding view of Sauteurs and its cathedral on top of Carib Leap. The town itself is picturesque and worth a brief tour with camera in hand. The drive up to the cathedral will bring you to Carib Leap, where the last remaining Carib Indians leaped to their deaths rather than be captured by their French pursuers. At the church, a workshop of the Young Grenadians

United Crafts Workers Association busily makes candles or batik that can be bought on the spot. These are teenagers trying to make a cooperative succeed—a worthy effort. In front of the workshop is an old cemetery and beyond an excellent view of Carriacou.

■ MORNE FENDUE
Home of Betty Mascol's Plantation House, where you should plan on having lunch. The great house was built of gray stone and wrought iron by Betty's father in 1908. There are several varieties of brilliant flowering shrubs featuring the biggest red poinsettias I've ever seen.

■ RIVE ANTOINE
Several miles outside of Morne Fendue, the road will emerge from the hinterland onto a windswept, palm-studded beach that curves around to some gigantic cliffs to the north. This is a good place to sit, cool off, and enjoy the view. If you swim, beware of the undertow.

Right up the road from the beach is the Rive Antoine rum distillery. After driving through fields of sugar cane—many charred from the annual harvest burning—you'll arrive at some old stone buildings and the distillery's huge waterwheel. This is one of the few remaining distilleries that looks and operates the way it did over 150 years ago.

There are four stages in the Rive Antoine distilling process. The first is the crushing station. It uses the big waterwheel and squishes the juice

The beach at Rive Antoine, Grenada.

from the cane stalks, then sluices the juice into the next stage—the boiling room. In this cavernous barn, five different tanks bubble the juice at different temperatures while birds fly in and out of the rafters adding their "seasoning" to the batch. It is then sluiced off again to the fermenting and storage room. After aging, it goes to the still to be boiled to its clear white state. Unfortunately, you can't sample it here due to strict Grenada laws regarding liquor taxes (the VAT). Only the customs man has the key. However, it's sold in just about any rum shop by the glass and in a few liquor stores in St. George's under the Rive Antoine label.

- PEARL'S AIRPORT
  This rock-strewn strip with cattle grazing on the side used to be the international airport. Noteworthy here are the burned-out remains of an Aeroflot and a Cubana Airways airplane. A reminder of what used to be.
- GRENVILLE
  A fishing and boat-building center with good waterfront/boat photo potential. Get out of the car and check it out. Then head south through the basket-weaving district. It seems like everyone is weaving. Stop and ask about the craft, maybe buy something, and ask to take a picture.
- GRAND ETANG
  It's been a long, hot day but you're almost home. Don't worry, you won't be hiking—just driving through Grenada's rain forest. Those hikes are for another day (see pages 165–166). There will be points along the snaking road from Grenville to St. George's with nice vistas of both the forest vegetation and St. George's in the distance.

GRENADA: KEY FACTS

LOCATION	12°N by 61°W 90 miles north of Trinidad 2200 miles southeast of New York
SIZE	133 square miles
HIGHEST POINT	Mt. St. Catherine (2756 ft.)
POPULATION	120,000
LANGUAGE	English
TIME	Atlantic Standard Time (one hour ahead of EST, no Daylight Savings Time)
ELECTRICITY	220/240 volts (50 cycles)
CURRENCY	The EC dollar ($2.64 EC = $1.00 U.S.)
DRIVING	On the left; valid driver's license okay
DOCUMENTS	Proof of nationality and ongoing ticket
BEER TO DRINK	Carib
RUM TO DRINK	Rive Antoine

GETTING THERE

The new Pt. Salines Airport is conveniently close to most tourist accommodations on the island. At this writing, there is no nonstop service to Grenada from the States but you can fly direct from the States on BWIA. Pan Am, American, Eastern, and Air Canada will route you there with connections. (The easiest way is to fly nonstops to Barbados or Trinidad, then hop a LIAT or Air Martinique puddle-jumper.) LIAT flies to Grenada from most islands in the West Indies chain. Taxis into the hotel area will cost between $25–30 EC (about $10–12 U.S.). Be prepared to be ambushed by cabbies when the customs door slides open. Do haggle—the competition is fierce and you should win. Don't let anyone grab your luggage until all financial matters are settled.

STAYING THERE

Almost all of the available accommodations can be found on the southwestern corner of the island from St. George's to the tip of L'Anse Aux Epines. I found prices higher than average here. Many of the accommodations are within walking distance of Grenada's most popular beach, Grand Anse. An exception is Betty Mascol's Plantation House in Morne Fendue, which has several interesting rooms for those who like being in the middle of nowhere (see page 129 for more information). There is a central toll-free Stateside number for the Grenada Reservations Clearing House, which handles most accommodations on the island: 800–CALLGND; in New York: (212) 840–6636; in Canada (800) 468–0023.

THE FLAMBOYANT (809) 444–4247
P.O. Box 214, St. George's, Grenada

The name alone is reason to stay here (it's actually the name of a brilliant flowering tree found in these parts). The Flamboyant is a complex of cottages on a hill with a terrific view of Grand Anse and St. George's. They are functional in design and come with one or two bedrooms, kitchen, living/dining room, and front porch to enjoy the view. The grounds are nicely landscaped and a footpath takes you on a five-minute walk to the beach. There is a supermarket about a mile down the road. Rates are NOT SO CHEAP for singles and doubles.

ST. ANNE'S GUEST HOUSE (809) 444–2727
Paddock, St. George's, Grenada, West Indies

Very popular with the seasoned international travel set (not to be confused with jet set), St. Anne's is the best deal on the island. Located in the hills of St. George's near the Botanical Gardens (it is *not* a ritzy neighborhood), there are fifteen clean and simple rooms, very good West Indian cuisine, and an interesting clientele. The beach is not close, there is no view, and assorted stray chickens and goats abound. Nevertheless, some people will only stay at St. Anne's so make your reservations early. Rates year round are DIRT CHEAP for singles and CHEAP for doubles (CP).

TWELVE DEGREES NORTH (809) 444–4580
P.O. Box 241, St. George's, Grenada, West Indies

A small, yet attractive complex of efficiency cottages on L'Anse Aux Epines whose main feature is a personal maid during the day. She arrives at eight A.M. cooks breakfast, launders, cleans, makes lunch, does light dusting, shops, makes drinks, prepares dinner, and is out the door at three P.M. (a tired woman). There is a private beach, pool, tennis court, ski boat, and Sunfish for your entertainment. This place has a high repeat business so reservations may be difficult. It's run by an ex-New Yorker. Rates are PRICEY for singles and doubles.

CALABASH (809)444–4234/4334
P.O. Box 382, St. George's, Grenada, West Indies

You can rent a suite with its own private pool for $350 U.S. a night. The twenty-one other suites are cheaper and have a maid who will serve you breakfast in your room. Located on 8 acres on L'Anse Aux Epines Beach, the design of the ten kitchenette-equipped cottages is best described as "contemporary." For the money you also get a lighted tennis court. Rates (excluding the pool suite) are VERY PRICEY for singles and WICKED PRICEY for doubles (MAP).

EATING THERE

There are not a lot of good restaurants on the island—yet. Some of the best are:

MAMMA'S, Old Lagoon Rd., Belmont (phone 2299)

Mamma's is the Whitman's Sampler of West Indian restaurants. There is no menu—just small plates that start arriving at breakneck speed and don't stop. As the plates start piling up, you're reminded of Lucy and Ethel trying to eat all the chocolates on the conveyor belt. There are all kinds of delights: callaloo soup, conch fritters, armadillo, manicou (possum), fish stew, breadfruit, tannia fritters, christophene, and on and on. The dishes change nightly. The decor is funky at best and the food is good, not great. The hand-painted shirts are a must buy. $$

LA BELLE CREOLE, Blue Horizon Cottage Hotel, Grand Anse (phone 4316)

Reputedly one of the best restaurants in Grenada, it features what could be called upscale West Indian food (local dishes with a Continental flourish). $$$

THE BOATYARD, Spice Island Marina (phone 4342)

The only reason I mention this haunt of the yachty set is that when I was there, Ted Kennedy sat at the next table. The food is dreadful but liquid dinners are the vogue among boaters anyway. $$

THE NUTMEG, on the Carenage, St. George's (phone 2539)

Their rum punch is fantastic, which may be the best reason to go here. The food is decent, the place clean, and the second floor offers pleasant views of the harbor. Their fish specials and lambi (conch) are recommended. A great spot for breakfast and lunch in town. $$$

BETTY MASCOL'S PLANTATION HOUSE, Morne Fendue (phone 9330)

A classic old plantation house located in the heart of Grenada's north country that's made of gray stone with wrought-iron grillwork and huge poinsettia plants in the circular driveway. A woman greets you and sends (orders) you to the washroom to freshen up. Then Betty Mascol—the proprietress—places an outstanding rum punch in your hand as she introduces herself and the other guests at the table. The cuisine is West Indian: callaloo soup, ox tail and tongue, seasoned rice, chicken, christophene, and a papaya custard and cream are usual fare, although she changes her menu when it suits her. The lunch is not cheap, but it's the only place in this town for sit-down. $$

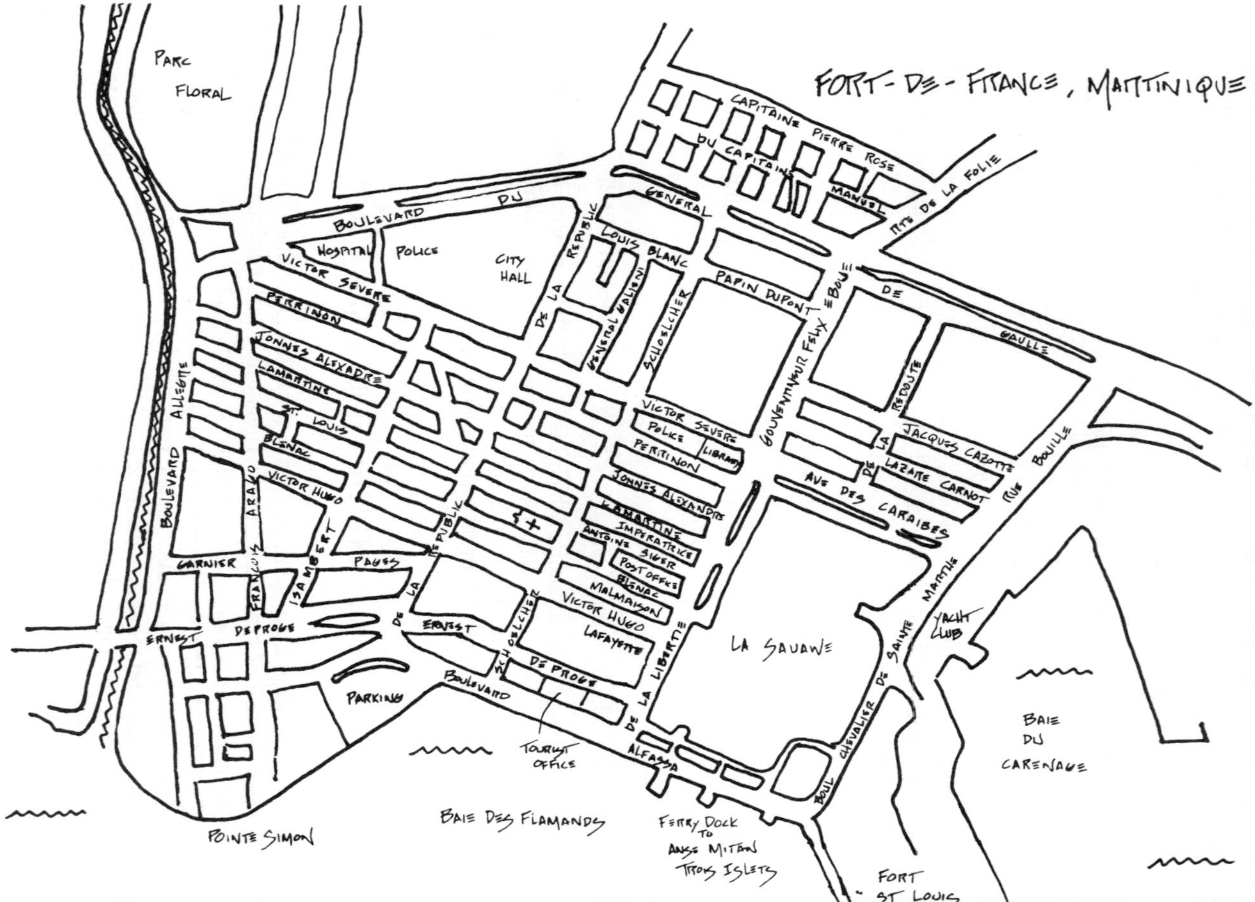
FORT-DE-FRANCE, MARTINIQUE
PARC FLORAL
CAPITAINE PIERRE ROSE
DU CAPITAINE
MANUEL
RTE DE LA FOLIE
GENERAL
BOULEVARD DU
HOSPITAL
POLICE
CITY HALL
DE LA REPUBLIC
LOUIS BLANC
PAPIN DUPONT
BOUL DE
GAULLE
VICTOR SEVERE
PERRINON
JONNES ALEXADRE
LAMARTINE
ST. LOUIS
BLENAC
VICTOR HUGO
GENERAL GALIENI
SCHOELCHER
GOUVERNEUR FELIX EBOUE
LA REDOUTE
JACQUES CAZOTTE
DE LAZARE CARNOT
AVE DES CARAIBES
RUE BOUILLE
VICTOR SEVERE
POLICE
LIBRARY
PERRINON
JONNES ALEXANDRE
LAMARTINE
IMPERATRICE
ANTOINE SIGER
POST OFFICE
BLENAC
MALMAISON
VICTOR HUGO
LAFAYETTE
BOULEVARD ALLEGRE
ARAGO
GARNIER
FRANCOIS
ISAMBERT
PAYES
DE LA REPUBLIC
ERNEST DEPROGE
DE ERNEST
SCHOELCHER
DE PROGE
BOULEVARD
PARKING
TOURIST OFFICE
DE LA LIBERTE
ALFASSA
LA SAVANE
MARTIN
DE SAINTE
BOUL CHEVALIER
YACHT CLUB
BAIE DU CARENAGE
POINTE SIMON
BAIE DES FLAMANDS
FERRY DOCK TO ANSE MITAN TROIS ISLETS
FORT ST LOUIS

CAFÉ SOCIETY "EN FRANÇAIS" IN MARTINIQUE

They are out there. A small but zealous group of Francophiles who can't get enough of Proust's mother tongue. Unfortunately for them, Paris is not the most inviting place to go in the winter. But there is a tempting option down here that combines the challenge of speaking French with a wonderfully warm climate.

Where is this stimulating, sophisticated tropical oasis? It's far away in the fashionable city of Fort-de-France, Martinique. As its name implies, it is the most French city in appearance, style, and attitude in these latitudes. Martinque is a full-fledged "department" of France, so everyone here is tuned into Paris, not Kingston. And this is a city that looks decidedly Mediterranean—many find it a smaller, more casual version of Nice. It features great restaurants, cafés, pâtisseries, lots of stores, and a central location that facilitates terrific day trips and perhaps overnights to all parts of the island. While the temperature is warm and sometimes hot in the daytime, the evenings can be a tropical dream (unless you become prey to some very nasty and aggressive mosquitoes—be sure to bring your favorite insect repellant).

The Martiniquaise may look like West Indians but they act like Frenchmen. You won't find the Liberation colors and many Rastas on the streets of Fort-de-Fance. You're more likely to see Yves Saint Laurent and Paris couture. This is definitely the most stylish and well-dressed city in

The waterfront of Fort-de-France.

the West Indies, if not the Caribbean. Expect a little—maybe a lot—of attitude and that French brusqueness.

The city of Fort-de-France (population 100,000) is located in the center of the island on the Baie des Flamands. It is surrounded by hills immediately to the north and east. Very large volcanic cones rise up in the distance to the north. Across the Baie is Anse Mitan and Trois Islets, the main tourist areas that are only a twenty-minute ferry ride from the downtown area. The focal point of the city itself is the Savane—a pretty, well-maintained 12.5-acre park with a statue of Empress Joséphine (Martinique's Jackie O.) as its centerpiece.

Fort-de-France is compact. Most activities are within walking distance from the Savane, which is where the recommended hotels are located. You will probably want to rent a car (also available right next to the Savane) for a few days so that you can venture out into the hinterland by day and return to civilization at night. This way you get the best of both worlds. Fort-de-France quiets down by around ten P.M., but there are cafés, salons de thé, and nightclubs that will take you into the night.

FORT-DE-FRANCE: KEY FACTS

LOCATION	14°N by 61°W 21 miles north of St. Lucia 26 miles south of Dominica 1965 miles southeast of New York
SIZE	417 square miles 50 miles long by 21 miles wide
HIGHEST POINT	Mt. Pelée (4656 ft.)
POPULATION	350,000 (Fort-de-France/100,000)
LANGUAGE	FRENCH!
TIME	Atlantic Standard Time (one hour ahead of EST, same as EDT)
ELECTRICITY	220 volts/50 cycles
CURRENCY	French franc (FF)
DRIVING	On the right; valid driver's license okay
DOCUMENTS	Passport or proof of nationality (w/photo) and ongoing ticket
BEER TO DRINK	Lorraine
RUM TO DRINK	La Mauny

GETTING THERE

Only two American carriers service Martinique. American flies three to four times a week nonstop from JFK. Eastern will fly direct via Miami. Air

Canada flies nonstop from Toronto and Montreal every Saturday. Air France occasionally flies out of Miami and has daily service to Paris. You can also connect from San Juan on Air France and American. Air Martinique and LIAT fly here from other Caribbean islands.

STAYING THERE

There is no shortage of beds on Martinique. But in downtown Fort-de-France, there are only three hotels worth mentioning—all located in a row right on the Savane. These are not deluxe hotels; the luxurious ones do not exist in the "centre-ville." (You'll have to go north a few miles to Schoelcher or across the Baie to Anse Mitan to find *them.*) However, the three in town are adequate, reasonably priced, and very convenient.

DANS LA CENTRE-VILLE

THE IMPÉRATRICE (011–596) 63–06–82
Place de la Savane, Fort-de-France 97200, Martinique, F.W.I.

Accorded three stars by the French government's official rating system (four is tops), the white-terraced Impératrice has probably seen better days but it does have lots of character. The lobby is tiny, you could easily walk by it. Adjoining it is a café and bar. The rooms have A/C and terraces overlooking the Savane—a good vantage point from which to watch the activity below while sipping some wine. Now the cons: make sure you check the beds before taking the room—some of the mattresses are as firm as Jello. Also note that the bathrooms don't have ceilings (they are just partitioned from the rest of the room), so be prepared to put your dignity aside. Finally, the telephones in the room are very troublesome. But the rooms are a decent size and the fresh-cut anthuriums are a nice touch.

Rates are NOT SO CHEAP for singles and doubles (CP).

LA MALMAISON (011–596) 63–90–85
Rue de la Liberté, Fort-de-France 97200, Martinique, F.W.I.

You have to look very carefully to find the entrance to this second-floor-lobby hotel. The rooms are grander than the Impératrice's, with firm four-poster beds, armoires, and floor-to-ceiling French windows. The best rooms are on the top floors and have terraces. All have A/C, phones, and TV (to improve your French). The hotel is rated two stars by the government. On the ground floor is a no-glitz café and pâtisserie that is a great spot to people-watch and count the number of languages you hear. While it caters mainly to non-Martiniquaise, it is a favorite hangout for the crews of various Navy boats that call on Fort-de-France.

Rates are NOT SO CHEAP for singles and doubles (EP).

THE LAFAYETTE (011–596) 73–80–50
5, rue de la Liberté, Fort-de-France 97200, Martinique, F.W.I.

This hotel doesn't have as much character as the Imperatice, although the beds are firmer. The rooms are fairly small and clean but nondescript, so try to get one with a terrace. Some of the upper-floor rooms have a great view of the harbor and Fort St. Louis (the standard old fortress that every West Indian city seems to have). Rated two stars by the French government, this is an acceptable alternative should the other two be full. The entrance to the hotel is on rue Victor Hugo.

Rates are NOT SO CHEAP for singles and doubles (EP).

DANS LES ENVIRONS

HOTEL CASINO LA BATELIÈRE (011–596) 61–49–49
Schoelcher 97200, Martinique, F.W.I.

Located a little over a mile from downtown (2.1 kms), this 215-room hotel bathed in white was *the* place to stay on Martinique and is trying to make a comeback with a much-needed facelift. The rooms are big, as is the price tag for staying here. But you'll find all the big-resort amenities like room service (for champagne cocktails) and a beauty salon (for the hair and nails). It has its own beach with the standard windsurfers, sailboats, and so on, as well as a large, comfy pool to lounge around in and see what everyone else is doing. For more exercise, there are six lighted tennis courts—the best on the island. There is a casino for those with loose change and a newly opened disco called the Palladium (Grace Jones did the honors on opening night).

Rates are VERY PRICEY to WICKED PRICEY for singles and doubles (CP).

EATING THERE

Here's where the fun begins and the pounds go on. There are no fewer than fifty major restaurants and cafés to choose from. This should keep you in café society for at least a week. Most feature what is termed "cuisine gastronomique"—French food with Creole, or West Indian flair. Be assured that as French food goes, it's delicious, especially at the establishments recommended. For a complete listing of all the eateries on the island, see the Tourist Board Office (63–79–60) on boulevard Alfassa (next to the Air France ticket office on the waterfront).

LES RESTAURANTS SUPÉRIEURS

L'ESCALIER (70–25–22)
19, rue de la Republic, Fort-de-France

A cosy and elegant restaurant with probably the best food in Fort-de-France. There is only one room and an enclosed balcony with maybe seven or eight tables. The decor of mustard-colored walls, wide-board floors, and crystal-adorned tables goes well with the waiters in black tie. A romantic must, as are les poissons et les viandes by Chef Crampont. $$$$

LA BIGUINE (71–40–07)
11, rue de la Folie, Fort-de-France

The ground floor offers a pub-style grillroom while upstairs is cuisine gastronomique. A popular place for non-Francophiles as the menus are in both French and English. Not to be missed is the shark cooked in tomato sauce and the iced local clams. $$$

LA GRANDÉ VOILE (70–29–29)
Boulevard Chevalier de Sainte Marthe, Fort-de-France

Located on the second floor of the Yacht Club with a very nice view of the ships on the Baie du Carenage, this is perhaps Fort-de-France's most famous restaurant. It's probably the most overpriced, too. Its fame makes it a big tourist gathering place, much like Pier 4 in Boston, Tavern on the Green in New York, Alioto's in San Francisco, and so on. $$$$$

LE BISTROT (71–33–06)
17, rue François Arago, Fort-de-France

A new and slickly designed restaurant that serves excellent traditional bistro fare and cuisine nouvelle. The decor is very art deco (and very downtown Manhattan), with white-and-black tile floors, marble tables, black wicker chairs, mirror wall panels, and half-moon smoked glass lamps. $$$

LE SECOND SOUFFLE (73–80–50)
27, rue Blenac, Fort-de-France

The true sign that you're not in the boonies is the presence of a strictly vegetarian restaurant. So Fort-de-France passes the test with the Second Souffle. Situated one flight up, this one-room, earth-toned establishment features a variety of dishes with a French and Creole accent, including a veggie souffle du jour. For single diners (for whom I have tremendous empathy!), there is a table of reading materials so you don't have to stare off into space (or, in my case, write on my ever-present notepad). $$

LA MARÉE (73-80–50)
44, boul. Allègre, Fort-de-France

This très Parisian à la Toulouse-Lautrec style café specializes in seafood dishes that change daily. Pink tablecloths, tiled floors, and lots of glass and mirrors make for a fun if not noisy atmosphere. The outside tables under the red awning are set among foliage and are a good spot for a glass of Beaujolais. $$

LE LAUREAT (70–63–29)
30, rue du Capitaine Manuel, Fort-de-France

An excellent choice for lunch, this simple Spanish-influenced restaurant offers a daily complete luncheon for FF 50–60. Note: Tuesday is paella day—not to be missed. You won't find many tourists here. Open only for breakfast and lunch. $$$

LA BAIE DES FLAMANDS (73–94–71)
Pointe Simon, Fort-de-France

This is a good, cheap, funky option for the budget-minded. Situated right on the harbor, it has nice views of boats, Fort St. Louis, and Anse Mitan across the Baie. It looks like a dump—plastic chairs and an eclectic decor—but the daily set menu features rather tasty Creole food for only FF 50. This is also a favorite hangout of the leathery looking yacht set. $$

CAFÉS AND SALONS DE THÉ

Are you just in the mood for a nice cold beer or a café au lait? If so, here are the best spots for refreshment and people watching.

- LA CARAFE—rue Lamartine, Fort-de-France
  A jazz club that's "au courant" and very local, what the Martiniquaise call "branche."
- TEA GARDEN—rue Victor Hugo, Fort-de-France
  Open very late with very pink decor.
- AUX DÉLICES BRETONNES—rue François Arago at Victor Hugo, Fort-de-France
  A dessert spot that's open late. Features crêpes.
- AU RENDEZVOUS—Avenue des Caraibes, Fort-de-France
  A great place opposite the Savane to watch the night strollers.
- LE NAUTILUS—69, rue Victor Hugo, Fort-de-France
  The balcony on the second floor overhangs rue Victor Hugo and is a very romantic place.
- MALMAISON—rue de la Liberté, Fort-de-France
  For daytime fun and pizza, this is worth checking out. It's opposite the Savane and the post office, so lots of foreigners stream in, including the crews from docked ships.
- LA FATTORIA—21, rue de la Liberté, Fort-de-France
  A more contemporary and slick day spot, with a more local crowd.
- JARDIN BRASILIA—Rond Point at Ave. Vietnam Heroic
  Slightly out of the way, but a new and very "branche," that is, trendy, place for fashionable Martiniquaise.
- PÂTISSERIES—everywhere
  Located on just about every corner downtown and the "de rigeur" way to grab a fast bite.

CLUBBING THERE

Unlike most of the West Indies, where nightlife consists of the hotel disco or the occasional skeletal steel band, Fort-de-France has a few exceptional clubs that feature both current French and English music. Note that like almost everything on a French island, most clubs are closed on Sundays. Check ahead of time. Among the best:

- HIPPO (71–74–60)
  24, boul. Allegre, Fort-de-France
  This is where you'll find a friendly mix of all types: Martiniquaise, French, black, and white.

■ MUST (60–31–06)
20, boul. Allegre, Fort-de-France
A popular club frequented primarily by white French people and tourists.

■ BAOBUB (no phone)
109, rue Ernest-Deproge, Fort-de-France
A large club acclaimed locally for its design. Very black.

■ PALLADIUM (61–49–49)
Hotel Casino Le Batelier, Schoelcher
Grace Jones (beloved by the French) opened the club. What more is there to say?

OTHER DIVERSIONS

BEACHES

Since you *are* in the Caribbean and surrounded by 80-degree crystal-clear water, why *not* swim? With a rental car you can enjoy the best "plages" that Martinique has to offer, including:

■ ANSE TRAUBAUD
Located on the southeastern corner of the island just past the beaches of Les Salines, it's actually part of the Baie des Anglais. This is Martinique's prettiest beach—a huge stretch of white sand (not common on this island) and large groves of shade trees. This is also a designated nude beach and the only beach you have to pay to access (FF 50 to a farmer who owns the land where you park). To get there heading north from Ste. Anne, take the dirt road that forks to the right off the main road about 1 km. north of the Club Med. Go about 5 kms. to the Baie des Anglais and head for the parked cars.

■ LES SALINES
The most famous of Martinique's white sand beaches, it's also more crowded and yet it's free, more easily accessed than Anse Traubaud, and is just minutes south of Ste. Anne.

■ LE DIAMANT
This long stretch of allegedly white sand (it looked gray to me) has good surf and stunning views of Diamant Rock. It's closer to Fort-de-France and near the photogenic village of Diamant. A swim here can be included with a pleasant "oooh-cruise" around the southwestern tip of the island. After a day at the beach, visit Anse D'Arlet, a very scenic

fishing village that inspired Gauguin and should inspire the photographer in you as well. The late-afternoon light is superb on the brightly painted fishing boats.

■ ANSE MITAN

If you don't want to deal with rental cars and driving, a frequently scheduled (usually on the hour) twenty-minute ferry ride will bring you right from the west end of the Savane to within a ten-minute walk to the beach. Now this is hardly a beach to write home about, but it's close, has sand, and is topless. Plan to return around sunset (generally around six P.M. year round) for a beautiful and wonderfully romantic ferry ride to Fort-de-France. On a 6:30 ferry, I experienced incredible sunset hues, the twinkle of the lights of Fort-de-France, and a full moon rising over the water. (Unfortunately for me, I was alone.)

TRIPS TO THE NORTH

■ ST. PIERRE

This city, once acclaimed as the Paris of the West Indies, was wiped out by the eruption of Mt. Pelée in 1902. The city never recovered its prominence, which was usurped by Fort-de-France. Of supreme interest to natural-disaster buffs is the Volcanological Museum. Here you'll find photos, melted glass, warped musical instruments from the once-grand city theater, and other lurid paraphernalia.

■ RAIN FOREST COASTAL WALK—Grand' Rivière Trail

For the fit, there is a six-hour, 15-mile walk through rain forest and volcanic topography that starts in Grand Rivière and ends in Prêcheur. Once there, you can haggle and hire a fishing boat to bring you back—or arrange to be picked up in Precheur. For more info, contact the Parc Naturel Régional de la Martinique (73–19–30), Caserne Bouille, rue Redoute de Matouba, Fort-de-France 97200.

ART GALLERIES

There are a number of art galleries in the city that are worth visiting. Of particular interest is the Galerie d'Art Pierre Subito at 51, rue Garnier Pages. There is some quality stuff here that isn't outrageously priced. Discuss Martiniquaise and Haitian art in French with Monsieur Subito; he is so impressed and pleased by Americans who can speak French that he may substantially drop the price. It's open weekdays from nine A.M. to noon and three to seven P.M. Saturday, he's open from nine A.M. to one P.M. On the same street at 30 rue Garnier Pages is the Galerie Singulière, featuring some excellent local pottery and sculpture.

THE **GOLF** OPTION

The first time I ever teed off, the ball careened to the right and over a hedge, narrowly missing a man who was on the adjacent putting green. That was just the beginning. After nine holes, I knew two things. One was that playing golf is a lot more difficult than I ever imagined. The second was why the golf course is a great place to make business deals: there's so much time between strokes.

In the colder latitudes, golf is a seasonal activity—but in the Caribbean the golf option is year round. Here are some magnificent courses, some very tough and demanding ones, too. If all you want to do is play golf, several islands offer enough courses to keep the fussiest connoiseurs happy. And if you just want to play once or twice, many other destinations have a golf option available.

There are four major golf destinations in the Caribbean. Two are in the Spanish-speaking territories of Puerto Rico and the Dominican Republic. In Puerto Rico are the deluxe sister hotels of Dorado Beach and Cerromar Beach—former Rock resorts now operated by Hyatt. Between them they offer four top-notch, eighteen-hole courses. Situated on a former grapefruit plantation, they include some of the best designed by Robert Trent Jones. In the Dominican Republic there is Casa de Campo, a 7000-acre resort on the southeast coast of the island that was developed by Gulf and Western and decorated in part by one of its occasional residents, Oscar de la Renta. It includes probably the most famous course in the Caribbean, Cajuiles I: this course will truly test your confidence and stamina. Designed by Pete Dye (and considered by many to be his best), it's one of the hardest courses anywhere, with seven holes bordering right on a ball-swallowing surf. Its sister course, Cajuiles II, is reputed to be even tougher.

The other two golf destinations are Jamaica and St. Croix. Both offer excellent courses and good variety. There are also several islands that, while not golf destinations, have some fine courses.

JAMAICA

There are numerous reasons to go to very beautiful and very dynamic Jamaica (see "The Hedonist Option," pages 77–84, and "The Cerebral Option," pages 114–120), but golf is one of the best. There are a total of nine courses on the island, three of which are marvelous and located within the Montego Bay area. This allows for a fair degree of variety, because each differs significantly from the next and they are all within a forty-five-minute drive from each other.

TRYALL GOLF AND BEACH CLUB
Sandy Bay Post Office, Hanover Parish, Jamaica
(809) 952–5110/5111
Stateside: P.O. Box 3492, Alexandria, VA 22302
(800) 336–4571/(703) 370–8377

This is Jamaica's best, and one of the finest courses in the Caribbean. Once a large sugar plantation, it is superbly maintained and a very scenic par 71. The course is a hilly 6407 yards long (Championship) and is full of water hazards. The third hole, a par 5, is virtually surrounded by water and hooks to the left. The fifth hole, another par 5, is almost a mirror of the third. The eleventh hole, again a par 5, is a narrower left hook that will definitely keep you on your toes. Signs of this property's former glory days are everywhere. The sixth tee, for example, has a 200-year-old waterwheel as its "set." Views of the turquoise Caribbean can be seen at every divit.

The club itself is very nice, and very expensive. The main building, reached through a U-shaped courtyard, is a symphony of pink, light blue, parquet, and chintz. It commands expansive views of the grounds and sea beyond. Your best bet is to stay in one of forty luxury, custom-made villas, each with its own pool and staff (including cook, chambermaid, laundress, and gardener). The three- and four-bedroom villas also come with a butler, bartender, and chambermaids.

Rates are OUTRAGEOUS (from $3000 U.S. per week for a two-bedroom villa to upward of $5000 U.S. per week for the four-bedroom units [EP]). If that's too much, The Tryall Guest House has forty-four rooms and rates that are RIDICULOUS per double room (MAP).

Down the road a few miles from Tryall is the Round Hill Hotel and Villas, P.O. Box 64, Montego Bay, Jamaica—(809) 952–5150 or (800) 237–3237 in the States. It is probably one of the top three luxury options in Jamaica (the other two being Tryall and Trident Villas and Hotel in very lush and very tony Port Antonio). This is where Paul McCartney, various Kennedys, and other notables hang their collective hats when in Jamaica. On rising ground, there are twenty-seven privately owned villas (really bungalows) painted white with green trim nestled among hibiscus and bougainvillea. Many of the villas have their own swimming pools and all are fully staffed with maids and gardener. There is also a building called Pineapple

House that has thirty-six rooms that are slightly cheaper. There is a private beach as well as three tennis courts when you're not on the links at Tryall.

Rates are RIDICULOUS for the Pineapple House for doubles (FAP) and RIDICULOUS to OUTRAGEOUS for the villas (FAP).

HALF MOON CLUB
P. O. Box 80, Montego Bay, Jamaica
(809) 953–2731
Stateside: 1320 S. Dixie Highway, Suite 1100, Coral Gables, FL 33146
(800) 237–3237/(305) 666–3566

WYNDHAM/ROSE HALL BEACH HOTEL AND COUNTRY CLUB
P.O. Box 999, Montego Bay, Jamaica
(809) 953–2650

About a half-hour away adjacent to each other on the other side of Montego Bay are Half Moon and Wyndham. While both are well maintained and par 72s, they are very different in design. The Half Moon course, designed by Robert Trent Jones, is a more traditional links layout and a power hitter's dream. It is long and narrow at 7143 yards (Championship) and consists mainly of straight fairways. There are four par-5 holes that will keep your drivers very busy. In contrast, the course at Wyndham, designed by Ian Smedley, is full of twists, hills, dips, and water hazards. Starting at an attractive English-colonial-style clubhouse containing the requisite dining room/bar and restaurant (and with the added flourish of a cannon in the courtyard), this tough course of 6598 yards (Championship) starts you off with a par-5 hook left that could wreck the rest of your game. The third hole, while short, requires you to place the ball over a pond about as big as this fairway and that ends only feet from the green. The eighth hole is considered the hardest; the left side is on the crashing surf and the green is a blind hole left of the tee. The back nine are full of obstacles and require real skill to finesse the ball to several blind greens. The fourteenth and fifteenth holes are twin toughies. The former features an uphill battle and a very tight right angle to the green. The latter has water hazards both fore and aft of the green, including a waterfall. (It was used in the 007 film *Live and Let Die.*) Wyndham has a great driving range, which slopes gently downhill and is set against the surf rolling in in the distance.

The Half Moon Club is considered a deluxe resort on Jamaica. While it's not top-drawer like Round Hill or Trident, it is just as expensive. It has a very good mile-long beach and thirteen tennis courts (four lighted) for serve-and-volley enthusiasts and four squash courts. Of the several types of accommodations the best value is the "superior" rooms. The food is excellent—naturally, you have to pay extra for it.

Rates for the Half Moon Club range from WICKED PRICEY for singles all the way to OUTRAGEOUS for singles and doubles (EP).

The Wyndham/Rose Hall Beach Hotel and Country Club is best appreciated for its setting and golf course. The hotel caters to the convention crowd and looks it. Its architecture is unattractive—big, pink (the company hallmark), rectangular buildings that aren't exactly in harmony with the natural setting. The parent company has another hotel in Kingston, which is much better suited to its surroundings and highly recommended.

Rates are less than the other deluxe resorts mentioned: they're still VERY PRICEY to WICKED PRICEY for singles and doubles (EP).

There are many other places to stay in the Mo Bay (as Montego Bay is called by Jamaicans) in every conceivable price range. Your best bet is to work with packages developed by Air Jamaica and other carriers—as you can realize significant discounts on both air fare and accommodations. Also, pay close attention to the location of the accommodations: if you want to be on the beach, you'll have to pay more. The actual city of Mo Bay is rather unattractive, hot, and busy, so be advised if your hotel is within city limits. My recommendation is to splurge and stay at Round Hill or Tryall—they're both wonderful and include all meals and other extras.

ST. CROIX

Golf and St. Croix share a notorious past. In 1972, on the island's best course, Fountain Valley, gunmen opened fire on the fairways, killing several golfers. No one here likes to talk about it, and most guidebooks don't mention it. At the time the attack was thought to be racially motivated, although there have been rumors that some developer was behind the killings to drive down land prices. Whatever the reason, the island fell into a ten-year tourism coma from which it is just now emerging. Probably in an attempt to overcome such bad PR and as a result of educational efforts, Cruzans (as residents refer to themselves) are the friendliest and most courteous residents of the U.S. Virgin Islands (in marked contrast to the people of St. Thomas—a most surly bunch).

There are two eighteen-hole courses on the island, Fountain Valley—now part of the Carambola Beach Resort and Golf Club, and the Buccaneer Golf Course. Both should provide enough challenge and interest to keep most golfers happy for a week. There is also a nine-holer at The Reef, (809) 773–9200.

CARAMBOLA BEACH RESORT AND GOLF CLUB
St. Croix, U.S. Virgin Islands 00820
(809) 778–3800
Stateside: (800) 223–7637/(800) 442–8198
(212) 586–4459

Fountain Valley was recently bought out by RockResorts to become part of the Carambola Beach Resort and Golf Club. It has undergone a major facelift and is one of the prettiest courses I have ever seen—situated in a verdant valley surrounded by mountains. In addition to the gorgeous surroundings, the course itself is beautifully landscaped with lots of ups and downs that aren't discernible on the scorecard. Designed by Robert Trent Jones about twenty years ago, it is 6827 yards long and a par 72. It has a driving range you'll need to use to warm up—the first four holes are tough. The first hole is a par 5 and a long hook right (526 yards for the Championship tee). The fourth hole also hooks right and is almost as long but is a par 4. The green on this hole sits between four traps right next to a pond—an overzealous shot will put your ball in the drink for good. The fifth hole, while very short, is surrounded by water and requires a well-placed shot or it's good-bye to another ball. The same holds true for the eighth hole. And water menaces the greens on the eleventh, twelfth (the designer's personal favorite), and fourteenth holes, too. The sixteenth hole is probably the most scenic, and potentially the most difficult. You

The 18th hole at Carambola, St. Croix.

must deal with a fairly significant dip in the fairway, a hook left, and a green that sits high on a knoll. The last two holes, while more straightforward, are both uphill battles. Fortunately, the "nineteenth" hole is wonderfully restful and refreshing, especially with a stiff cocktail in hand. The clubhouse is fronted by a long, high-ceilinged loggia that overlooks the first and last fairways and is a very pleasant place to relax (and collect the money you won on your game).

The golf course is only part of the Carambola Resort. The rest lies over the mountain in undoubtedly the most stunning setting on St. Croix. The white-sand beach curves west into mountains that drop into the sea. The design of the red-roofed resort is reminiscent of Malliouhana on Anguilla, except on a much larger scale. There are multilevels of an open-air pavilion with white walls, light blue beams, and terra-cotta tiles that follow the land's downhill sloping contours. The accommodations are off to the sides of the central building in several smaller units. Though tastefully decorated, they could be larger—one of my only complaints about the resort (the other is that it altered forever St. Croix' most beautiful beach).

For golfers, Carambola offers a package that is very tempting. Called the Carambola Golf Plan, for about $1500 U.S. per person (double occupancy) you get eight days/seven nights "deluxe sea-view" accommodations, all meals, unlimited green fees (which here run $32 U.S. daily) and use of a golf cart (usually $22 for eighteen holes), and such priceless perks as a Carambola golf visor and three golf balls. Of course, you also get to use the resort's other facilities, including four tennis courts and the fabulous beach.

THE BUCCANEER
P.O. Box 218, Christiansted, St. Croix, USVI 00820
(809) 773–2100

The Buccaneer's golf course is very different from Carambola's. Designed by Bob Joyce, it's more of a links-type layout emphasizing placement as opposed to power. It's also a short eighteen at 6117 yards (Championship) and a par 71. The hilliness and openness of the course allow for terrific views of the Caribbean and, on clear days, St. Thomas and St. John are visible to the north. The best vista is probably on the green of the third hole, which sits on top of a rounded grassy knob right on the water. Water hazards are not as much of a factor here, although they create problems on the sixth, tenth, thirteenth, and fifteenth holes.

The Buccaneer used to be the premier resort on the island before the advent of Carambola. This pink palace sits high atop a hill, a feudal fortress overlooking its territory. There are three beaches, eight tennis courts (the best tennis facility on the island and one of the best in the Caribbean), spa and health club, and even riding stables. The accommodations are quite good—the best are the beachfront rooms.

Rates are VERY PRICEY to RIDICULOUS for singles and doubles (EP).

SPRAT HALL PLANTATION
P.O. Box 695, Frederiksted, St. Croix, USVI 00840
(809) 772–0305
Stateside: (800) 843–3584

PINK FANCY
27 Prince St., Christiansted, St. Croix, USVI 00820
(809) 773–8460
Stateside: (800) 524–2045

There are two alternatives that are cheaper yet still special. Both have been around for at least 200 years. Sprat Hall has a very peaceful setting on rising ground north of Frederiksted, while the Pink Fancy offers an in-town location for those who like to shop till they drop.

Sprat Hall was built sometime in the late 1600s and is the only plantation that wasn't burned in the slave revolt of 1848. It has been in the same family for sixteen generations—quite a claim on an island that has been ruled by seven different powers. The Great House is very stately and painted white. The furnishings inside are almost all antiques—sixteen generations worth of collecting are evident throughout. The living and dining areas are an unusual yet comfortable combination of well-worn furniture and formal rooms. The four rooms upstairs are outstanding, with huge four-poster beds, painted wide-board floors, antiques, and a constant breeze. There are other rooms in an "annex" that are more standard hotel fare and forgettable (always beware of the word "annex" when making reservations). Sprat Hall does have its own beach club on pretty, uncrowded Rainbow Beach as well as stables adjacent to the Great House.

Rates are PRICEY for singles and doubles for the Great House rooms (EP). (P.S.: no smoking is allowed in the Great House.)

The Pink Fancy is a small, charming, and very picturesque white-and-pink-shuttered "inn" in an unsightly neighborhood. There are thirteen efficiency rooms rather attractively furnished in four buildings that are joined together by multilevel terraces and walkways. In the center courtyard is a small pool and bar where drinks are on the house for guests. It is within a short walk of all the shopping and dining possibilities in Christiansted, and there are many. Guests here may also want to hop the Virgin Islands Seaplane Shuttle, which is down the street, for a day trip to the beautiful beaches of St. John or Tortola, as there really isn't a beach close by. But the Pink Fancy's main assets are its charm and convenient location.

Rates are VERY PRICEY for singles and doubles (CP).

ELSEWHERE IN THE CARIBBEAN

BARBADOS

Barbados, the land of plenty to do (see "The Windsurfing Option," pages 185–193), is also the home of the Sandy Lane Golf Club, (809) 432–1405, a 6576-yard (Championship), par-72 eighteen-hole course. It is actually two courses, the front nine and the back nine, connected by a cartway. This is not one of the tougher courses around the Caribbean, but it will keep your game in good shape.

SANDY LANE HOTEL & GOLF CLUB
St. James, Barbados, W.I.
(809) 432–1311 Stateside: (516) 625–0333

While golf may be your *raison d'être* for staying at the Sandy Lane, there are other reasons why the Sandy Lane may appeal to you. This is particularly true if you're into luxury, as it is considered one of the Caribbean's poshest resorts (see "The Ten Most Luxurious Resorts in the Caribbean," page 24). Made of white coral stone and set on 380 acres in the chi-chi parish of St. James, this elegant hacienda-style hotel has one of the best and most elegant designs of any resort in the tropics. Its focal point is an extraordinary building where a double balustrade embraces an open-air terrace adjoining the Sandy Lane's stunning beach. What a place for a party! The beach is partially shaded by stately trees and beach umbrellas. There are chaises for comfort and white-jacketed waiters to ensure a steady flow of pina coladas. Waterskiing, windsurfing, sailing, and snorkeling are available at the beach for a fee.

Off the beach, the Sandy Lane has an excellent tennis program with five courts (two floodlit) and instruction. It also has a reputation for excellent service and a friendly staff. There are eighty-two double rooms, twenty-seven suites, and three penthouses—all furnished in a Romanesque white and gold motif and with balconies overlooking the Caribbean. The gardens are beautifully planted and maintained. Of course, this place isn't cheap!

Rates are OUTRAGEOUS for singles and doubles (MAP).

There are two nine-hole courses on the island. The Rockley Resort, (809) 427–5896, in Christchurch, has a very friendly staff and caters to execs from nearby Bridgetown. Heywoods, (809) 422–4900, in St. Peter, is popular with patrons of this resort and those staying on the northern section of the desirable west coast.

TOBAGO

You wouldn't think that one of the best courses in the Caribbean (and some say the world) would be tucked away on the relatively remote island of Tobago (see "The Privacy Option," pages 11–18), but it is. The Tobago Golf Club, (809) 639–8871, part of the Mt. Irvine Bay Hotel, is a Caribbean links-style course that is 6793 yards long (Championship) and a par 72. It's a tough course all around, despite the lulling landscape of gentle rolling hills and turquoise Caribbean. Especially infamous on these coconut-tree-studded fairways is the ninth hole, with a hook right past a water hazard, and a green that seems the size of a postage stamp. There's no relief until the "nineteenth" hole, as number eighteen will torment you with a sharp hook left, a water hazard, and a humiliating finish by the golf club.

GOLF LISTINGS FOR OTHER ISLANDS

- ST. THOMAS
  Mahogany Run (18 holes—Tom and George Fazio)
  Mahogany Run Golf and Tennis Resort, P.O. Box 1224, St. Thomas, USVI 00801
  (809) 775–5650
- ST. KITTS
  Royal St. Kitts Hotel and Casino (18 holes—Robert Trent Jones)
  P.O. Box 406, Frigate Bay, St. Kitts, W.I.
  (809) 465–8651
- MARTINIQUE
  Golf de l'Impératrice Josephine (18 holes—Robert Trent Jones)
  Trois-Islets, Martinique, F.W.I.
  (011–596) 76–32–81
- GUADELOUPE
  Golf International de St. François (18 holes—Robert Trent Jones)
  Golf International, St. François, Guadeloupe, F.W.I.
  (011–596) 84–41–47

WHAT ABOUT TENNIS?

Just about every large hotel in the Caribbean has a tennis court or access to one. However, if you're a tennis freak, be warned that the smaller islands will have fewer courts or limited access. So be sure to ask when making reservations at some remote destination.

These resorts will particularly appeal to tennis buffs:

- BUCCANEER—St. Croix
  Eight Laykold courts—two lit for night play.
- SANDY LANE—Barbados
  Eight hard courts—four lit.
- CURTAIN BLUFF—Antigua
  Three hard and one clay court—tournament in the spring.
- HALF MOON CLUB—Jamaica
  Thirteen Laykold courts—four lit. Also, video-taped lessons and four squash courts.
- CERROMAR/DORADO BEACH—Puerto Rico
  Twenty-one Laykold courts between the two resorts—two lit. (Cerromar has the most courts.)
- CASA DEL CAMPO—Dominican Republic
  Thirteen clay courts—six lit and four lit Laykold courts.
- PALMAS DEL MAR—Puerto Rico
  Fifteen hard courts and five Har-Tru—four lit. Tennis packages available.

THE **OUTDOORS** OPTION

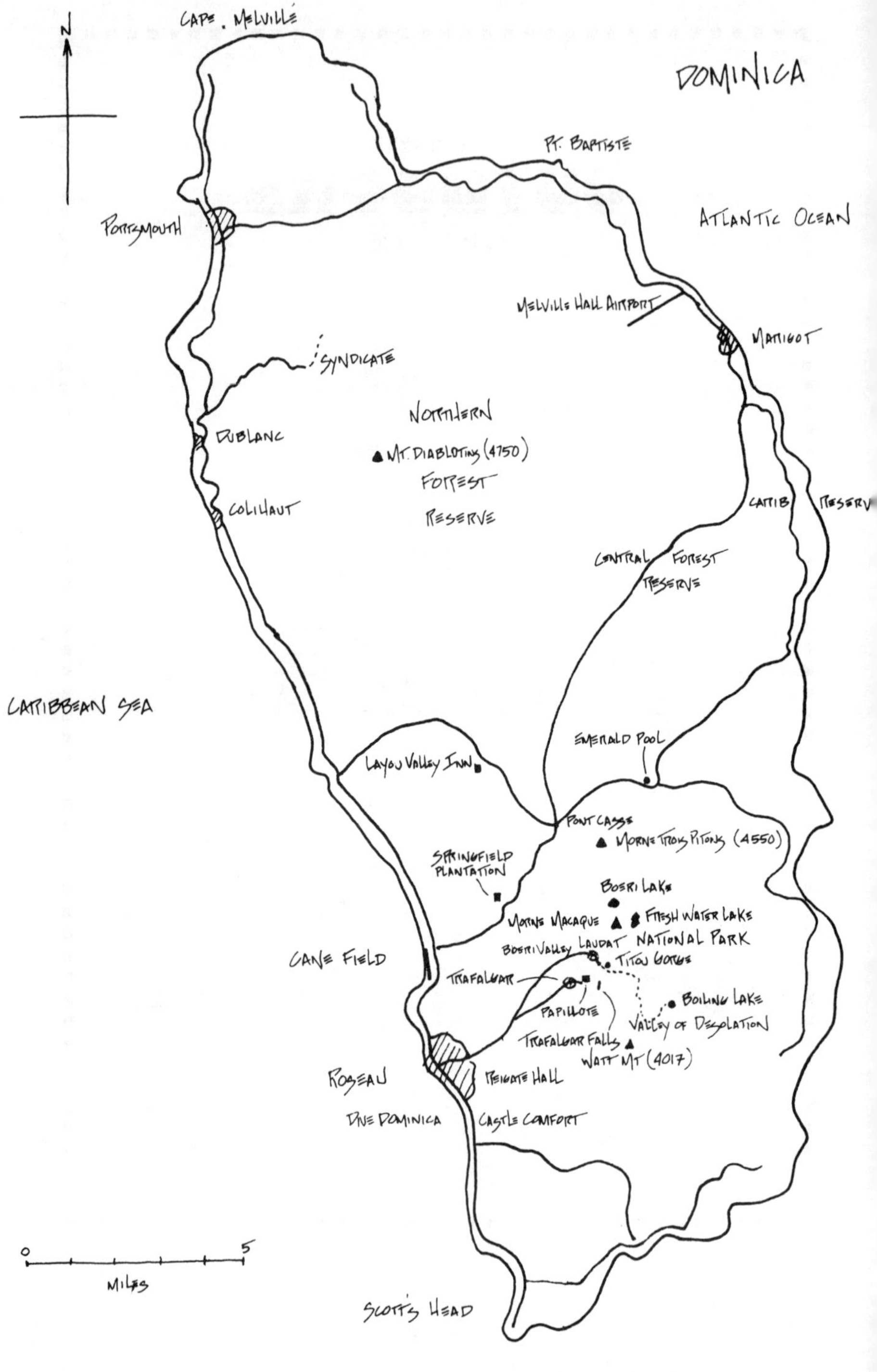
N
CAPE MELVILLE
DOMINICA
PT. BAPTISTE
PORTSMOUTH
ATLANTIC OCEAN
MELVILLE HALL AIRPORT
MARIGOT
SYNDICATE
NORTHERN
MT. DIABLOTINS (4750)
FOREST
RESERVE
DUBLANC
COLIHAUT
CARIB RESERV
CENTRAL FOREST RESERVE
CARIBBEAN SEA
EMERALD POOL
LAYOU VALLEY INN
PONT CASSE
MORNE TROIS PITONS (4550)
SPRINGFIELD PLANTATION
BOERI LAKE
MORNE MACAQUE
FRESH WATER LAKE
BOERI VALLEY
LAUDAT
NATIONAL PARK
CANE FIELD
TITOU GORGE
TRAFALGAR
BOILING LAKE
PAPILLOTE
VALLEY OF DESOLATION
TRAFALGAR FALLS
WATT MT (4017)
ROSEAU
REIGATE HALL
DIVE DOMINICA
CASTLE COMFORT
0
5
MILES
SCOTT'S HEAD

EXPERIENCING THE POWER OF NATURE IN DOMINICA

Everyone here has a hurricane story. On August 29, 1979, a megatempest named David pummeled the southern half of Dominica for six hours. Winds up to 200 MPH left 40 dead, 60,000 homeless (that's 80% of the island's population), and removed up to 6 feet of topsoil in places. It was total devastation. But a visitor today would be hard pressed to see any signs of this.

That's because everything grows in Dominica. This is the lushest, most verdant island in the Caribbean. When David wiped out square miles of trees, Nature grew back at a rate that is hard to believe. We're talking full-grown vegetation, not saplings or upstarts. And what Nature couldn't restore, aid from the U.S., France, Venezuela, and other countries did. Housing has been replaced; roads have been rebuilt and are in better shape than before the hurricane.

Much of Dominica is rain forest. Its volcanic, mountainous topography traps moisture from the trades and converts it into 200–300 inches of rain a year. The color green takes on a whole new meaning here, with so many shades it puts even Ireland, the Emerald Isle, to shame. Dominica does have beaches, but they are of the black-sand variety (which, when it sticks to your leg, looks like dirt), and the prettiest are on the windward side with dangerous undertows. Dominica's unique beauty is in its mountains. This is where the rain forest thrives, where waterfalls and thermal springs abound, and where the walking and hiking are the best in the Caribbean.

Dominica is also quintessentially West Indian. Roseau, the capital, is not pretty, cute, or charming. Rather, it's hot, crowded, and fairly dirty—with architecture that is more functional than attractive. This is part of its special character—that is decidedly Caribbean. Roseau is very market-oriented, geared to satisfying the needs of islanders, not tourists. This is particularly refreshing, as is the friendliness and openness of the people, especially in the small mountain villages.

There is a place to stay on Dominica called Papillote that combines the island's natural beauty with the warmth and friendliness of the locals. Sitting suspensefully under the perfect cone of a dormant volcano known as Morne Macaque, it is truly integrated into its surroundings; from the hot-water springs running through the compound and the botanic gardens, to

**Trafalgar Falls,
Dominica.**

the peacock and peahen and the ever-present residents of Trafalgar (the village down the street). The five rooms (five more are planned) are simple and comfortable. Time here is meant to be spent outdoors. There is a pavilion where meals are served and where it's very pleasant to sit anytime. Two hot-water pools constructed by a Canadian artist out of indigenous stone feature sculptures of magical serpents that spew hot mineral water, which feels good after a day of hiking. Papillote is ideally located next to a vast wilderness area.

It's also right next to Trafalgar Falls, a series of *huge,* narrow, vertical waterfalls. A twenty-minute walk and fairly easy rock scramble will bring you to the base of "Papa" falls ("Mama" is the medium-sized one on the right and "Baby" is the smallest one way up on the left). Once there, you can carefully slip into a pool of cool mountain water and work your way against a slight current to the left of the falls. Here you'll see mustard-orange-colored rocks, which is where the hot springs flow into the stream. Maneuver your way under this water—it's not too hot—and enjoy a natural Jacuzzi. The further up you climb, the hotter it gets. Basking in hot water, while tons of water gush and tumble by 5 feet away, you'll think you've found a bit of heaven. Before you leave Papillote, you will be asked a dozen times if you want a guide to the falls. You don't need one. There's a trail leading up to it, though you will come to the stream and think you've come to a dead end. You haven't—just ford the stream and follow the rocks and "path" to the left. You'll have to climb a little, but it's not very hard. Unfortunately, the beauty of the falls and their proximity to Roseau and Papillote's restaurant have made this destination popular with tourists. Best advice: go early in the morning or late afternoon (light's best then, too) for more solitude and privacy.

But Trafalgar Falls is really just kid's stuff. The real hiking is further up the valley. Here you'll find Caribbean wilderness in the National Park. There are several hikes that should appeal to serious walkers.

The best is the hike through the Valley of Desolation to the Boiling Lake. It sounds Dante-esque and indeed there are places along the way that seem right out of the *Inferno.* But there are also intensely green mountains, lush rain forest, and fabulous vistas that take you through several climate zones in one day. If you only have one hike in you, do this one. It's very strenuous, as you'll be walking for at least six hours at a fast pace. But if you are in decent shape, you'll never forget the hike. There aren't cliff faces to climb—just several mountains to go up and down. The trail is very narrow and can get very muddy, so the going can be tricky. You won't recognize your Reeboks after this one—hiking boots are better.

You will need a guide for this hike. While the trail can be followed, it's just too long and isolated to risk getting disoriented. A guide will cost about $80–100 EC (about $35–40 U.S.) and can be found in the villages of

Laudat and Trafalgar. Two guides who are particularly good are Irvin and Robbie from Trafalgar—they can be reached by contacting Papillote.

You must bring water. I recommend at least a 1.5-liter plastic container of Carib Spring water (available at any store in Dominica) per person. Also take along some high-energy food to replace the thousands of calories (wishful thinking) that it feels like you're burning.

The starting point for the Boiling Lake hike is the village of Laudat. This is about as high and as close to the park as you can go. From here you will have stunning views of Trafalgar all the way down to Roseau and the sea. It's also a very scenic twist-and-shout drive up to this pretty little spot. (You will want to be driven as you'll need your strength for the walk ahead.) When you start your hike from Laudat, follow the signs to Roxy's (a guest house) and take the left before you start going down the hill. This road will lead you to a fork: take a left and follow the concrete aqueduct. This is part of Trafalgar's hydroelectric project. If you do walk on the aqueduct, be prepared to play balance beam. Some sections are about 10 feet above ground and you're walking on about an 8-inch-wide piece of concrete. You then come upon a pipe bridge with planks and cables to make it passable. A left after the crossing will bring you to a concrete wall and the start of the Titou Gorge (more on that later). Just before the gorge there is a trail of stone steps going up to the right. This is the trailhead to the Boiling Lake. Once you leave the gorge it's a pretty steady uphill climb, not terribly difficult but very steady. At this point, the trail is in good shape and fairly clear—some roots and rocks to step over but it's obvious it has been well trodden. After about forty-five minutes of this you will arrive at what is called the "Breakfast River" by the locals (so named because it's a good place to rest and fuel up. The hard stuff begins on the other side). Here is where you will hear the mountain siffleur—one of the most exotic-sounding birds I've ever heard—which only lives at these elevations. A tiny, brown bird that's almost impossible to see, it trills a beautiful, symphonic five-note song that ends on a high note.

After the pit stop, get ready to climb stairs for the next hour. It's a very steep trek up a narrow trail to the summit. This ascent/descent is the real kicker in the hike—and you have to do it twice! You will arrive at the top dripping with sweat, only to almost suffer hypothermia from the stiff breeze. The view is reminiscent of vistas afforded by the Rockies or Cascades, except that the ocean in the distance is that incredible light blue. Now you're ready to go down into the Valley of Desolation (sounds like a Joni Mitchell song). The descent is slow, muddy, and slippery. But when you look up, the view is unbelievable: a massive green sweep of valley with high, jagged mountain peaks and thermal vents sending wisps of steam into the air. Off in the distance and hidden by a peak, the Boiling Lake's giant caldron bubbles away, sending a huge plume of white vapor several hundred feet into the air. The wonderfully fragrant smell of sulphur is everywhere. Talk about sensory overload!

Once in the valley, you'll go along a rocky river bed with a hot-water stream flowing down it. The color of the water will change as you get further into the valley (due to the mineral content and how it has stained the rock below). You'll see water that's black, gray, white, green, and light blue. Where it's open to the sky and elements, it's cool and breezy. But at the bottom, the vegetation is dense and it's hot and humid.

When you finally reach the Boiling Lake, after a few more ups, downs, and a traverse across a rock-strewn slope, you will feel very remote and isolated. You *are.* The lake itself is situated in a crater. It's fairly large, about 100 yards across, and very round. It is the second largest of its type in the world (the biggest is in New Zealand). The water is a milky white and it *is* boiling. The rising steam combines with the cool ocean breeze to create a warm mist that envelops you. This is a good spot to rest and eat lunch, but don't get *too* comfortable because it's an equally long and arduous hike back.

To cool off once you've begun the return journey, take a dip in the first stream you encounter. There are several warm-water pools upstream of light blue warm water (from the mix of minerals) with little waterfalls and other touches of Nature's kitsch that make swimming very pleasant. Since it's unlikely you'll encounter anyone, whip off your clothes for a fun skinny-dip and splash around.

The Valley of Desolation, with the flume of the Boiling Lake in the center.

You return to Laudat the same way as you came. But the different perspective allows you to see things you might have missed before. One thing you will definitely notice is the fatigue in your legs, so take it slow and hit the brakes. The descent down the muddy trails can be treacherous. But you have the Titou Gorge to look forward to—a wonderful reward for a hard day's work.

The Titou Gorge lies at the base of the trail and would actually go unnoticed if you didn't know it was there. It's a part of the hydroelectric project based in Trafalgar. When you reach the concrete aqueduct, take a right, and in about a hundred feet, you'll see a pool of water that leads into a gorge. Jump into the cool-but-oh-so-very-refreshing-after-walking-and-sweating-for-seven-hours water and swim into the gorge. What you see at water level is truly beautiful. Deep-light-blue or medium-green water—depending on the amount of sunlight—rock walls that rise up at least 50 feet creating natural halls and chambers, and a roaring waterfall at the gorge's end. Unfortunately, this fall is hard to photograph unless you have a waterproof camera or play waterpolo and are used to propelling yourself upright with your feet. The waterfall does create a strong current, particularly as you get closer to it. Once you enter the waterfall room, it's fun to walk up the right side of it about 5 feet—it's not at all difficult—and sit behind the fall in the space Mother Nature has thoughtfully provided. The vantage point here is one of total hydration—memorize it for the next time you're stuck on a rush-hour subway in mid-July. Swimming out is anticlimactic, so I turned around and made a second approach—it's pretty difficult to get tired of this one.

From the Titou Gorge, it's only about fifteen to twenty minutes to Laudat. Upon arrival, head down to Roxy's Mountain Lodge for an ice-cold Carib or lime squeeze. The bar is very nice, recently redone with a lot of hand-hewn wood and a super stereo system. Roxy's is also a cheap, clean guest house for those on a tight budget.

There are several other hikes in the National Park as well as in the National Forest Reserve in the north of the island. In the National Park, an easier walk than the Boiling Lake journey will take you along a road to the Fresh Water Lake, a pristine and very tranquil lake that is swimmable. For those who would rather let their fingers do the driving, a four-wheel-drive vehicle like a Suzuki Samarai (which are available all over the Caribbean) can take you right up to the lake. A little more remote is the Boeri Lake, where the water is very heavy and hard to swim in. The Boeri Valley, downstream from the lake, is still an essentially uninhabited wilderness area that's ideal for orienteering and bushwacking. Before attempting it, check with the Forestry Department to make sure you won't get lost for days or run into some Dreads living in the woods. Fortunately, there is nothing poisonous on Dominica to worry about. The Boeri Valley can be reached by a forty-five-minute climb from the Midland Falls to Stinking Hole. This window to the Boeri Valley is located about halfway between the junction of the Laudat-Trafalgar road and Laudat.

To the north of the island, the National Reserve offers hiking up Dominica's highest mountain, Mt. Diablotins. The trailhead begins in Syndicate, which is also the place to view the imperial parrot (also known as the Sisserou) and the red-necked parrot. There aren't many of these species left and the ones that are are protected and under study by a team of British birders. They have built a viewing platform over a gorge that should only be scaled by those with no fear of heights (it's precariously perched on a tree that leans several hundred feet over the gorge). The best time to see the birds is early in the morning or around dusk. They are loud squawkers so you will be able to tell them from other large birds. To reach the viewing area and the trail to Mt. Diablotins, take the west coast road north from Roseau. Go 4 miles north of the town of Colihaut. As you pass a school on your left and then, just around a bend, a white house with red trim, take a sharp right and follow this road until you come to a grapefruit orchard on your right (there will be a small house on the left). Turn left on the dirt road and right again at the next junction. You are now on a banana plantation road that borders the National Forest Reserve. Go for

AUGUST 29, 1979

No one has a better hurricane story than Anne Gray Jean-Baptiste, the owner (along with husband Cuthbert) of Papillote—a very simple and naturalist accommodation surrounded by waterfalls in the mountains east of the island's capital, Roseau. When hurricane David struck, Anne was two weeks away from opening a supper club—one of four buildings on her property. Reports indicated a severe hurricane was expected to make landfall on Martinique or St. Lucia, Dominica's neighbors to the south. But around nine A.M., the winds began to roar. As Anne and Cuthbert were listening to the latest update, the roof blew off. Within an hour, all four buildings were leveled. The Jean-Baptistes found themselves lying in 2 inches of water under a crawl space created by the collapsed roof and the only remaining upright wall. To make matters worse, dozens of helpless baby bats from the eaves were screaming and drowning in the water. Because Papillote is located high up at the rear of a box canyon, all during the hurricane the winds bouncing off the canyon walls created periodic tornados that literally tore up the valley. Each time one hit, the cracks in the remaining wall grew wider and longer. Had one more come up the canyon, the wall would have collapsed and it would have been curtains. During those six hours, Anne thought she would never survive. Even after such a harrowing experience—and the destruction of every last bit of Papillote—Anne found the experience absolutely thrilling. Being subject to the sheer force of nature is one of the risks—rewards—of living in an environment such as this.

about one-half mile until you pass a tiny concrete bridge and a little banana shed on the left just beyond the bridge. Park your car before the bridge and well out of the way of the occasional banana trucks that pass by. Walk past the shed for about 300 yards until the road bends to the left. At this point you will notice a trail on the right through banana trees. This will lead you to the parrot viewpoint and the trail to Mt. Diablotins. When you're on this trail for about ten minutes, you will notice a trail on the right—this is the trailhead to Mt. Diablotins. Continuing straight for another ten minutes, you will reach the gorge and the small platform for the parrots. There are plans to build an information center about the birds and the Forest Reserve, which will make finding your way around a lot easier. It is both a good idea and island etiquette to contact the Forestry Department before venturing inland. They also have detailed maps and information that are very helpful. They can be reached by phoning 2731 or stopping by at their headquarters in the Roseau Botanical Gardens.

DOMINICA: KEY FACTS

LOCATION	15°N by 61°W 30 miles south of Guadeloupe 26 miles north of Martinique 1924 miles southeast of New York
SIZE	29 miles long by 16 miles wide 300 square miles
HIGHEST POINT	Mt. Diablotins (4750 ft.)
POPULATION	75,000
LANGUAGE	English
TIME	Atlantic Standard Time (one hour ahead of EST, same as EDT)
ELECTRICITY	220–240 volts/50 cycles
CURRENCY	EC dollar ($2.64 EC = $1.00 U.S.)
DRIVING	On the left; local permit needed with your valid license—$12 U.S.
DOCUMENTS	Passport or proof of nationality and ongoing ticket
BEER TO DRINK	Carib
RUM TO DRINK	The "house" overproof

GETTING THERE

Dominica is not the easiest place to reach. Neither of the two airports can accommodate jets, so you will have to make connections from San Juan (American or Eastern to Air Caribe International), St. Thomas and St. Croix (LIAT), Antigua (Pan Am, American, or Eastern to LIAT), Guadeloupe (American, Eastern, or Air Canada to LIAT and Air Guadeloupe), Martinique (American, Eastern, or Air Canada to LIAT and Air Martinique), or Barbados (LIAT). It is possible to leave New York at eight A.M. and be in Dominica by 5:15 P.M. the same day.

STAYING THERE

There is a surprisingly good choice of accommodations for such a relatively undeveloped island. Most are located near or around Roseau, the capital. Among the best:

PAPILLOTE (809) 448–2287
P.O. Box 67, Roseau, Dominica, West Indies

This is my first choice for those who want to be one with nature. The place is geared to the outdoors, located high up in the mountains where the air is noticeably cooler. There are botanical gardens, two outdoor hot-water pools, and Trafalgar Falls is a twenty-minute walk away. The sound of rushing water is everywhere. The rooms are simple but comfortable and there are plans for a visiting masseur/masseuse to knead out those aches and pains the hot pools don't. Staying here will give you a good chance to meet Dominicans from all walks of life, as the Jean-Baptistes are very popular among the locals. It is very convenient to the best hikes on the island and Anne Gray Jean-Baptiste is very enthusiastic about showing plant lovers around. She is also completing plans to steer the day-tourist traffic away from the hotel so they won't interfere with guests' privacy. Since you are miles away from the nearest restaurant, the MAP plan makes sense. While the food is good West Indian fare, the menu could be more imaginative and varied (just how many times can you have lime delight for dessert?).

Rates are CHEAP for singles and NOT SO CHEAP for doubles (add $20 U.S. for MAP).

SPRINGFIELD PLANTATION (809) 448–1401
P.O. Box 41, Roseau, Dominica, West Indies

Built in the English colonial style, this hotel features big rooms and antique furnishings. There are nine guest rooms and cottages available to guests and a river-fed pool. It is located near the entrance to the National Park at an elevation of 1200 feet so there are great views and cool, mountain air.

Rates are NOT SO CHEAP for singles and doubles (CP). MAP (recommended) is $15 U.S. extra per person.

LAYOU VALLEY INN (809) 449–6203
P.O. Box 196, Roseau, Dominica, West Indies

Not to be confused with the Layou River Hotel (not recommended), this is a great place for those who want total solitude or for "stay-at-home" types. It is really in the middle of the island and, consequently, in the middle of nowhere. It's very clean with ten tastefully furnished rooms that have private baths. Sitting 1500 feet up on the backbone of Dominica, there are great views. The management has a naturalist philosophy akin to Papillote's, and will help you with hikes, walks, and so on.

Popular with French tourists, rates are CHEAP for singles and NOT SO CHEAP for doubles (CP). Add $20 U.S. for MAP (recommended).

REIGATE HALL HOTEL (809) 448–4031
Reigate, Dominica, West Indies

The ne-plus-ultra of Dominican hotels, this resort overlooking Roseau features pool, sauna, tennis court, games room, and gymnasium along with deluxe accommodations. Owned and operated by a flamboyant type who drives a Rolls-Royce around Dominica, this is my choice for those who must be pampered (or as much as you can be pampered on Dominica—Dominicans are not accustomed to servicing others). Rates are NOT SO CHEAP to PRICEY for singles and doubles (CP only).

POINT BAPTISTE (809) 445–7322
c/o Ms. Geraldine Edwards, Calibishi, Dominica, West Indies

A restored big house and cottage on the north coast just east of Calibishi, it has both a black- and white-sand beach. This is an ideal alternative for a large group that wants to be on the sea and still have access to the mountains. You will need a car. The price for the house is negotiable.

EATING THERE

In most cases, you will elect to use the MAP plan at your hotel or guest house. But you may want a night out on Roseau, so here are your best choices:

LA ROBE CREOLE (phone 2896)

Reputed to be the best restaurant on the island, it is certainly the most famous. It's small and attractive, made of gray stone and heavy wood.

Their specialties include shrimp in coconut with garlic butter, various kebabs, and an extensive snack menu. The food is quite good, although when I was there, the menu was limited and service was slow. $$$

THE ORCHID (phone 3051)

A typical West Indian restaurant in both appearance and cuisine, it's basically a large room with a high, sloped, squared-off ceiling replete with swirling fans. The menu changes daily but always features a local fish and meat dish. $$

GUIYAVE (phone 2930)

Another West Indian restaurant that serves a mean rum punch and is popular with the business-lunch set. $$

GRENADA SPLASHDOWN

High up in the lush mountains of Grenada is a series of obscure waterfalls called the Seven Sisters. You can hear them for most of your hike through the dense and moist vegetation. Once you arrive, the sight of the lower falls is stunning. So is the feeling of falling 30 feet over one into a pool of cold water. Sound like your kind of fun? Read on.

The Seven Sisters are located in the Grand Etang National Reserve—a series of peaks and valleys in the middle of Grenada. The hike itself will take about three hours round trip including the time spent getting up the nerve to jump over the falls. It is recommended that you hire a guide as the trailhead and trail up to the falls is hard to find and follow. Henry Tours (phone 5313/$20 U.S. per person) will take you up and provide the encouragement to jump ("There's no other way down!").

It will take about an hour to reach the base of the falls. The walk down isn't difficult but it *is* muddy. It will take you first through cultivated terrain of banana, cinnamon, and nutmeg trees, then down narrow ledge trails into denser vegetation thick with swinging vines for the Tarzan in you. You may see a monkey or two, although I didn't. The real fun begins when you reach the base of the falls. You strip down to your bathing suit, or to nothing if you prefer to be truly one with nature, and commence on a really steep climb up the banks of the falls—bushwacking to the top of the Sisters. Admiring the view, you then realize that the way down is going to be wild—like going down the rapids without a raft.

The water is almost cold but perfect after the hot sticky climb. The rocks on the bottom can be slippery, but if you take them slowly you'll have no problem. Most of the gorges are calm so you won't be swept over the falls. In one spot, there is a very narrow sluice where you have to maneuver rather gingerly above the rushing water to get through. The grand finale is the highest fall—a 30-foot-plus sheer drop into a churning pool below. Quarry jumpers will think this is a piece of cake. But those of you who have any degree of acrophobia will have your doubts. The best way to approach it is to go quickly. The longer you wait the harder it is to make the big leap. It will be necessary to jump in a sitting position as the pool is not very deep. Be sure to push out so that you will clear the ledge. The feeling of falling into the unknown is unforgettable. Hitting the water feels like you've been through the "hot oven" in a major way. The pain lasts only a moment and the final waterfall will seem like kid's stuff—only about 12 feet or so. You'll jump this one with pleasure.

GETTING THERE/STAYING THERE

See "The Cerebral Option," pages 127–129.

WALKING AND HIKING IN ST. LUCIA

For those who love the outdoors but think camping is slumming it with nature, there is St. Lucia. This island, wonderfully diversified in vegetation, climate, and geography, has excellent and accessible trails that are both beautiful and invigorating. Yet it also has all the creature comforts necessary for an eighties' lifestyle.

These amenities are concentrated in St. Lucia's northwest corner. Here you'll find the rather unattractive city of Castries, which does have most services you might want. A majority of the island's hotels are located north of the city, on a calm and attractive, though certainly not pristine, stretch of beach. There are also accommodations and resorts around the island's two other major towns, Soufrière and Vieux Fort. These have much more West Indian character and ambience than Castries as well as far more dramatic natural settings.

But the beauty of St. Lucia lies in the countryside, the villages, and its rugged coast and interior. Here the feeling is reminiscent of a more tranquil, unhurried era—a marked contrast to the bustle of Castries. Yet it's all easily accessible by car. And the visuals are truly phenomenal. The lush green expanse of the banana plantations, a cricket game on the east coast, the incredible Pitons, and the center's tropical wilds can all be experienced in one day.

While you can see a lot of St. Lucia by car, it doesn't allow you to get very close. Fortunately, there is a well-developed system of walks and hikes that enable you to do so. These access the entire island and can be reached by rental car, tours, and in a few instances by public minibus.

THE TEN BEST BEACHES IN THE CARIBBEAN

This was a tough list to whittle down to ten, but here goes:

- **SANDY CAY—Carriacou**
  A deserted island with palm trees, white sand, and great snorkeling reefs about a mile off of Hillsborough.
- **MAUNDAYS BAY—Anguilla**
  The prettiest beach on this island of cream-colored beaches.
- **CATTLEWASH—Barbados**
  Pink sand, boulders, surf, and no hotels on the eastern shore.
- **NEGRIL BEACH—Jamaica**
  An experience in itself.
- **TRUNK BAY—St. John**
  Despite the crowds, this is the prettiest beach in the Virgins.
- **ENGLISHMAN'S BAY—Tobago**
  A remote beach tucked away on Tobago's north shore.
- **ANSE COLUMBIER—St. Bart's**
  A Rockefeller built his house here, so you know it must be the best beach on the island.
- **BREWER'S BAY—Tortola**
  Just north of beautiful Cane Garden Bay, it's just as pretty but not as developed.
- **LONG BEACH—St. Martin**
  Home of La Samanna, it stretches off into the setting sun.
- **PRINCESS MARGARET BEACH—Bequia**
  A wonderful little beach on this wonderful little island with lots of bobbing boats to watch.

N
ST. LUCIA
PIGEON ISLAND
CAP ESTATES
GROS ISLET
RODNEY BAY
ST LUCIAN
EAST WINDS INN
EDGEWATER BEACH HOTEL
VIGIE AIRPORT
CASTRIES
MARIGOT BAY RESORT
PITON FLORE WALK
PITON FLORE
ATLANTIC OCEAN
BARRE de L'ISLE WALK
DENNERY
CARIBBEAN SEA
MT. GIMMIE
ANSE CHASTENET
SOUFRIERE
HUMMINGBIRD
FOND ST JACQUES RD
MAHAUT RD.
MICOUD
PETIT PITON
DASHEENE
RAIN FOREST WALK
GROS PITON
CHOISEUL
HEWANORRA AIRPORT
CLOUD'S NEST COTTAGES
MARIA ISLANDS
VIEUX FORT
CAPE MOULE A' CHIQUE
0
5
MILES

THE WALKS

For those who desire minimal exertion, there are three short walks cooled by breezes or the shade of the forest. Any one is within an hour's drive from wherever you are on St. Lucia, making the entire expedition a half-day affair.

In the north, above Gros Islet, there is Pigeon Island, connected to the mainland by a causeway. This is a very short walk with several marked trails around the point. There is a small entrance fee for the National Trust, which maintains the park. The "island" will appeal to history buffs. It was first used as a pirate's ambush point, then weathered hundreds of years of English/French squabbles, and also served as a whaling station and the retreat of an obscure English actress, Josset Agnes Huchinson. The visitor's center will have all the gory details. Pigeon Island will also appeal to bird watchers who, if they happen to be around after a heavy storm, may see a large number of exotic sea birds blown in from all over the Caribbean.

The second walk is right on the main west-to-east coast highway, between Castries and Dennery. It is a *very* short loop called Barre de L'Isle (about a quarter-mile long), and not very interesting. Another trail branches off by the picnic table gazebo to Mt. LaCombe. It's a pleasant 2.5-mile round-trip walk that takes you along a ridge with some nice north/south views. This trail is also noteworthy because it is by far the easiest forest walk to access.

The third walk is an excursion to the Maria Islands off the southeast corner of St. Lucia. This is the only place in the world where the Maria Islands ground lizard and the Couresse snake can be found. Tours can be arranged through the Maria Islands Interpretive Center (24094) on the highway near the Hewanorra Airport. While you're in that area, there is a very short walk offering fantastic views of the southern end of the island on Cape Moule à Chique. To get there, drive through Vieux Fort up to the lighthouse and walk behind it until you reach a cliff and the vista point.

THE LONG WALKS

Muddy shoes are the vogue here. These walks are for those who really enjoy getting into more remote areas. Each walk will average between three and four hours exclusive of travel time. Plan to carry some refreshment, wear cool clothes you can sweat in, and bring your camera.

In the north, there is a good walk around the northern tip of St. Lucia from Cap Estates. There is a path and the Cariblue Hotel (28551) occasionally organizes tours for anyone interested. The headlands to the east can also be interesting, but in almost all cases you'll need a four-wheel-drive vehicle to get close enough. If you do try this, don't leave any valuables in your jeep and don't carry any—practically all hikes are in uninhabited areas.

Moving further south to the north-central part of the island, there is an excellent walk at Forestiére called Piton Flore. As it is located within the Forest Reserve, you *must* get permission from the Forestry Department in Castries before embarking (phone 23231). This trail, actually a loop in and out of Forestiere, used to be highly traveled but Hurricane Allan changed that, toppling trees to make passage much more difficult. Begin by parking your car at the Forestiere school (just after the town—you can't miss it). The vehicle is safer there. Directly in front on your left will be a Caribbean pine plantation. Keep going down the road and you'll pass several houses on the right. Eventually you'll come to a flatter area where you will see a house on the left that is actually a Forestry Department rest house. There may or may not be someone living there (an employee in the field). Next to the house you'll see and hear a pumping station. If you take the steps down to the pumping station, you'll find yourself on a trail that will lead you around a loop and bring you back to the top of the stairs. It will take about two hours to walk the loop, providing some superb glimpses into the rain-forest habitat. An alternative to walking the entire loop is to keep walking straight past the pumping station (do not go down the steps). This will put you on the lower part of the loop. Follow this path for about a half-hour until you come upon an old concrete block house on the right. Behind this, there are steps that lead up to Piton Flore and a TV tower. The walk up, about a half-hour, is quite strenuous. The top, though, offers some terrific views of the east and northern coasts. From the top of Piton Flore back to your car, the walk will take you a little over an hour.

The main rain-forest walk is down in the south-central part of the island. It links the Fond St. Jacques road, west of Soufrière, with the Mahaut road, which is east of Micoud. The trail actually traverses the entire island and originally was the major trading route for the Arawak and Carib Indians. It is clear all the way across and makes for a very interesting walk, about three and a half hours from end to end. By law you must go with a guide from the Forestry Department, although exceptions can be made if you work it out in advance.

The trail, called the Rain Forest Walk, can be accessed on either end. The most enjoyable way to get to the Walk is from the west, as the drive down from Castries takes you through Anse La Raye, Canaries, and Soufrière and is wonderfully scenic. From the road you can see the Pitons, which have become the symbol of St. Lucia—two twin volcanic cones that rise almost 3000 feet out of the water. When you get to Soufrière, don't be surprised if lots of young men insist on guiding you to the volcano. Just be firm. Your best bet is to ask an older man or woman how to get to the Still restaurant. On the way to the Still, you'll pass the cathedral on your left. Follow the road until you arrive at the restaurant, which features local cuisine and is a great spot for lunch. You'll also pass the sulphur springs—actually part of a dormant volcano whose waters were cherished by Louis XVI. Today it's billed as the world's only drive-in volcano. You can tell you're near it when you start smelling rotten eggs. If you've seen a sulphur spring at a national park out West, don't bother with this one. If you do choose to go, be prepared to be surrounded by Rastas selling trinkets or their services as trail guides for the springs (which is a rip-off—you don't need one). Don't let their official trail-guide T-shirts fool you, and don't leave anything valuable in the car.

Continue inland on the road past the Still restaurant—on the entire stretch there are only two turnoffs. At the first fork, after about two miles, bear right (or down) and keep driving for approximately another two miles where the road forks again. Bear left (or uphill)—this will bring you to the village of Fond St. Jacques. You'll know you're there when you see an enormous church. Keep on going—the road will get progressively worse—but you can make it with the average rental car. Soon you'll come upon some fabulous views, on the left-hand side, of Mt. Gimmie—St. Lucia's highest peak. And the scenery gets better and better with each mile. Eventually you come to a lily farm that grows a very exotic, pinkish-red flower called anthurium. Ahead the road turns into a track but you can still drive it. Go straight down until you come across a clearing with a sign that reads "Designated a Nature Reserve." There will also be a small hut on the right. This is the forest reserve house and may or may not be occupied. Park the car in the clearing ahead of you. The road continues, but it's not motorable: it now becomes a trail and is the beginning of the Rain Forest Walk. If you walk this trail for about three and a half hours you'll eventually come to the road on the other side (there is another clearing and "designated" sign). That's the end of the walk. It's probably a good idea to walk to the halfway point and then turn back, as the entire end-to-end round trip takes seven hours—and you still have the long drive back. (You'll know you're halfway when you come across the Quilesse Forest Reserve, a clearing with rest houses.) The exception is if you've arranged for someone to meet you on the other side, or if you switch car keys with another party midway to rendezvous back at the hotel—great if you can do it.

If you aren't up for the very scenic but tedious drive down the west coast, the hike can be accessed much faster via the east coast highway. Just before you get to Micoud there is a turnoff for Mahaut. Keep driving straight inland on what looks like the main road. Pay no attention to several turnoffs along the way. Keep on driving until you can drive no further and happen upon the "designated" sign.

On this hike you will see both natural and planted forestation. The planted part, consisting mostly of blue mahoe (a tree hibiscus from Jamaica) and Honduras mahogany (from Belize), is basically a thin strip about 100 feet on either side of the trail. You can tell it's planted because there is usually only one species per grouping. Beyond that is indigenous vegetation. There are scattered strips of natural forestation along the trail, recognized by the denser and varied species. Benches are provided so you can rest and enjoy the flora. The Forest Department strongly urges that you not leave the trail as you can get very lost very easily.

Quilesse, especially at dawn or dusk, is a bird watcher's heaven. If you're quiet and patient you may see from thirty to forty species of birds. With luck you may see the rare green St. Lucian parrot—recognized by its loud squawking. There are only about 200 left in the world. Fortunately, they are on the rebound, having doubled their population in the last ten years—thanks to the diligence and dedication of the Forestry Department. There are also three varieties of hummingbirds: the very small Antillean crested hummingbird (the male has a gold crest), the green-throated Carib and the purple-throated Carib. You'll also see the broad-winged hawk—a smaller predator—and various species of doves. And if you're really lucky, you may see the St. Lucia oriole, readily distinguishable by its black-and-orange markings. The small bird with a bright reddish tail that flits out to snag moths and flying insects is the stolid fly catcher. Other species flying about include Adelaid's warbler, the Antillean peewee, and the mangrove cuckoo. And there are more that your guide or a good birding book will point out. You might, if you're fortunate, see a boa constrictor. You needn't worry about the deadly pit viper—that's found in the island's drier scrub areas and is nocturnal.

There are three tour companies that will take you down the east coast route for this walk, each on different days of the week. You can book one at any hotel through St. Lucia Representative Services, also known as St. Lucia Reps (22332), Barnard Travel (22214), and Carib Touring Ltd. (22689). It will cost about $70 EC (about $26 U.S.), which includes everything and spares you the hassle of driving and parking. Depending on road conditions, some may drop you off in Mahaut and drive around to meet you at Fond St. Jacques. You'll have to check with the tour operators when you book.

Much has been written advising tourists not to swim in the fresh water on St. Lucia due to a microsopic parasite called the blood fluke that burrows into your skin and does horrific things to your body. This should be clarified. Researchers from the Rockefeller Institute came to the island in the seventies and virtually wiped out the problem. You *can* swim in the fast-moving mountain streams, if you can find water deep enough, because the snails, which host the parasite through several stages of its development, cannot exist there. It's only in the slow-flowing flat coastal rivers, which you really wouldn't think of getting near anyway, where the possibility of exposure may exist.

THE HIKES

The last two vigorous walks—I'll call them hikes—are exhilarating climbs that on completion will give you a real sense of accomplishment. The first is the grueling hike up Mt. Gimmie, the tallest mountain on the island at 3117 feet. It can be arranged through the Forestry Department if several days' notice is given. This is a very long and hard hike—it will take you four hours just to reach the base, and an hour after that. It should only be attempted in the dry season (the summit is surrounded by clouds otherwise).

The other hike, not under the jurisdiction of the Forestry Department, is up Petit Piton—the smaller of the two dramatic volcanic cones (2438 vertical feet) on the west coast. This is a very strenuous yet rewarding hike, about two and a half hours up and one and a half hours down. You won't need rope, but don't try it if you suffer from any degree of acrophobia. It is exactly like climbing stairs for two and a half hours. There are two particularly difficult stretches where you must use hand-holds and walk across a rock ledge. It's not dangerous, just scary. Get up there before it gets hot (around noon) and carry water. Bring very little else except maybe your camera, and wear *good* walking shoes. To find the trail, go to the police station in Soufrière and ask them to help you find a guide who will take you up. It will cost you about $80 EC (about $30 U.S.) whether you are one or ten. It's a hard climb for the guide as well, so the charge is reasonable. Negotiate before you start, and tell him that the negotiated fee is for the group, not per person—repeat it at least two or three times.

It should be stressed that all hikes into the Forest Reserve must be sanctioned by the Forestry Department for several reasons. The first is that the Department lacks the manpower and facilities for large-scale manhunts and it's very easy to get lost in the dense vegetation. Second, there is illicit marijuana farming going on and woe to the hiker or tourist who stumbles upon that. The Forestry Department, by the way, is not too keen on camping—you'll have to clear that with them well in advance. To reach the Forestry Department, call 23231, or (809) 452–3231 overseas, or write: Forestry Department, Ministry of Agriculture, Castries, St. Lucia, West Indies. Allow two weeks for the letter to reach its destination.

ST. LUCIA: KEY FACTS

LOCATION	14°N by 61°W 21 miles south of Martinique 26 miles north of St. Vincent 2020 miles southeast of New York
SIZE	238 square miles 27 miles long by 14 miles wide
HIGHEST POINT	Mt. Gimmie (3117 ft.)
POPULATION	140,000
LANGUAGE	English
TIME	Atlantic Standard Time year round (one hour ahead of EST)
ELECTRICITY	220/50 cycles AC
CURRENCY	The EC dollar ($2.64 EC = $1.00 U.S.)
DRIVING	On the left; local permit needed with valid driver's license.
DOCUMENTS	Proof of nationality and ongoing ticket
BEER TO DRINK	Heineken
RUM TO DRINK	Admiral Rodney

GETTING THERE

There are two airports on St. Lucia. The most convenient is Vigie, which is within walking distance of downtown Castries and very close to most hotels on the island (between $5–10 U.S. in a taxi). Only small planes fly here: LIAT, Air Martinique, St. Lucia Airways, Caribbean Airways, and other interisland airlines. The international flights and jets land at the newer Hewanorra Airport, about an hour from Castries by car or taxi (about $35 U.S.). Winlink flies a shuttle to Vigie from Hewanorra and it doesn't cost much more than a cab. BWIA, Pan Am, Eastern, and Air Canada fly direct to Hewanorra.

STAYING THERE

St. Lucia has a well-developed tourist trade with plenty of accommodations. Unfortunately, hotels are often expensive—you might do best to book a package deal. There are a few good, cheap places to stay that make up in character what they lack in grace. The most convenient and liveliest part of the island is in the northeast quadrant. Staying here will allow you to explore and still have somewhere to drink and dance at night. The other areas, Marigot Bay, Soufrière, and Vieux Fort, are for those who want a sense of isolation.

THE NORTHWEST QUADRANT

This is the strip of beach that starts at Vigie, just north of Castries, and goes all the way to the northernmost point. Recommended are:

- THE EDGEWATER BEACH HOTEL (809) 452–4872
  P.O. Box 1114, Castries, St. Lucia, West Indies

At first glance, the small motel-like one-story structures look as if they have seen better days. On closer inspection, they *definitely* look like they've seen better days. In fact, it is just this side of rundown. But it's clean, right on Choc Beach, and cheap for St. Lucia. It also has a wonderfully warm ambience, thanks to the manageress, Jane Tipson. You won't feel like a tourist here; lots of locals hang out at the bar, most of them eating pizzas—the best on the island.

Rates are CHEAP for singles and doubles.

- EAST WINDS INN (809) 452–8212
  La Brelotte Bay, Castries, St. Lucia, West Indies

This smallish "cottage-motif" hotel is on a very nice beach with excellent snorkeling and pretty parrots in cages. The accommodations are clean and not very fancy.

Rates are NOT SO CHEAP for singles and PRICEY for doubles.

- THE ST. LUCIAN (809) 452–8351
  Reduit Beach, Castries, St. Lucia, West Indies

If you want all the amenities of a large resort hotel, this is the place for you. A former Holiday Inn, the accommodations are standard in decor and size. The beach is very good and the free watersports add variety and value. It's also within walking distance of Rodney Bay (see "The Dinghy Crawl," page 110).

Rates are PRICEY for singles and VERY PRICEY for doubles.

- THE SUNDALE (809) 452–4120, Choc. Castries, St. Lucia, West Indies

- THE MODERN INN (809) 452–4001, Castries, St. Lucia, West Indies

Two modest guest houses near the beach that are clean, inexpensive alternatives for the budget-minded.

Rates are DIRT CHEAP for singles and CHEAP for doubles.

■ MARIGOT BAY RESORT (809) 453–4357
P.O. Box 101, Castries, St. Lucia, West Indies

Acclaimed as one of the most beautiful harbors in the Caribbean, it probably was before all the development and boats. While the accommodations are pleasant—cottages are tastefully appointed and spacious—I would feel claustrophobic staying here for a week. The exception is for those participating in the diving program, which will get you out and about. This is also the headquarters of the Moorings yacht charters to the Grenadines. Staying here for a night or two is usually part of the charter package. There is no decent beach—a major drawback. The resort includes the Hurricane Hole Hotel—the best value—and the Marigot Bay Inn and Hillside Villas (complete with an escalator-type tram). A water taxi (free of charge to all) connects the two complexes on either side of the tiny bay.

Rates are PRICEY for singles and VERY PRICEY for doubles at the Hurricane Hole and the Inn, VERY PRICEY for singles and doubles at the Hillside Villas.

■ ANSE CHASTENET (809) 454–7354/7355
P.O. Box 216, Soufrière, St. Lucia, West Indies

With a truly stunning view of the Pitons, this is a perfect location for the Piton/Mt. Gimmie hikes and the rain-forest walk. It is also a great spot for scuba, one of the best on St. Lucia. And if you're wondering where to go to have an illicit affair, this is the place. There are all types of accommodations, from deluxe suites with plunge pools to white octagonal villas with verandas. Furnishings are simple but tasteful. Unfortunately, the beach is of the volcanic variety (the sand is gray, not white) and there are over a hundred steps to get down to it. Don't forget anything in your room or you'll be exhausted by the time you return.

Rates are PRICEY to VERY PRICEY for singles and doubles.

■ DASHEENE (809) 454–7444
Soufrière, St. Lucia, West Indies

If the combination of dramatic views, dramatic architecture, and dramatic prices appeals to you, then Dasheene will, too. Perched 1000 feet above sea level and Lord Glenconner's Jalousie plantation, the resort sits between the two Pitons and affords great views of both. The contemporary design allows the western wall, including the bedroom, to be completely open to the terrace and the view. There is no beach, but the resort has privileges at Anse Chastenet. A spring-fed pool (from the volcano) is available for those who want to take the waters.

Rates are OUTRAGEOUS for both singles and doubles (MAP).

THE SOUTH

■ THE CLOUD'S NEST BEACH COTTAGES (809) 454–6226
P.O. Box 233, Vieux-Fort, St. Lucia, West Indies

These funky cottages are on the beach and just steps away from the Club Med (formerly the Halcyon Days Hotel). The beach is nice and the cottages are very close to Hewanorra Airport and the Maria Islands, but don't expect much more. There are also cheaper rooms at the hotel in Vieux-Fort—a monument to kitsch, including an extraordinary collection of British royal memorabilia. Somehow the tackiness and wild color-scheme of the place work to lend it charm and character. At least stop in for a drink and check it out—there are nice views of the harbor and town from the porch.

Rates are CHEAP for the beach cottages and hotel.

EATING THERE

There are several good restaurants that offer West Indian food as well as other cuisines. Try one of the following:

■ THE GREEN PARROT (23399/23167/23168)

Located on the Morne Fortune overlooking Castries, this is a St. Lucia institution. The menu features West Indian dishes served with a Louisiana Creole flair—try the Stuffed Pussy (in season). No joke, it's on the menu. There are floorshows on Wednesdays (Princess Tina bellydances) and Saturdays (Chef Harry entertains with limbo). $$$$ Be sure to visit the Curio Shop when at the Green Parrot. Chef Harry also operates ANSE JAMBETTE, which is highly recommended for lunch. It is located near Canaries and accessed by land or sea (the latter is more fun and available in an all-inclusive lunch excursion). $$

■ SAN ANTOINE (24660)

Also on the Morne Fortune, people go here as much for the ambience as for the food. Built on the ruins of an old hotel destroyed by fire in the sixties, it has been beautifully restored. The views of Castries are spectacular. $$$$

■ HUMMINGBIRD (47232)

The restaurant of choice in Soufrière, it features West Indian cuisine and a dining terrace overlooking the Pitons. If you're lucky, they may have some fresh-water mountain crayfish that are delicious. $$$

■ CHAK CHAK (46260)

Cheap and good West Indian food in Vieux-Fort—a local favorite. $

■ THE LIME (no phone number available) and EAGLE'S INN (20650)

The former is a brand-new, attractive restaurant on Rodney Bay and the latter serves West Indian cuisine at the inlet to Rodney Bay. Both have good local food at reasonable prices. $$

OTHER ACTIVITIES

■ TRIM'S RIDING STABLES, Cas-en-Bas (28273)

A laid-back stable where you can ride any way you want, located on the northern tip of the island in Cap Estates.

■ CHOISEL SCENIC DRIVE

A beautiful drive through the lovely seaside village of Choisel and continuing along the coast to La Pointe Beach on the island's southwest corner. Also in the area is the "St. Lucian Stonehenge," man-made stone formations that have been tentatively carbon-dated at 2500 BC. Contact the Tourist Board (24094) for more info. The locally published book *Historic Sights* is available at most bookshops and tourist stands for $10 U.S. and provides history buffs with more detailed information.

CAMPING IN COMFORT ON ST. JOHN

At some point the Rockefellers probably owned a chunk of all this country's most beautiful property, including the land that became Yellowstone National Park in Wyoming and Acadia National Park in Maine. Can you imagine being that wealthy? Fortunately, they gave the land to the public for everyone's enjoyment.

In another instance of philanthropy, Laurence Rockefeller bought 5000 acres of land in 1954 on St. John in the U.S. Virgin Islands and donated it to the National Park Service. The following year President Eisenhower signed the bill creating the Virgin Islands National Park. Today, it is nearly twice as large, having grown to 9500 acres.

St. John is by far and away the nicest U.S. territory in the Caribbean. Because of the National Park, it is also one of the more unspoiled and handsome islands. There are trails to hike, ruins of the old Annaberg sugar plantation to explore and a variety of programs conducted by the park rangers to enjoy. And there are two campgrounds, one private (Maho Bay) and one public (Cinnamon Bay), that allow you to live close to nature without the usual sacrifices in comfort and amenities inherent in camping.

Probably the best reason to come to St. John is to swim, and snorkel. It has some of the most beautiful beaches anywhere as well as some of the last undeveloped stretches of sand in the Caribbean. There are also terrific reefs for snorkeling within an easy swim of the shore. As with any beautiful and scenic public property, there will also be many people. While the more renowned beaches (such as Hawksnest, Trunk Bay, and Cinnamon Bay) are gorgeous, they can be crowded—at least crowded enough to ruin your idea of a deserted Caribbean beach. But there are smaller and little-known beaches where you still might fulfill your fantasy. These include Jumby Bay, Salomon, and Honeymoon Beach on the north coast, and Salt Pond Beach on the south coast. Finding these beaches may take a little patience and determination (see map), but they're worth the effort. The reefs are easily accessed and not hard to find (you can see them in the water from the beach). There is a marked underwater trail at Trunk Bay, but this is exciting only for beginners. Fantastic snorkeling can be found off Hawksnest Beach, Cinnamon Bay, and Waterlemon Cay in Leinster Bay.

About two-thirds of St. John is national park. The remainder is primarily composed of the towns of Cruz Bay and Coral Bay, on the western and eastern ends of the island respectively. To explore the whole island, it's a good idea to rent a jeep: some of the less-traveled roads are very rough. If you don't want to deal with driving, especially on the left, most of your shopping, dining, and bar needs can be met in Cruz Bay—the biggest town on the island, a brief hitchhike or taxi ride from the campgrounds. When in town, don't miss Meada for a fine West Indian lunch, and the Backyard or the Purple Line for a couple of cold ones.

Just north of town is the Caneel Bay resort, one of three Rockresorts in the Virgin Islands. The veranda bar is a very pleasant spot for a cocktail. The beach at Caneel is not very large or private and is restricted to use by hotel guests (although the latter rule never stopped me before). But do stop by for a drink.

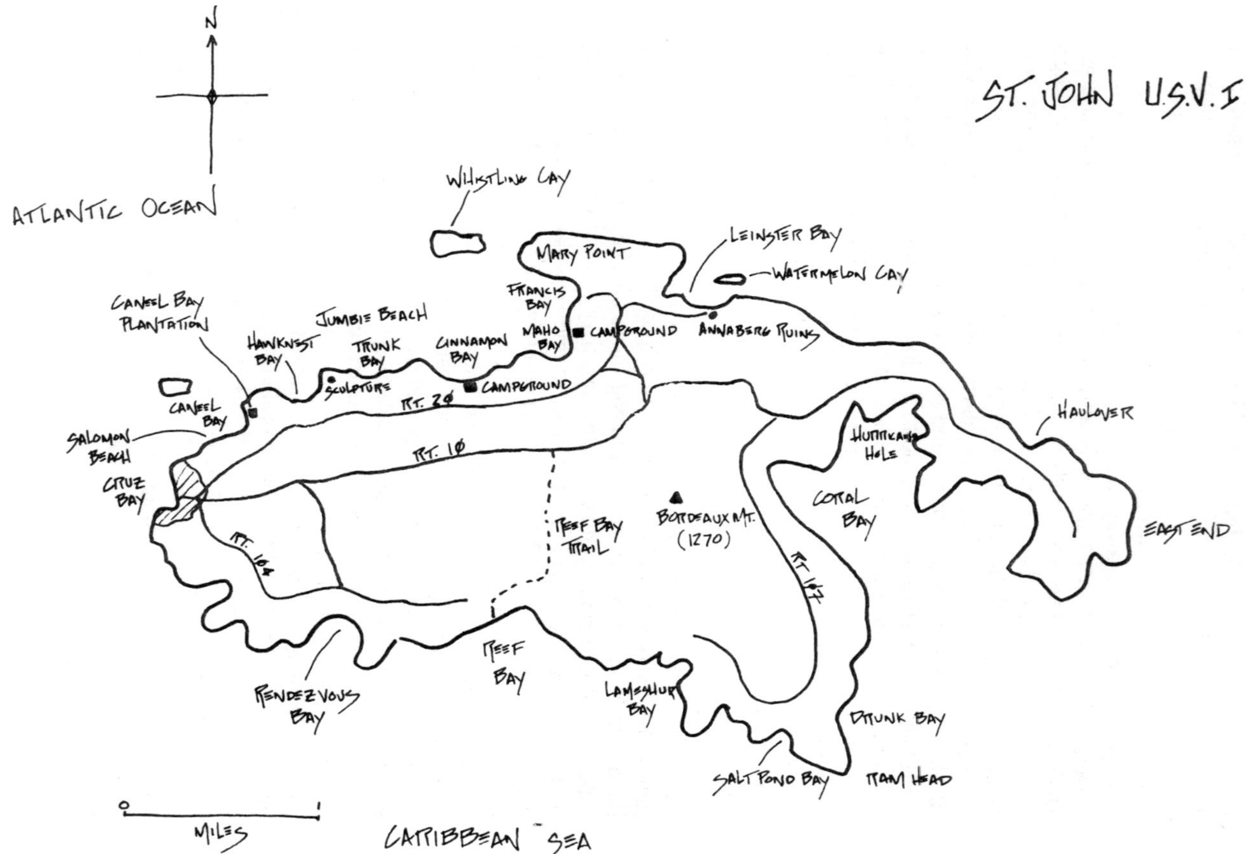
ST. JOHN U.S.V.I.
N
ATLANTIC OCEAN
WHISTLING CAY
MARY POINT
LEINSTER BAY
WATERMELON CAY
FRANCIS BAY
MAHO BAY
CAMPGROUND
ANNABERG RUINS
CANEEL BAY PLANTATION
JUMBIE BEACH
HAWKNEST BAY
TRUNK BAY
CINNAMON BAY
SCULPTURE
CAMPGROUND
RT. 20
CANEEL BAY
SALOMON BEACH
RT. 10
CRUZ BAY
HURRICANE HOLE
HAULOVER
CORAL BAY
EAST END
REEF BAY TRAIL
BORDEAUX MT. (1270)
RT. 104
RT. 107
REEF BAY
RENDEZVOUS BAY
LAMESHUR BAY
DRUNK BAY
SALT POND BAY
RAM HEAD
0
MILES
CARIBBEAN SEA

THE CAMPGROUNDS

Camping on St. John is not your typical camping experience. First of all, the weather is about as perfect as can be—no cold, rainy days to put a damper on your fun. Next, there is the warm, clear water and palm trees right at your doorstep. Finally, you don't have to rough it; you can choose accommodations that allow you to be outdoors without the usual aggravations. Here are your choices:

CINNAMON BAY CAMPGROUND (809) 776–6330
P.O. Box 720, Cruz Bay, St. John, USVI 00830
Stateside: (800) 223–7637/(800) 442–8198/(212) 586–4459
Rockresorts Reservations, 30 Rockefeller Plaza, Room 5400, New York, NY 10112

Now you can say you stayed at a Rockresort without spending a fortune. Located on the north coast of the island and on one of St. John's "big three" beaches, this well-managed campground is affiliated with the National Park Service. There are cottages, tents, and bare sites available, all within a few hundred feet of the water. My recommendation is to stay in one of the forty cottages on the grounds. They are clustered in blocks of four, with the best (that is, closest to the water and offering a view) situated in the "nine" and "ten" blocks. The cottage is really just a 15-foot-by-15-foot room, with two of the walls consisting only of screens with adjustable shades for privacy (the walls that separate your "cottage" from the one next door are made of concrete, as is the floor). Though very basic (remember, you are camping), it is actually quite pleasant for two people. The furnishings, while sparse, are comfortable. There are twin trundle beds (with linens), a table, and four canvas captain's chairs under spot lighting. Cooking is done on a propane stove or charcoal grill outside and there is a cooler, water container, and utensils. Outside, there is a backyard patio and picnic table. The bathrooms are communal with cold water. It's rustic but functional and very rewarding, especially when you fall asleep to the jungle sounds you hear through the screen walls.

The campground has a commissary and a very attractive outdoor dining pavilion called The Rain Tree, where meals are available three times a day. There is a watersports center on the beach, with windsurfing, sailing, scuba and snorkel gear available. The campground also offers a weekly dive package.

The park rangers conduct a weekly program of slide presentations, hikes, and snorkeling trips. Of particular interest is the Reef Bay Trail hike that takes five hours and leads you past old sugar mill ruins, ancient petroglyphs, and culminates in a boat ride back to town. You'll need reservations for this: 776–6201.

Rates for two people are NOT SO CHEAP for cottages and tents (there is only a $6 U.S. difference between the cost) and DIRT CHEAP for bare sites. Reservations should be made months in advance and you are limited to a two-week stay. Sometimes there are cancellations, so it's worth a shot to call at the last minute.

MAHO BAY CAMPS (809) 776–6240
P.O. Box 310, Cruz Bay, St. John, USVI 00830
Stateside: 17 E. 73rd St. New York, NY 10021

Of the two campgrounds, Maho Bay is smaller, more intimate, and more deluxe. Situated about 8 miles out of Cruz Bay and a few miles past Cinnamon Bay, it consists of tented cottages connected by a series of wooden walkways. Each unit has a view of the bay, yet the dense vegetation provides privacy. There are double beds (or twins) with linens, electricity, reading lights, a convertible couch, table and chairs, a cooler, utensils, and Coleman stove. Like Cinnamon Bay, the bathrooms are communal.

The management here is very ecology-minded, hence the boardwalks so as to not disturb the ground growth, the organic toilets to save water, and the help-yourself herb garden. The campground is surrounded by national park, so there's lots of room and ample opportunity to commune with nature. There is an open-air dining pavilion and breakfast and dinner are available daily. A small, expensive commisssary is on the grounds for that quart of milk you forgot to buy at the supermarket in Cruz Bay. Maho Bay has its own beach and a fully equipped watersports center.

Rates are NOT SO CHEAP for two people. Reservations should be made months in advance.

PRIVATE HOMES FOR PRIVATE VACATIONS (809) 776–6876
c/o Mary Phyllis Nogueira, Mamey Peak, St. John, USVI 00830

An acceptable alternative if the campgrounds are full or if you require a tad more comfort and luxury. Mary has over ten homes available for rental, including some with pools, Jacuzzis, and Jeeps. Prices should run you under $1000 U.S. per week, with some rentals available for under $500 U.S.

GETTING THERE

One of the reasons why St. John is so popular, besides its beauty and the park, is that it's easy to reach. You can fly nonstop to St. Thomas from the

States on American, Pan Am, or Eastern, and connect, via taxi, to a ferry from either the waterfront in Charlotte Amalie—a cheaper taxi ride—at 9:00 A.M., 11:00 A.M., or 5:30 P.M., or from Red Hook. The Red Hook ferries run almost hourly from 6:30 A.M. until 11:00 P.M. The ride will take about forty minutes from Charlotte Amalie and twenty minutes from Red Hook.

To arrive in style, you can fly the Virgin Islands Seaplane Shuttle, (800) 524–2050/(809) 773–1776, from San Juan, St. Thomas, or St. Croix. Flying "the Goose" is an experience! You board on land and then the plane literally drives into the ocean. There are no pontoons—the belly of the fuselage becomes a boat hull. You take off and land, on water, to the howl of the engines in a cloud of sea spray. Once you've landed, the wheels flip down and the plane drives up a ramp to the terminal. These planes can also land on a runway and will leave you near the Park Visitor's Center in Cruz Bay.

ST. JOHN: KEY FACTS

LOCATION	18°N by 64°W 3 miles east of St. Thomas 1400 miles southeast of New York
SIZE	20 square miles
HIGHEST POINT	Bordeaux Mt. (1270 ft.)
POPULATION	3000
LANGUAGE	English
TIME	Atlantic Standard Time all year
ELECTRICITY	110 AC (60 cycles)—same as U.S.
CURRENCY	U.S. dollar
DRIVING	On the left; valid driver's license okay
DOCUMENTS	None for U.S. or Canadian citizens
BEER TO DRINK	Beck's
RUM TO DRINK	Cruzan Gold

THE **Windsurfing** OPTION

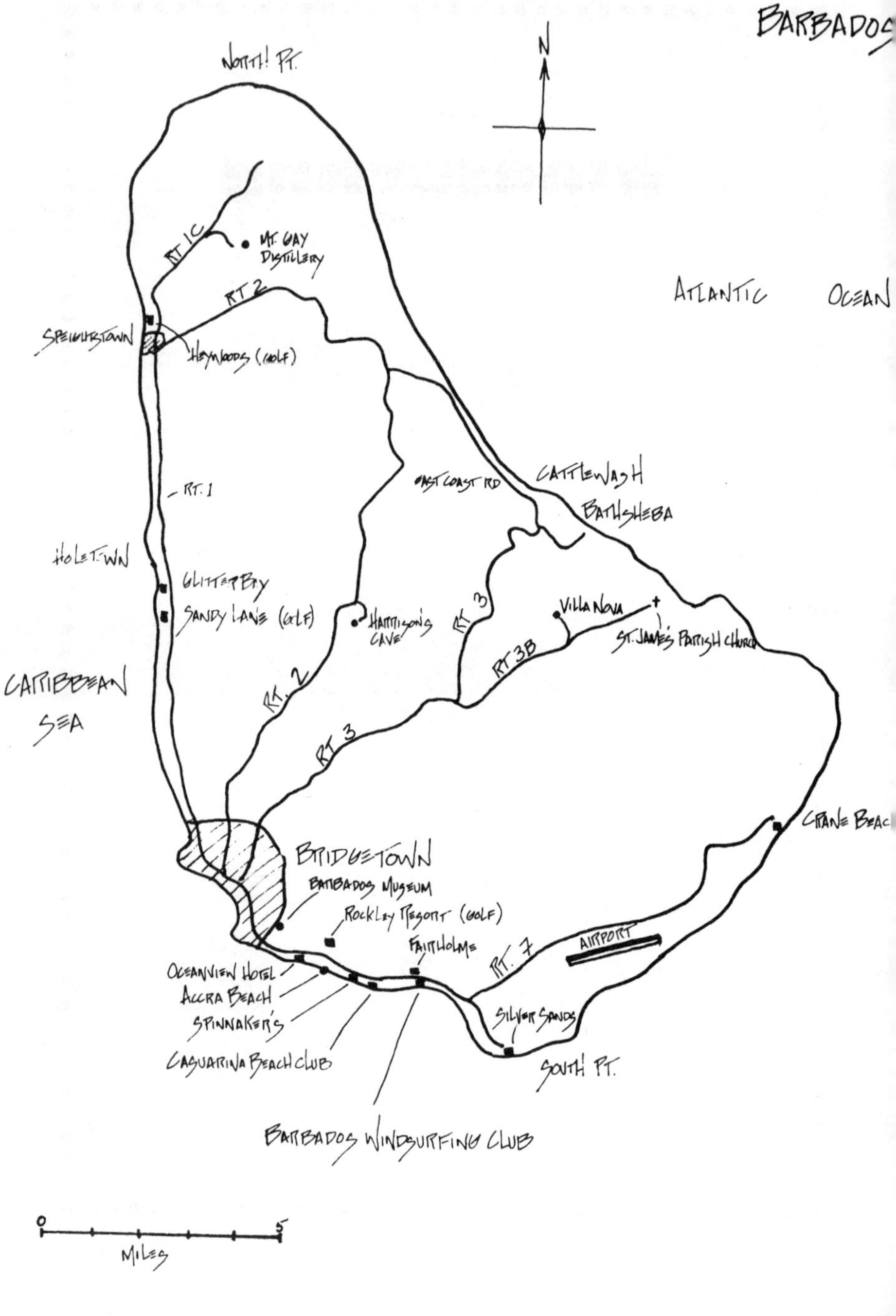

BARBADOS
NORTH PT.
N
RT. 1C
MT. GAY DISTILLERY
RT. 2
ATLANTIC OCEAN
SPEIGHTSTOWN
HEYWOODS (GOLF)
EAST COAST RD
CATTLEWASH
BATHSHEBA
RT. 1
HOLETOWN
GLITTER BAY
SANDY LANE (GOLF)
HARRISON'S CAVE
RT. 3
VILLA NOVA
ST. JAMES'S PARISH CHURCH
RT. 3B
CARIBBEAN SEA
RT. 2
RT. 3
CRANE BEACH
BRIDGETOWN
BARBADOS MUSEUM
ROCKLEY RESORT (GOLF)
FAIRHOLME
AIRPORT
RT. 7
OCEANVIEW HOTEL
ACCRA BEACH
SPINNAKER'S
SILVER SANDS
CASUARINA BEACH CLUB
SOUTH PT.
BARBADOS WINDSURFING CLUB
0
5
MILES

WINDSURFING ON BARBADOS

With everything else Barbados has to offer, the fact that it is also the windsurfing capital of the Caribbean is almost lost in the shuffle. Steady strong wind and surf conditions on the southern tip of the island combine to make optimal boardsailing. Add to that sunny skies, warm water, and Barbados' other amenities, and it's easy to understand why so many vacation here, or even spend a season hanging ten.

The Barbados Windsurfing Club (BWC) in Maxwell was founded on the same philosophy as a ski lodge. Exercise all day in the fresh air, then gather together around the hearth with a hot toddy (in this case, rum punch) to exchange tales of adventure, tips on equipment, and room numbers. Partners Andy Voss and Paul Rapson, both avid windsurfers, found a hotel for sale on the beach in 1982 and put their philosophy to work.

The club is a beehive of activity and a great place just to hang out and people-watch. The camaraderie that was a goal of the founders is evident everywhere. This is truly a windsurfer's haven, not only for muscle-hard champs but for all ages (although the demographics definitely skew to the younger side).

The style is fab-fifties block-and-balcony and the room decor is Americana. The beach has some coral cobble and reefs to dodge and is not the best that Barbados has to offer. But the club's bar and "family room" make up for its few deficiencies. If you're not on your board, you're at the bar. If the Bajan bartender has his way, and he usually does, calypso music is on the stereo. The bar is open on two sides to the ocean, providing the best vantage point for viewing the action on the high seas. There is always a breeze to ventilate the accommodations and wiggle the bar glasses from the overhead rack to a crashing demise. People come and go constantly. Yet it's very common just to hang out all day and not even bother getting wet.

The club is *not* for the windsurfing novice. This is dictated more by wind and surf conditions than by club policy. It's just too hard to learn with the wind ripping the boom out of your arms and the waves shaking your board like an earthquake. There are calmer places on the island better suited for beginners. The prerequisite for the BWC is that you can make a beach start in moderate conditions—the point being that if you can make it through the breakers you'll be okay. This loosely translates to a classification of intermediate—those who have windsurfed before and made it back to the starting point in a good breeze without assistance.

Affiliated with the club, and by far its biggest asset, is the Club Mistral. Sponsored by Mistral of Switzerland, one of the leading manufacturers of equipment, it provides state-of-the-art equipment and top-notch instruction for intermediates to experts. This solves the serious windsurfer's problems in regard to transport, customs officials, and spare parts. And Mistral has designed its equipment to meet the challenge of the local wind and surf conditions.

Mistral has two facilities on Barbados that correspond to each location's level of difficulty. The Mistral operation at the club offers several different kinds of boards and three different sail rigs. The staff can tailor a board and rig to accommodate both your abilities and the day's weather. The conditions at the Silver Sands shop (located on the southern tip of the island and the site of the Suzuki Fun Board Championships) are strictly for experts (the equipment provided reflects that). Here you'll find shorter boards that are big on speed, surf jumping, and wave riding. The instruction offered at the Sands focuses on improving the highly developed skills of boardsailors who want to make the leap to expert.

But for the majority of windsurfers who want to improve, the Mistral shop at the club is the best place to get instruction. It offers a weekly program of one lesson per day that covers the essential elements of the sport as follows:

Monday	beach starts (one hr.)
Tuesday	water starts (two hrs.)
Wednesday	jibing (two hrs.)
Thursday	water starts (two hrs.)
Friday	jibing (two hrs.)

All lessons begin at 10:30 A.M. sharp so your equipment must be ready. Classes usually have up to five people. Lessons for tacking and use of the harness are available on request as is private instruction. It is not necessary to stay at the BWC to participate in any instructional program. Rates at press time are by no means cheap, starting at $45 BDS ($22.50 U.S.) per hour, $75 BDS for two hours, and $270 BDS for six hours. Larger instructional packages are negotiable.

If all you want to do is rent a board, they have many combinations that will suit individual abilities and current conditions (you won't be stuck with a light-air sail when it's blowing a gale). Rates at press time are as follows:

one hour	$24 BDS	($12 U.S.)
two hours	$33 BDS	($16.50 U.S.)
half-day	$40 BDS	($20 U.S.)
full day	$70 BDS	($35 U.S.)
two days	$125 BDS	($62.50 U.S.)
three days	$170 BDS	($85 U.S.)
one week	$280 BDS	($140 U.S.)
two weeks	$510 BDS	($255 U.S.)
three weeks	$600 BDS	($300 U.S.)
four weeks	$700 BDS	($350 U.S.)

There is a rescue boat poised at the ready should any equipment—or you—break down.

For those with the competitive spirit, the BWC will set up races for any group that shows interest. With the BWC's encouragement, resident experts often give advice or on-the-spot seminars at almost any time. So don't be surprised if someone approaches you with helpful hints. There is usually someone around to offer repair and breakdown tips should you bring your own board. Various windsurfing videos are shown at night for anyone interested. So you can totally immerse yourself in the sport if you want to.

What about the beginner? What does he or she do? The BWC will gladly put them in touch with an instructor who operates out of the calm Sandy Beach Lagoon near the Carib Beach Bar at Worthing. This is actually where windsurfing started on Barbados. The water is shallow and very flat—ideal for learning. Novices are welcome to stay at the BWC for the windsurfer camaraderie, although there are other hotels right on the lagoon that would be more convenient.

The BWC is a club run *by* windsurfers *for* windsurfers. In keeping with this philosophy, the BWC will tailor any package to your needs—including the arrangement of any equipment and instruction from Mistral. Because they feel that windsurfers are individualists, they are *very* flexible. If you just want dinner every third night and champagne on ice every morning, they'll come up with a package.

BARBADOS: KEY FACTS

LOCATION	13° N by 59° W 100 miles east of St. Vincent 2200 miles southeast from New York
SIZE	166 square miles
HIGHEST POINT	Mt. Hillaby (1116 ft.)
POPULATION	280,000

LANGUAGE	English
TIME	Atlantic Standard Time year round (one hour ahead of EST)
ELECTRICITY	110 AC/60 cycles
CURRENCY	BDS dollar ($1.99 BDS = $1.00 U.S.)
DRIVING	On the left, local permit needed (with valid personal driver's license and fee)
DOCUMENTS	Proof of citizenship w/photo (U.S. & Canada) and ongoing ticket
BEER TO DRINK	Banks
RUM TO DRINK	Cockspur

GETTING THERE

You know Barbados loves tourists when you arrive at the sparkling Grantley Airport—the best in the Caribbean. All the major carriers fly nonstop or direct here: American, Pan Am, and Eastern from the States, BWIA and Air Canada from Toronto and Montreal. LIAT, Air Martinique, and Caribbean Airways service the other islands.

STAYING THERE

There are no fewer than sixty-five hotels and eleven guest houses on the island. With that phenomenal number of choices, there is something for everyone. For windsurfers, the area to focus on is the south coast in the parish of Christ Church—where conditions are best (although most of the finest hotels are located on the west coast). If you book your vacation as part of a package, try to get accommodations on the south coast to minimize driving time.

THE BARBADOS WINDSURFING CLUB (809) 428–9095/7277
Maxwell, Christ Church, Barbados, West Indies

The spot that's hot for windsurfing and windsurfers. On the beach, of course. Club Mistral is on the premises. Prices are NOT SO CHEAP—PRICEY for singles and doubles.

THE FAIRHOLME (809) 428–9425
Maxwell, Christ Church, Barbados, West Indies

A five-minute walk from the BWC, the Fairholme is a clean, quiet, and much cheaper alternative to the Barbados Windsurfing Club. While the common rooms are very spartan in their faded, fabulous-fifties furnishings, the rooms in the main house are surprisingly comfortable and attractive. All have private baths, ceiling fans, and firm double or twin beds. There are newer efficiency apartments in a separate wing but they lack the main house's character and style. The garden and pool in the back are pleasant. The proprietress is a very kind woman named Joyce Noble, who also runs the restaurant. The Fairholme is very popular with Europeans, especially the Dutch and Germans.

Rates are DIRT CHEAP for singles and CHEAP for doubles.

SPINNAKER'S (809) 428–7308
St. Lawrence Gap, Christ Church, Barbados, West Indies

The ideal choice for beginners as it is right on the Sandy Beach Lagoon. The rooms are pleasant and comfortable—many have balconies overlooking the water. Its location is also central to the nightlife of the St. Lawrence Gap. The restaurant is quite good and the staff are very friendly. A popular spot with the Dutch.

Rates are NOT SO CHEAP for singles and doubles.

CASUARINA BEACH CLUB (809) 428–3600
St. Lawrence Gap, Christ Church, Barbados, West Indies

A large resort with spacious grounds in the midst of the heavily developed south coast. The atmosphere is relaxed and there are some real perks that make this typical-looking beach hotel a value, including an Olympic-sized swimming pool, air-conditioned squash courts, tennis courts, and a very nice beach. The rooms have balconies with standard big-hotel decor.

Rates are PRICEY for singles and doubles.

GLITTER BAY (809) 422–4111
St. James, Barbados, West Indies
Stateside: c/o Robert Reid Assoc., 845 Third Ave., New York, NY 10022
(800) 223–6510/(212) 832–2277
Canada: c/o Robert Reid Assoc., 12 Redstone Path,
Etobicoke, Ontario M9C 1Y7
(416) 622–8813

This stucco Moorish-style luxury resort, while a tad out of character with Bajan architecture and inconveniently located for windsurfing on the west coast, is still a very deluxe place to stay should comfort and service be your first priority. Built on the grounds of the former Cunard estate (the

Great House is now the reception and administration area), the beach/pool/bar area is terrific, as is the service.

Rates are WICKED PRICEY for standard rooms to OUTRAGEOUS for one-bedroom suites on up (singles and doubles—EP).

CRANE BEACH HOTEL (809) 423–6220
St. Phillip, Barbados, West Indies
Stateside: c/o Robert Reid Assoc., 845 Third Ave., New York, NY 10022
(800) 223–6510/(212) 832–2277
Canada: c/o Robert Reid Assoc., 12 Redstone Path,
Etobicoke, Ontario M9C 1Y7
(416) 622–8813

The first thing you notice on entering Crane Beach is a profusion of little signs saying "Do Not (sic) . . ."—obviously aimed at the onslaught of tourists that walk the grounds each day. It's too bad, because it dulls the sheen on this extraordinary place. Set on a bluff overlooking one of the nicest hotel beaches in the Caribbean (and there are great waves for bodysurfing, too), the hotel and its white-columned pool are stunning. The Estate Mansion, or main building, has some magnificent high-ceilinged suites in its old wing that overlook the Atlantic (the hotel is on the Atlantic or windward side). There is an "annex," the Crane Bank House, down the beach, which offers significantly cheaper and uninspiring rooms for those on a budget.

Rates are VERY PRICEY to WICKED PRICEY for singles and doubles (EP) in the Estate Mansion, and NOT SO CHEAP to PRICEY for singles and doubles in the Crane Bank House (EP).

SANDY LANE

See "The Golf Option," pages 150–151.

DOING THERE

If you want a break from the boards, Barbados has more to do than almost any other island in the Caribbean. The tourist industry is so highly developed, everyone seems to be in on the act. And the Barbados government makes a point of educating it citizens on the value of the tourist dollar. A banner strung across a major access road to Bridgetown, the capital, says it all: "Tourism is our business. Let's do our part." Bajans are very friendly despite the hordes of tourists who stream through Barbados (almost 400,000 a year). One gets the feeling that they view tourists as they do rain—a necessity to keep the island growing.

There are three free weekly newspapers geared to the tourist: *The*

Visitor, The Sun Seeker, and *What's On in Barbados.* All are crammed with activities that cater primarily to the standard tourist crowd. Avoid them.

There are two tourist attractions worth your while. The first is the Harrison Caves in the parish of St. Thomas (432–8048/8049). An electric trolley runs through these fascinating caverns of stalactites, stalagmites, and running/dripping water to the accompaniment of a guide reciting a rote speech that must have been written for morons. I couldn't help but get the feeling that I was on an ride at DisneyWorld. Yet these caves are real, and if you can get past the tourist b.s., it's very interesting. Admission is $10 BDS. The other attraction is the *Atlantis II* (436–8929), a submarine that takes you down 150 feet to view marine flora and fauna day and night. It can hold twenty-eight people and has sixteen 2-foot viewports (eight on each side) and one large viewport on the bow. With a group of friends and a few cocktails, this could be lots of fun. Costs will run about $100 BDS per person.

Other activities of interest: Cricket (the Bajan national sport) at the Kensington Oval in Bridgetown. The season usually runs from May through December, though cricket is played locally year round (check the local papers for current matches). Crop Over, held in July and early August, celebrates the completion of the sugar-cane harvest. This is Barbados' version of Carnival, with calypso bands, tons of food, and a grand finale called "Kadooment Day." There are also tours of Bajan Great Houses sponsored by the Barbados National Trust that feature weekly "open houses" of private estates as well as five permanent-trust properties (phone: 496–2421). And for outdoor enthusiasts, there is the Outdoor Club of Barbados (Sturdee House, Bank Hall, St. Michael, Barbados, W.I., phone: 436–5328). The club is run by an intrepid bunch of individuals who conduct some 5-mile day hikes along old Carib trails around the island that will take you through rain forests, over cliffs, and along deserted beaches (Barbados does have a few left, including a long stretch of pink sand on the east coast called Cattlewash). Each day of the week covers a different hike. The cost is $140 BDS ($70 U.S.), which includes transportation from your hotel, three meals, snacks and beverages (local produce and cuisine). If you're tired of the board and beach, try this one.

Barbados, unlike most other islands its size, does have nightlife. The place to go for live music and dancing is an old converted house on the beach in Christ Church called Rachel's (there *is* a dress code: no shorts). A younger, more rambunctious crowd frequents the Warehouse, which also has live music and dancing. For a publike atmosphere that's hardly mellow, you can crawl into the St. Lawrence Gap and slug down a few Banks at The Ship Inn. Probably the most fun is visiting the eateries on Baxter St. in the wee hours of the morning. There are always people awake and they will keep you in stitches. Pop in to Enid's and ask for "pot hot"—some tasty local chicken.

THE **Hip** OPTION

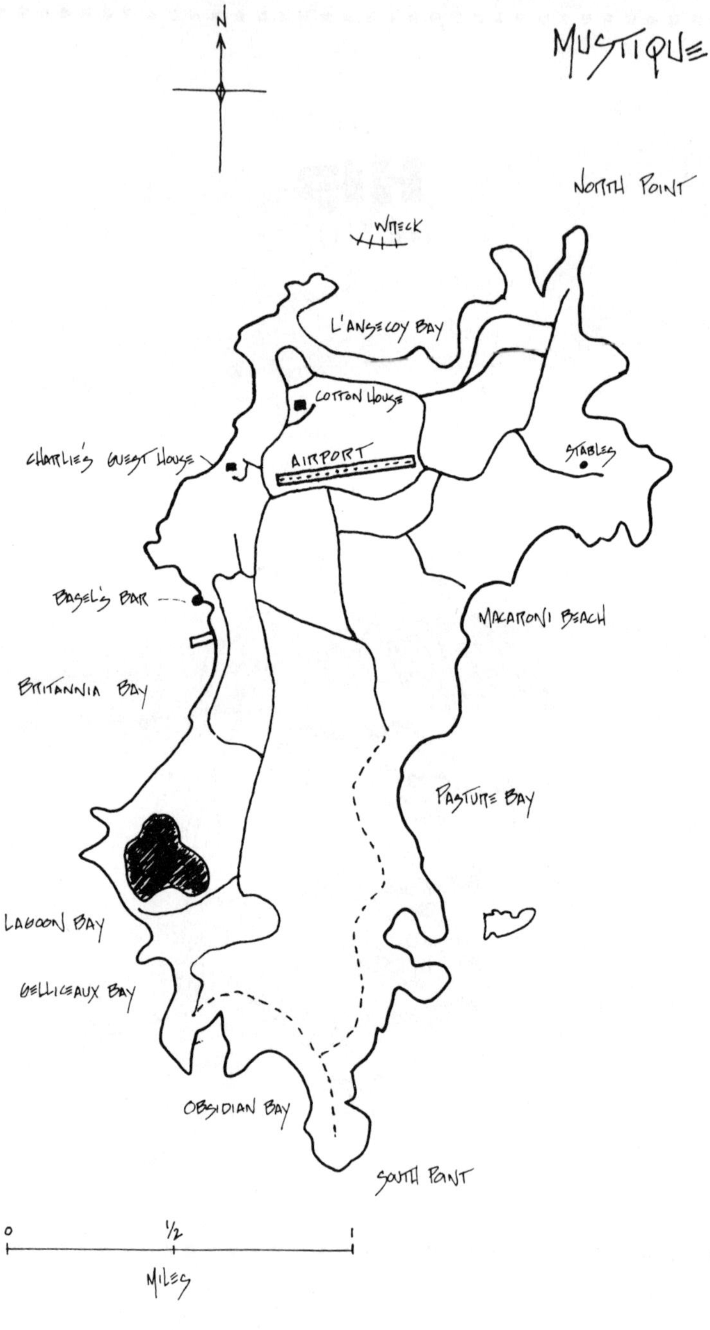
MUSTIQUE
N
NORTH POINT
WRECK
L'ANSECOY BAY
COTTON HOUSE
CHARLIE'S GUEST HOUSE
AIRPORT
STABLES
BASIL'S BAR
MACARONI BEACH
BRITANNIA BAY
PASTURE BAY
LAGOON BAY
GELLICEAUX BAY
OBSIDIAN BAY
SOUTH POINT
0
1/2
1
MILES

SLUMMING IT ON MUSTIQUE

You can't miss it. It sits like the House of Zeus atop Mount Olympus. It's the first thing you see approaching Mustique, the absurdly miscast Italianate mansion of Harding Lawrence—the founder of Braniff—and advertising queen Mary Wells. Yours to love for a cool ten million. Down the road is HRH Margaret's Les Jolies Eaux—the notorius playpen of Koo and Andy. Welcome to Mustique, vacationland of the rich, famous, and even more rich.

Owned by the Mustique Company, this is the Caribbean's Trump Tower or Costa Smerelda. It is opulent. Many of the villas resemble separate miniresorts in the Victorian-gingerbread mould, elevated to the appropriate grandness. Besides the Cotton House, there are only about fifty houses on the island. A glance at the property titles would reveal a global representation of the fabulous and fortunate.

Don't know somebody with a villa? Then you can stay at the Cotton House on the northwest corner of the island. It's discreetly tasteful, the nineteen rooms tucked into two plantation houses and three whitewashed, almost Swedish-looking cottages. All details are looked after, as to be expected. The pool is small, but who swims anyway? The main activity here is to have a drink or maybe a bite to eat, sit by the pool, and see who shows up. Visually, the pool ensemble is stunning. Designer Oliver Messel framed it with the remnants of an old sugar-mill warehouse, its jagged edge outlined against the sky. The pool itself conjures up memories of the Clampett's pool in the TV show "The Beverly Hillbillies." Looking from the pool to the north, you can see the tennis courts and rooftops of a famous rock legend's compound. The beach in that direction, L'Ansecoy Bay, is very pretty and looks out on the wreck of the *Antilles*, a French cruise ship that ran a reef in 1971.

If Cotton House doesn't fit your style or budget, there is an alternative: Charlie's Guest House. And what an alternative! If it weren't on Mustique, Charlie's would be a dump to avoid at all costs. It's still a dump. But for $35 single and $50 double, you can actually stay on Mustique, which is remarkable. This minicompound is situated at the virtual end of the sloping airport runway. As you walk up the driveway, you're greeted by three Dobermans, which, I was later assured—on my perch in a nearby tree—are harmless. Before my arrival, a woman from Bequia had told me that Charlie's reminded her of a kennel and now I know why. There are also countless cats, rabbits, and caged birds. The rooms are in two low-slung buildings that form what could loosely be described as a courtyard. The five small rooms have a definite sixties flair, in keeping with the style of the English woman named Virginia who runs Charlie's. If you *really* want to be chic on Mustique, this is the place.

The hub of activity on this tiny island is most certainly Basil's Beach Bar. Located on Brittania Bay along with Basil's Market, Boutique, and Water Sports Center, it's a favorite with both the yachting set and occasional celebutantes. Basil himself is reputed to be Mustique's version of Mandingo. His thatched-roof-beach-bar-on-stilts also serves lunch or dinner (not surprisingly the prices aren't posted—don't be afraid to ask). On Wednesday nights there is usually a jump-up with pan bands from Bequia or St. Vincent. It's very possible you'll recognize someone—the tip-off is their bodyguard(s). Basil's T-shirts are great collector's items and can be bought at Basil's Boutique.

The island is small, comprising only 1350 acres. It can be seen fairly easily by walking or hiring a scooter for $25 U.S. a day (inquire at Basil's). You can also hire a taxi at $25 U.S. for an hour—which should be enough time for a cursory tour of the island. Or you can walk. Starting from Basil's, go left up the hill and down until you can go no further. Take a left and you'll pass a church/community center on your right, then the runway, and in the distance Cotton House. Proceed left up a dirt road where you'll see a sign directing you to Charlie's. Follow the road to the Cotton House, pick up a map at the office, and have a drink by the pool (notice the groovy

Some of the accommodations at Cotton House, Mustique.

ashtrays). After a few cocktails, ignore the boutique in the windmill (cute, but no Cotton House T-shirts) and walk down by the tennis courts, bearing right. This will take you past a bird sanctuary and to the horse stables. If you don't want to ride, take a left and a quick right at the eastern end of the runway. Turn left on the first road you come to, which will lead you to Macaroni Beach—the island's best—a curved beach of off-white sand, palm trees, and a few thatched huts to give you shelter. Time-out for a swim. When you're ready, head back the way you came: turn left at the end of the road and left again at the end of the next. This road will take you past Pasture Bay (too rough for swimming) and onto a dirt road that leads to South Point. This is where you'll find Les Jolies Eaux, winter retreat of Princess Margaret. Heading north, you'll past Obsidian Bay and Gelliceaux Bay. At Gelliceaux you'll find the island's best snorkeling at the bay's northern end. This is also a great spot for a swim as by now you'll probably be quite hot. The road continues to Lagoon Bay with more good snorkeling reefs and finally back to Brittania Bay and Basil's.

GETTING THERE

Somehow Mustique's developers squeezed a runway on the island that can only receive small planes. The easiest way to get here is to fly to Barbados (serviced by American, Pan Am, Eastern, Air Canada, and BWIA) and connect via charter service with Mustique Airways. There are also several scheduled flights a day from St. Vincent, St. Lucia, Grenada, and Martinique on LIAT or Air Martinique. If you are on Bequia or another Grenadine, you can hire a boat to take you over for a day trip. From Bequia, it will cost between $100–150 U.S.—depending on your negotiating skills—for the round-trip hire of boat and crew. It makes sense to fill the boat with a group (usually up to ten), since the cost is the same for one or ten. This is a great way to see the island if you can't afford Cotton House and can't stomach Charlie's.

WHERE TO STAY

If you really want to do Mustique with panache, you can rent one of the palatial villas from the Mustique Company for $2000/week and up. Contact: The Mustique Company, Mustique, St. Vincent, West Indies. (809) 456–4777.

Or you can stay at:

THE COTTON HOUSE (809) 456–4777
Mustique, St. Vincent, West Indies
Stateside: David Mitchell & Co., 200 Madison Ave., New York, NY 10016
(212) 696–1323

The island's only true resort, the accommodations and pool are lovely as is L'Ansecoy Beach. The hotel offers minibus service (with box lunches) to Macaroni and other island beaches. There are also watersports (windsurfing, scuba, and snorkeling) as well as horseback riding and tennis.

Rates are RIDICULOUS for singles and OUTRAGEOUS for doubles, FAP (fabulously affluent plan—accommodations, three meals a day, afternoon tea, room service, and all the hotel's facilities).

CHARLIE'S GUEST HOUSE (809) 458–4621
Mustique, St. Vincent, West Indies

Slumming it on Mustique. Located next door to Cotton House, the funky accommodations can give you a terrific view of the bellies of in-coming aircraft. But it *is* affordable and it *is* on Mustique.

Rates are CHEAP for singles and NOT SO CHEAP for doubles.

ATTITUDE AND FABULOUSNESS ON ST. BART'S

Years ago, before St. Bart's became the ultrachic retreat it is today, the only bar in town was Le Select—a one-room affair jammed with memorabilia and the crews of visiting yachts. Jimmy Buffet's "Cheeseburger in Paradise" lyric got its inspiration from the hamburger stand that shares the outdoor patio with Le Select. Remarkably, the Select and Cheese are still intact today, a pocket of sanity on this isle of vanity. Step outside, and you're in the Caribbean's version of the Hamptons-times-ten.

There's no doubt that St. Bart's is the most expensive public island down here. There are certainly resorts that are more expensive, and more exclusive (for example, Mustique), but you can't pay more for what you get, especially when the dollar is down. Going out to eat here—the major evening pastime—almost requires an armored truck. What was once a sleepy hideaway for the Rockefellers, Rothschilds, and Biddles is now the glitz capital of the New York and L.A. creative elite.

St. Bart's is also the most un-Caribbean of Caribbean islands. It's almost as though the ten-minute flight from St. Martin traveled at Warp One and landed in Cap D'Antibes in the Med (St. Bart's is part of the French Department of Guadeloupe). Most shocking, particularly after spending time on the other islands, is the population, which is almost totally white. And there is no poverty—no one-room houses with water from a public tap. Perhaps this is why it's so popular with rich Americans—over 90% of the visitors are from the U.S. There's no unsightliness or destitution to make them feel guilty about enjoying their wealth. The French themselves find St. Bart's too expensive, although when the rates go down around Easter, there's an influx of Parisians.

This hilly island is tiny—not even 10 square miles. Most of the terrain is fairly dry and developed. This is not a place for enthusiasts of the wild kingdom. Most activity centers on the water, the stomach, and the right side of the brain. There are twenty-two beaches—six are quite good, one is nude. There are over fifty restaurants, most specializing in cuisine gastronomique, which is basically French food with Creole flourishes. And there are several bars and cafés, places to see and be seen, and a disco called Autour du Rocher.

People say they come to St. Bart's to get away from it all. Hah! One of the main attractions of the island is running into other people you know from the States. A prime example is Christmas here, the hottest ticket you can find in the Caribbean. Everyone who is anyone is on the island, at someone's house—never at a hotel. Life consists of house-hopping and dinner parties. Celebrity name-dropping is the name of the game. By day, many hang out at their pools while the more adventurous may go to a beach.

You may detect just a touch of cynism in this particular report. If this is what people want, you say, why not let them enjoy it in peace? That's true—and the island is pretty, clean, and sophisticated. It's just that with all the Caribbean has to offer—the staggering beauty, richness of life, and kaleidoscopic images—why, I ask myself, is St. Bart's so popular? Why do people return year after year to this highly overrated and way-overpriced speck in the sea? Because it's fabulous, that's why. And when a place becomes fabulous, there's no need for explanation. If that doesn't make sense, you're probably better off in one of the truly "hip" places like Bequia or Tobago.

The island, which is very small (only a third the size of St. Thomas), is split into two sections by the airport. On the smaller western section, there are two nice beaches—the Anse des Flamands and Anse de Columbier. Flamands is really a beautiful beach despite its steep rake and the

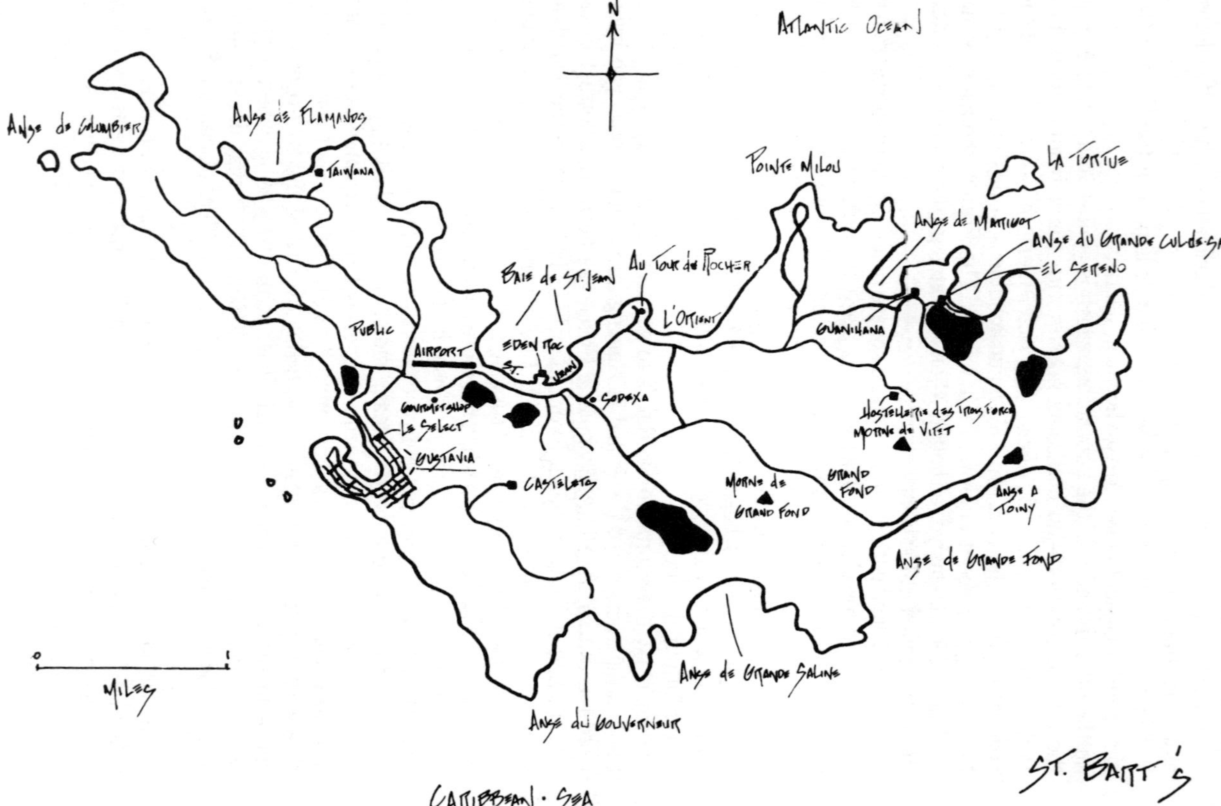
N
Atlantic Ocean
Anse de Columbier
Anse de Flamands
Taiwana
Public
Airport
Baie de St. Jean
Eden Roc
St. Jean
Au Tour de Rocher
L'Orient
Pointe Milou
La Tortue
Anse de Marigot
Anse du Grande Cul-de-Sac
El Sereno
Guanahana
Hostellerie des Trois Forces
Morne de Vitet
Sodexa
Gourmet Shop
Le Select
Gustavia
Castelets
Morne de Grand Fond
Grand Fond
Anse a Toiny
Anse de Grande Fond
Anse de Grande Saline
Anse du Gouverneur
0
1
Miles
Caribbean · Sea
St. Bart's

presence of several hotels. Columbier, also known as Rockefeller's beach, is more remote—about a half-mile walk from Le Petit Anse. This is one of the island's best and a favorite of visiting yachts. Besides these beaches, there's not a lot to see on this side.

East of the airport is where you'll find most of the action. St. Jean, with its beach, is the focal point of the island (even more so than Gustavia, the capital). Everyone goes through St. Jean at some time during the day. The beach features several hotels and restaurants as well as watersports centers, and the area itself has the highest concentration of hotels, restaurants, and stores on the island. If you're staying in a house (recommended), the beach here is good only for meeting people. You'll find them to the west of Eden Rock (the big promontory in the middle)—especially by the Mistral Windsurfing Center and the Filao Beach hotel pool. Off the beach, the major people-spot is the shopping center at the east end. Plan on having a brew at La Creole (but don't eat there, the food is awful) or the café au lait at the ice cream shop up the street just past La Louisiane (skip the ice cream—that's one dish the French have yet to master).

Heading east out of St. Jean is a very pleasant drive that takes you around a loop that winds through the hills and around the windward side. There's a very pretty, small beach on the right end of Anse de Marigot. It used to be fairly deserted until someone built a hotel next to it. The stretch of road that hugs the Anse à Toiny is very scenic, with hilly pastures rising up on the opposite side. Once you pass through Grand Fond, take a left at the sign for Salines. Go all the way to the end of the road (a salt pond will be on your right—and dunes in front of you) and park where you can. Follow the path and you'll quickly arrive at St. Bart's nude beach (after passing a weathered sign saying "Nudity Prohibited"). Almost everyone here is either topless or naked, so you may feel uncomfortable if you don't remove something—even if it's just to swim. Otherwise your neighbors will think you came to gawk at them. It's not hard to strip down, just remember when you used to do it in the seventies. Around the point to the west is another good beach, Gouverneur, a smaller version of Salines (and not nude). To reach it, however, involves driving all the way back to Gustavia and up the hill past Castelets for almost two miles.

Gustavia (on the other side from St. Jean and the airport) is the capital, where the two banks are located as well as Le Select. It's very pretty and very clean for a Caribbean capital. The harbor is U-shaped with most of the shops and restaurants located on the north side. Coming into town from the airport (take a left at the intersection of the Cross), you will encounter a hairpin turn. This offers a great photo opportunity of the town. Continue on and park when you pass by Le Select. Stroll around, browse, then go in and have a Heineken. Welcome to the real St. Bart's.

ST. BARTS: KEY FACTS

LOCATION	17° N by 62° W 15 miles southeast of St. Maarten 1693 miles southeast of New York
SIZE	9.6 square miles
HIGHEST POINT	Montagne de Vitet (922 ft.)
POPULATION	3056
LANGUAGE	French
TIME	Atlantic Standard Time (one hour ahead of EST, same as EDT)
ELECTRICITY	220 volts/50 cycles
CURRENCY	French franc (FF)
DRIVING	Valid U.S. or Canadian license okay
DOCUMENTS	Passport or proof of nationality and ongoing ticket
BEER TO DRINK	Heineken
RUM TO DRINK	Any from Guadeloupe

GETTING THERE

Landing at the aptly named St. Bart's Aerodrome la Tourmente is one of the most thrilling aerial experences in the Caribbean, topped only by the cliff approach of Saba. The nineteen-seater STOL aircraft (usually a Dehavilland Twin Otter) flies stomach-wrenchingly low over a notch in the mountains, then dips down fast to the runway. With trees and cars rushing past your window, the plane seems to bounce on the runway as the pilot hits the brakes so hard that you lurch forward in your seat.

There are several airlines that do this regularly. From St. Maarten's Juliana Airport, one of the Caribbean's primary gateways, Winair has at least four flights daily. Air St. Barthélémy has the latest flight from Juliana at five P.M. From St. Thomas and San Juan, Virgin Air flies daily and Air St. Barthélémy does on certain days (check schedules), as does Coastal Air Transport from St. Croix. Air Guadeloupe has daily flights from Pointe-à-Pitre, Guadeloupe.

STAYING THERE

For those in the know, which is what everyone who comes to St. Bart's thinks they are, the thing to do is rent a house or bungalow from SIBARTH Realty, BP 55, St. Barthélémy, 97133, F.W.I. (011–590–27–62–38). Renting a house will also save you a considerable amount of money on food as you won't have to go out to eat all the time.

The woman to speak to here is Brooke Lacour—the power broker of rental properties on the island. She handles over 80% of available accommodations (probably because she maintains a stateside office). Call (800) 932–3222 or write: Wimco, 28 Pelham St., Newport, RI 02840.

Book as early as possible, especially for the Christmas season. The toniest section seems to be Pointe Milou—a breezy headland with some very *Architectural Digest*–type homes. Rentals for a week in high seasons generally run between $2000–5000 U.S., although there are some places to be had for more or less. Kudos for those who can get one with a pool. Many of the homes can sleep up to eight, so with a group the cost becomes less prohibitive.

If you're not fortunate enough to wrangle an invitation or a house and still want to go here, there are a number of hotels that are quite good and expensive. Even the low end will run you about $100 a night during high season. Listed below are the best of the high-, low-, and medium-price ranges:

TAIWANA (011–590) 27–65–01
St. Barthélémy 97133, F.W.I.

Talk about accommodations with attitude, this place takes the cake! In all my travels, this is the only hotel that wouldn't even let me walk around the premises, let alone look at a room, even though I explained that I was a travel writer. There is no brochure or rate sheet for Taiwana, just a small white card with its name and address. And this is the only place I saw with mirrored windows on the guest cottages.

Located at the right end of the pretty beach of Anse des Flamands, the complex is small and insular, with a small pool, red tennis court, and a color scheme of oranges and purples. The interiors are probably very tasteful, but I could only see my own reflection when I tried to look in.

Rates are OUTRAGEOUS for singles and doubles.

CASTELETS (011–590) 27–61–73
B.P. 60, St. Barthélémy 97133, F.W.I.
Stateside: (212) 319–7488
c/o Jane Martin, 717 Fifth Ave., 13th Floor, New York, NY 10022

Perched way up the mountain from Gustavia, Castelets is worth mentioning only because it's an institution and the restaurant is the best and among the most expensive on the island. While the rooms are very tasteful, there are better places to stay that are much more convenient to the water and action. And the pool is about the size of a blow-up model from the five-and-dime.

Rates are VERY PRICEY for singles and doubles in the club accommodations and WICKED PRICEY to OUTRAGEOUS for doubles in the better villas (CP).

GUANAHANI (011–590) 27–66–60
St. Barthélémy 97133, F.W.I.
Stateside: (800) 235–3505/(212) 308–3330
First Resort Corp., 307 E. 56th St., New York, NY 10022

This very expensive, brand-new resort opened in December 1986 on the end of the west peninsula of Anse du Grande Cul-de-Sac. It's big by St. Bart's standards and similar to the Manipany on the western end of the island, yet better and prettier (for resort lovers only). However, the plantings need a couple of years to grow and provide more privacy between units. Everything is white, white, white with pastel accents. There are two overpriced restaurants located on the premises.

The best units are the ocean-front cottages on the bluff to the right. Each has a tiled terrace with a fridge and hotplate set up outside—vaulted ceilings with fans, A/C, queen-size beds, wood and canvas furnishings and terrific double-sinked/bidet'd bathrooms. You can also get units with their own pools. There is a beautiful pool/Jacuzzi/bar-cabana similar to the Messel design of Cotton House on Mustique. A reef keeps the water calm for swimming and snorkeling. The watersports center (sailing, waterskiing, scuba, and fishing) is located on the beach. The beach itself is adequate—a short walk around the point to Marigot will reveal the best beach in the area. Two artificial-grass, lighted tennis courts round out the recreational facilities.

Rates are WICKED EXPENSIVE for singles and RIDICULOUS for doubles (CP).

EL SERENO BEACH HOTEL (011–590) 27–64–80
B.P. 19, Saint Barthélémy 97133, F.W.I.

This is billed as a blue-and-white dream; I wouldn't go that far. But it *is* a good and cheaper alternative to the above—it's actually less than $200 a night for a double room in season! "Située au coeur de la baie de Grand Cul-de-Sac," this très French hotel is right on the water with an interesting bar/pool that has islands, bridges, and a garden in the middle (not good for laps). There are twenty bungalows with individual walled gardens, A/C, video, fridge, and safe for your jewels in each room. The restaurant, La Toque Lyonnaise, serves an excellent buffet.

Rates are VERY PRICEY for singles and WICKED PRICEY for doubles (CP).

HOSTELLERIE DES TROIS FORCES (011–590) 27–61-25
St. Barthélémy 97133, F.W.I.

Now this is a wonderful place. Set high up in the windward mountains with views of the water to the east, it is St. Bart's cosmic alternative. Owner Hubert Delamotte, an astrologer in a big way, has designed rooms to match each sign of the zodiac. Each room is in a separate or shared bungalow with nice detail and gingerbread trim as well as special features to compliment the personality traits of each sign. The Aquarius Room, for example, is water-focused with little color (because Aquarians don't need color—especially in the bathroom). Most of the rooms have four-posters and double hammocks on the porches. Currently there are rooms for eight signs; the remaining four are in the works.

There is a pool and an excellent restaurant (with organic veggies) on the premises. The bar is very comfortable and the whole place is just well done and NOT AT ALL PRETENTIOUS, like so many other establishments on this island. Mr. Delamotte is also into yoga and meditation, and welcomes all lifestyles to his holistic retreat.

Rates are VERY PRICEY for singles and double (MAP).

EDEN ROCK (011–596) 27–60–01
St. Barthélémy 97133, F.W.I.

Set on a rather large rock promontory in the middle of St. Jean beach, this is about the cheapest place you'll find on the island. It's also St. Bart's oldest hotel and in many ways it looks it. The Rock could use a good infusion of cash to give it a much-needed facelift, but a "pull-and-tuck" would jack up the price considerably. So despite the masonite walls and occasional patched plaster, it still has a great aura about it. After all, Greta Garbo stayed here, and the builder-owner was the first person to land a plane on the island. Many of the rooms have porches that hang right over the water—a nice place to sleep at night (the twin mattresses aren't heavy) and to watch the activity on the beach with binoculars. If you don't mind funky, then you won't mind Eden Rock.

Rates are PRICEY to VERY PRICEY for singles and doubles (CP).

EATING THERE

With over fifty restaurants on an island of barely 10 square miles and 3000 people, dining is a major sport here. The following establishments are among the best:

■ CASTELETS (27–61–73)
Morne Lurin
The best on St. Bart's. It has been for a long time and will probably continue to be for a long time. Quite simply, the food and view are fabulous—and so is the bill. $$$$$

■ LE BRIGANTIN (27–60–89)
Rue Jean D'Arc, Gustavia
Occupying the former Gustavia Yacht Club, this tastefully appointed restaurant specializes in seafood. An outdoor garden is très romantic and the bar quite convivial. $$$$$

■ LA CREMAILLÈRE (27–63–89)
Rue du Général-de-Gaulle, Gustavia
French in both cuisine and atmosphere—the desserts are extraordinary. $$$$$

■ PELICAN (27–64–64)
St. Jean
Franco-Japanese right on the beach in St. Jean. $$$$

■ CLUB LAFAYETTE (27–62–51)
Grand Cul-de-Sac
A lovely setting among pink-and-green decor about 50 feet from the water. Lunch only; try one of their planteurs (rum punch), then chow down on a grilled lobster with homemade sorbet for dessert. $$$$

■ AUTOUR DU ROCHER (27–60–73)
L'Orient
Jimmy Buffet's place not only has the island's leading (and some say only) nightspot, but a highly regarded French restaurant as well. $$$$

■ HOSTELLERIE DES TROIS FORCES (27–61–25)
Vitet
Cuisine gastronomique with cosmic blessings—the motto is "Food Is Love." The food and the atmosphere here are superb. $$$$

FOR RENTERS ONLY

There are two supermarkets on the island: the Gourmet Shop at the airport "mall" and Sodexa at the St. Jean "mall." Of the two, I prefer the Gourmet Shop. There are also two excellent catering services:

- CHEZ TATIE (27–61–61)
  Public
  An institution in herself, Mme. Tatie is generally regarded as the best chef of local West Indian/Creole/French food. Her space does not accommodate many but she does prepare meals to go—a great boon to renters. Her specialty is colombo—a spicy stew. $$$

- RÔTISSERIE BERTRAND (27–63–13)
  Rue Lafayette and rue du la Roi Oscar II, Gustavia
  Another "to go" establishment of très gourmand dishes and your foie gras. It's not cheap by any means but they will prepare a mean dinner with a day's notice. $$$$

DON'T MISS

For certified divers, the diving off St. Bart's, while not very deep (80 feet max.), offers bountiful marine life. There are two shops that will take you there. Make sure you bring your own fins and mask:

- SCUBA DIVING CLUB, "la bulle" (the bubble), St. Jean Beach at "Le Camp"
- ST. BARTH'S WATER SPORTS AND SCUBA DIVING (27–66–16), corner of rue Oscar II and Guadeloupe in Gustavia

For windsurfing enthusiasts, there are several outfits that have quality boards to rent. Noteworthy are the Mistral Club on St. Jean Beach and Club Lafayette on Grand Cul-de-Sac.

BEQUIA

Sitting at the bar at Frangipani enjoying a "Happy" Hairoun, the Vincentian brew, I unwittingly revealed to the woman next to me that I was a travel writer. She stiffened and brusquely requested that I not write anything about Bequia. "We don't need or want any more tourists," she said with

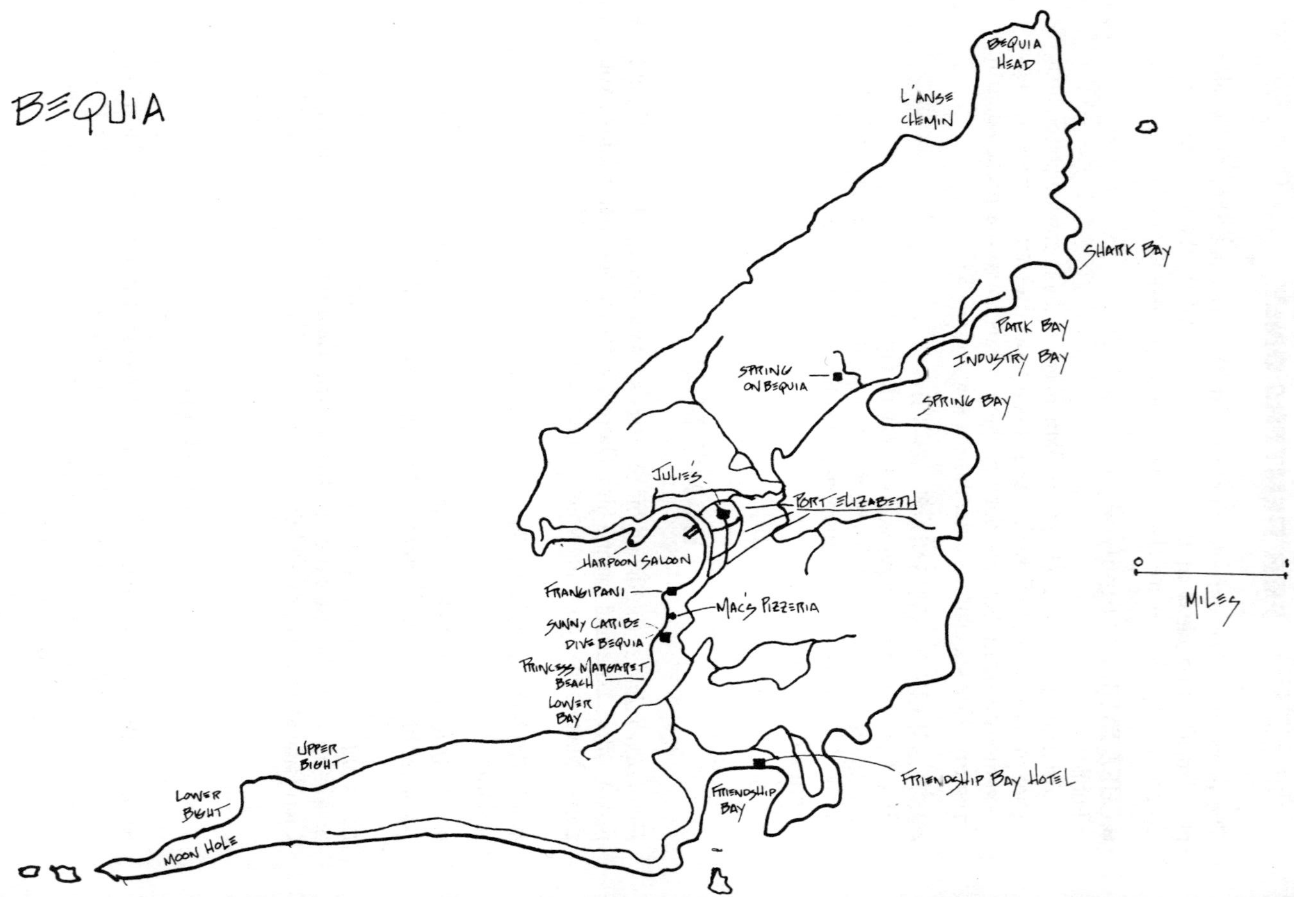
BEQUIA
BEQUIA HEAD
L'ANSE CHEMIN
SHARK BAY
PARK BAY
INDUSTRY BAY
SPRING ON BEQUIA
SPRING BAY
JULIE'S
PORT ELIZABETH
HARPOON SALOON
FRANGIPANI
MAC'S PIZZERIA
SUNNY CARIBE
DIVE BEQUIA
PRINCESS MARGARET BEACH
LOWER BAY
UPPER BIGHT
LOWER BIGHT
MOON HOLE
FRIENDSHIP BAY
FRIENDSHIP BAY HOTEL
0
1
MILES

conviction. It's a typical response of a seasonal resident who wants to slam the door in the face of any new arrival. But as I got to know Bequia, I began to agree with her. This island is extraordinary—I would hate to see it spoiled. So it is with great reluctance and profuse apologies that I bring Bequia to light.

The best way to describe Bequia is that it is the quintessential Caribbean experience—a harmony of all the elements that make the islands special. It is pretty, clean, and small enough to get to know intimately. The local residents are very friendly and responsive. There are handsome beaches, good restaurants, lots of bars, shops, and accommodations that are very reasonably priced. A sea orientation and yachty element add the perfect touch to the island's ambience.

For such a small place it's surprisingly lively. It's easy to spend a week here and not be bored. The action revolves around the waterfront of Port Elizabeth, starting at the ferry dock and winding around the Harborwalk to Princess Margaret Beach (also known as Tony Gibbons Beach). Here you can browse in a small but intelligent bookshop, buy some fresh fruit and vegetables from Rastas, have a few drinks, check out the brown coral jewelry from sidewalk vendors, dance to pan music, eat lobster pizza, go scuba diving, buy clothes and T-shirts, have more drinks, and go for a swim at a very pretty beach—all in a half-mile stretch.

There are walks that will take you to just about anywhere on the island in an hour or less. Port Elizabeth, where the recommended hotels are, is not only the island's hub but its center as well—all roads lead to town. The walks are fairly easy, up over the hills to the other side.

My favorite walk is to Industry. Leaving town on the road to Spring, you will climb and descend the hill and come upon an old sugar-mill ruin overgrown with hibiscus and bougainvillea on the left—a good photo opportunity. It is then a very pleasant walk through tall coconut trees, acres of them, with the usually deserted Spring beach off to the right. The road follows the curve of a bluff offering terrific views of Petit Nevis and Mustique. It quietly descends into more coconut groves and Industry beach. There is a bar at the beach to quaff a rum punch before heading back, and the swimming is also quite good. For the industrious, there is a hike from there to Bequia Head on cowpaths. This should be attempted only with ample daylight. People do get lost, so be sure of the way back and wear good walking shoes.

Another area worth exploring is "Moon Hole," an interesting and innovative development on the western end of Bequia. Designed by Tom Johnson, it strives to blend with its natural surroundings and to a great degree it succeeds. The stone used in the walls matches the cliffs and gullies where they are built. At first sight it looks as though the developer ran out of money. The complex looks unfinished; there is no glass where windows should be, no color except for gray stone and metal. Yet that is the architect's intention—to achieve harmony with the striking natural setting. The centerpiece of this creation is Moon Hole, a huge natural arch that, it is said, frames the full moon. Underneath the arch is a terraced, Victorian-style house. It is all gray and adorned with bright white whalebones and other marine accents. It's a bit odd, but still stunning. To get there, take the road to Friendship and at the top of the hill follow the right fork (the left takes you down to the Friendship Bay Hotel—noteworthy for its swinging bar chairs). The road will hug the coast through La Pompe and Paget Farm, where it seems every house is painted powder blue. Keep going and you'll eventually reach Moon Hole. Be as discreet as the designers were—this is *not* meant to be a tourist attraction.

For those susceptible to cabin fever, there are a variety of diversions. First, there's Dive Bequia (83425), a *very* laid-back operation in the most "for sure" Southern-California style. Run by Bob Sachs and Anne Gröne, they offer anything from snorkel trips, resort courses, and PADI certification to night dives and underwater videos of yourself doing a Lloyd Bridges imitation. They have great T-shirts for sale, too.

There is also a St. Vincent day trip that will both please and exhaust even the most energetic—a hike up the Soufrière volcano on the northern end of the island. Be sure to bring good walking shoes, water, energy snack, and a windbreaker or sweatshirt. It's cool and windy at the top and after the sweaty hike it will make your teeth chatter.

You leave at 6:30 A.M. on the *Friendship Rose*—an auxiliary schooner that will get you to Kingstown by eight A.M. On arrival in Kingstown, you will be met by an onslaught of cab drivers. This is the time to be a shrewd and hard-nosed negotiator. Talk to several drivers, finding one whom you won't mind spending the day with, whom you can understand, and who seems to know what he's talking about. By speaking to many drivers, you'll get a good idea of the going rate and a mutually agreeable price range. At press time this was about $240 EC (about $90 U.S.), which should be all-inclusive and *not* per person. Reconfirm the price and what's included at least two or three times. It'll sound stupid but it will prevent the driver from sneaking in hidden charges. You may also want to see the vehicle; it's a long drive to the starting point over roads that aren't in the greatest shape.

The drive itself will take about one hour. You'll have to switch to a Jeep for the half-hour bounce up to the trailhead. (The cab driver will have the Jeep connection arranged.) It is then a three-hour, fairly strenuous hike to the crater rim and summit. And rim is no exaggeration. You actually crawl up to the edge of the crater and peer over about a 1000-foot sheer drop to the floor of the volcano. There used to be a rather large crater lake that is now only a semblance of its former self. If you carefully walk, or crawl, along the rim to the right from the top of the path, you will find a rope pegged into the ground. It was put there by researchers who go down to take measurements on the activity of this very active volcano (it last erupted in 1979). You can climb down via the rope (with some sort of protection for your hands) to roam around the crater. *Before* doing this, tug on it a few times to make sure it's still in good shape. Otherwise you'll end as a postscript on the hometown eleven o'clock news. Obviously, the climb back up to the crater rim will be very tiring—make sure you are strong enough and have the energy to do it.

After you've taken your pictures and refueled, the return climb will be easier. Leave no later than 1:00 P.M., allowing two hours for the descent. If you keep to this timetable, you should be able to make the 4:15 P.M. boat back to Bequia. If you don't, there's always the Kingston Park Guest House (see page 216) and the superb Botanical Gardens. The gardens are among the oldest in the Western hemisphere and this is where Captain Bligh of *Mutiny on the Bounty* fame planted the Caribbean's first breadfruit tree.

BEQUIA: KEY FACTS

LOCATION	13° N by 61° W 9 miles south of St. Vincent 2050 miles southeast of New York
SIZE	7 square miles 5 miles long by 3 miles wide
HIGHEST POINT	Belle Pointe (881 ft.)
POPULATION	5000
LANGUAGE	English
TIME	Atlantic Standard Time (one hour ahead of EST, no Daylight Savings time)
ELECTRICITY	220–240 DC/50 cycles
CURRENCY	The EC dollar ($2.64 EC = $1.00 U.S.)
DRIVING	On the left; local permit needed with valid driver's license
DOCUMENTS	Proof of citizenship and ongoing ticket
BEER TO DRINK	Hairoun
RUM TO DRINK	Any Vincentian brand.

GETTING THERE

There is no airport on Bequia; the only access is by boat. Three boats service the island exclusively—the most fun is the *Friendship Rose* (on the *Rose* they hoist the sails). Up-to-date schedules are available from the Tourist Board: (809) 457–1502.

WHERE TO STAY

There are several *very* reasonable places to stay that are quite satisfactory. Prices on Bequia are still much lower than the more tourist-oriented island. Who's complaining?

SUNNY CARIBÉE PLANTATION HOUSE (809) 458–3425
Bequia, St. Vincent, West Indies

Ideally situated between a stellar beach and the diversion of the waterfront, this is an excellent value for those who want pleasant surroundings for not a lot a money. The establishment is a symphony of pink and turquoise. Make a point to stay in the cabanas, particularly those that border the coconut-tree-studded common. Each cabana has a small veranda, comfortable and attractive furnishings, ceiling fan, mosquito netting, and hot water (a luxury here). You also get a fridge (of the dorm-room mould) in your cabana if desired. The main house is all pink with a wraparound, arched veranda. Meals are served here and are very good (the MAP route may be worth it). There is a small but attractive, raised, kidney-shaped pool and the standard beach bar. Dive Bequia is located on the grounds, too. A small beach is tucked in front of the bar with chaise longues, but it's worth the five-minute walk over the point to HRH Maggie's Beach.

Rates are CHEAP for singles and NOT SO CHEAP for doubles. MAP is $20 extra per person.

THE FRANGIPANI (809) 458–3255
Bequia, St. Vincent, West Indies

If you like being the center of attention, especially with the yachty set, then the Frangipani is for you. It sits on a point in the middle of the Harborwalk and has people marching by all day long. The main house, with its trademark red roof, has several rooms furnished with mahogany antiques (Room 4 has a majestic four-poster and a corner view of the harbor). The newer "garden" rooms are made of stone and wood with sundecks. On Thursday nights there is a BBQ and buffet with decent pan bands for jumping. Get there early; the music stops around eleven P.M., as does most activity on Bequia. It's owned by the P.M. of St. Vincent—Pat "Son" Mitchell.

Rates are NOT SO CHEAP.

JULIE'S GUEST HOUSE (809) 458–3304
Bequia, St. Vincent, West Indies

Julie's is the best deal in the Caribbean. For $44 EC (about $17 U.S.), you get a single or double room *and* breakfast and dinner. The rooms are very simple with firm platform double beds, mosquito nets, blond wood, bright wall colors, and private baths (no hot water). The food is good West Indian fare, again, very simple. You really enjoy eating because the whole place is such a bargain that the food seems *free*.

Julie's is not on the beach but one block in from the harbor in a residential neighborhood. You'll hear dogs barking and roosters crowing at all times (especially as you try to fall asleep). The "lullaby of Bequia" usually starts with either an all-dog or all-rooster chorus. They sing a duet which builds to a cacophony and then, spent, gradually winds down. You get used to it.

The people who stay here are an interesting bunch and are usually repeaters. This is *not* a place to be antisocial. There is a bar where a bunch of Julie's friends listen to the cricket matches. The staff are courteous and very friendly, especially when you introduce yourself. If you are with a group of three or four persons, you can get the cottage in the back. It has a yard with goats and chickens grazing through the mango and breadfruit trees.

Rates are DIRT CHEAP (MAP).

OTHER HOTELS

- THE OLD FIG TREE (809) 458–3201
  Simple, motel decor on the Harbor Walk. CHEAP.

- FRIENDSHIP BAY HOTEL (809) 458–3222
  Nice beach but too expensive. I'd rather be in town. PRICEY for singles/VERY PRICEY for doubles (MAP).

- SPRING ON BEQUIA (809) 458–3414
  An interesting design and tranquil setting on rising ground but dead and expensive. Rates are PRICEY for singles and VERY PRICEY for doubles (MAP).

STAYING THERE—ST. VINCENT

Should you miss the boat or have an early-morning flight out of St. Vincent, there are a few good places to stay in Kingstown. Don't forget to visit the Botanical Gardens and to eat at the French Restaurant (that's what it is called.) The rest of the town is forgettable.

THE UMBRELLA BEACH APARTMENTS (809) 458–4651
Villa, St. Vincent, West Indies

Lovely accommodations and a favorite of those on the guest house circuit, this establishment has private baths, all watersports and a location on the beach. Rates are CHEAP.

KINGSTOWN PARK GUEST HOUSE (809) 456–1532
P.O. Box 41, Kingstown, St. Vincent, West Indies

Located on a hill overlooking the town and Bequia beyond, this converted old plantation house gets raves from guests. The quarters are clean, cheap, and include good West Indian cuisine. It's only about a ten-minute walk to town and is less than 3 miles from the airport. Rates are DIRT CHEAP for singles and doubles (MAP).

HERON HOTEL (809) 457–1631

An easy walk from the ferry dock, this is a great spot to stay if you want to catch the early boat. The comfortable rooms—in pale tones with wood floors surrounding a courtyard—provide refuge from the not-very-scenic neighborhood. Rates are CHEAP for singles and NOT SO CHEAP for doubles (MAP).

YOUNG ISLAND (809) 458–4826
c/o Ralph Locke, 315 E. 72nd St., New York, NY 10021

If it's luxury you want and spending lots of money proves it, there's Young Island. Billing itself as "an exclusive, private island resort," it's hardly that. A Chappaquidick-sized swim and you're practically in downtown Kingstown. But it is one of those service and sunshine places that are la mode for some. I'd rather be on Bequia. Rates are RIDICULOUS for singles to OUTRAGEOUS for doubles (MAP).

DON'T MISS

BEQUIA BOOKSHOP

Located on the waterfront across from the park, it features an excellent collection of West Indian writers and a good general selection. And if it's maps and charts you're into—this is the place. It is owned by a very knowledgeable and polite ex-Bajan named Ian Gale, a good person to talk to about Caribbean authors. The Bequia Bookshop T-shirt is an intelligent collector's item (as are books).

MAC'S PIZZERIA

They have lobster and fish pizza that is unusually good—it's been made almost world famous by the yachty set. Perched on the Harborwalk with a breezy veranda, it features a healthy array of food, from pita-bread sandwiches and quiche to banana bread and home-made yogurt. Tuesday nights Mac's throws a BBQ and jump-up with live bands.

For Drinks

- THE HARPOON SALOON—for sunset cocktails and a great view of the harbor.
- DE REEF—in Lower Bay and on Sunday afternoons.
- FRANGIPANI—the hub.
- GREEN BOLEY—next to Mac's on the Harborwalk Cocktail Crawl.
- FRIENDSHIP BAY—the swinging bar chairs are fun and the Cactus Delight cocktail makes them even more fun.

GLOSSARY

Accommodations: Lodgings/rooms/accommodation.

Bareboat: A sailing-boat hired without captain or crew.

Buttondown: A buttondown shirt, used to suggest a 'preppy' look or style.

Camcorder: A video camera.

Combo: Combination (as in combo pizza).

Cookies: Biscuits.

Crash: To sleep (as in crash out on the beach).

Funky: Pleasantly eccentric or out of date.

Gas station: Petrol station.

Jam on: To dance or to party.

Pop: A soft drink.

Schlepping: Carrying.

Skinny dip: Nude bathing.

CARIBBEAN SUPERLATIVES

Best beach—SANDY CAY, Carriacou

Best luxury hotel—MALLIOUHANA, Anguilla

Best hotel—HOTEL DES TROIS FORCES, St. Bart's

Best guest house—JULIE'S, Bequia

Best West Indian restaurant—MAMMA'S, Grenada

Best continental restaurant—CASTELETS, St. Bart's

Best pizza—MAC'S PIZZERIA, Bequia

Best beer—CARIB (Trinidad)

Best rum—COCKSPUR (Barbados)

Best rum punch—BETTY MASCOL'S PLANTATION HOUSE, Grenada

Best bar—A-FRAME, St. Lucia

Best nightclub—ABRACADDABRA'S, Antigua

Best dive sight—THIRD ENCOUNTER, Saba (110 ft.)

Best golf course—DORADO BEACH, Puerto Rico

Best port of call—NORTH SOUND, Virgin Gorda

Best hike—BOILING LAKE, Dominica

Best tennis—BUCCANEER, St. Croix

Best windsurfing—BARBADOS WINDSURFING CLUB, Barbados

Best hip destination—BEQUIA

Best shopping—CHARLOTTE AMALIE, St. Thomas

Best Carnival—PORT-OF-SPAIN, Trinidad

Best reggae music—KINGSTON, Jamaica

Best calypso music—PORT-OF-SPAIN, Trinidad

Best pan music—PORT-OF-SPAIN, Trinidad

TOURIST BOARD ADDRESSES

ANGUILLA
Caribbean Tourism Association,
20 E. 46th St.,
New York, NY 10164
(212) 682–0435

ANTIGUA

(U.S.)
Government of Antigua and Barbuda,
Department of Tourism,
610 Fifth Ave.,
Suite 311,
New York, NY 10020
(212) 541–4117

(CANADA)
Government of Antigua and Barbuda,
Department of Tourism,
60 St. Clair Ave. E.,
Suite 205,
Toronto, Ont. M4T 1N5
(416) 961–3085

(UK)
Antigua and Barbuda Tourist Office,
15 Thayer Street,
London, W1
(01) 486–7073

BARBADOS

(U.S.)
Barbados Board of Tourism,
800 Second Ave.,
New York, NY 10017
(212) 986–6516

(CANADA)
Barbados Board of Tourism,
20 Queen St. W., #1508
Box 11,
Toronto, Ont. M5H 3R3
(416) 979–2137

(UK)
Barbados Board of Tourism,
263 Tottenham Court Road,
London, W1
(01) 636–0090

BRITISH VIRGIN ISLANDS

(U.S.)
BVI Tourist Board,
370 Lexington Ave.,
New York, NY 10017
(212) 696–0400

(CANADA)
BVI Tourist Board,
801 York Mills Rd., #201,
Don Mills, Ont. M3B 1X7
(416) 446–1121

(UK)
British Virgin Islands,
Tourist Bureau and Information Centre,
48 Albemarle Street,
London, W1
(01) 629–6353

DOMINICA

Caribbean Tourism Association,
20 E. 46th St.,
New York, NY 10164
(212) 682–0435

GUADELOUPE/ST. MARTIN/ST. BART'S/MARTINIQUE

(U.S.)
French West Indies Tourist Board,
610 Fifth Ave.,
New York, NY 10020
(212) 757–1125

(CANADA)
French Government Tourist Office,
S.O.F.T.,
1981 Avenue McGill College #490,
Montreal, Quebec H3A 2W9
(514) 288–4264

GRENADA (Carriacou)

(U.S.)
Grenada Tourist Board,
141 E. 44th St.,
New York, NY 10017
(212) 687–9554

(CANADA)
Grenada National Tourist Office,
143 Yonge St., #102,
Toronto, Ont. M5C 1W7
(416) 368–1332

(UK)
Grenada National Tourist Office,
1 Collingham Gardens,
London, SW5
(01) 370–5164

JAMAICA

(U.S.)
Jamaica Tourist Board,
866 Second Ave.,
New York, NY 10017
(212) 688–7650

(CANADA)
Jamaica Tourist Board,
2221 Yonge St., #507,
Toronto, Ont. M4S 2B4
(416) 482–7850

(UK)
Jamaica Tourist Board,
Jamaica House,
63 St James Street,
London, SW1
(01) 499–1707

PUERTO RICO

(U.S)
Puerto Rico Tourism Co.,
1290 Avenue of Americas,
New York, NY 10019
(212) 541–6630

(CANADA)
Puerto Rico Tourism Co.,
10 King St. E., #501,
Toronto, Ont. M5C 1C3
(416) 367–0190

SABA

Saba Tourist Office,
1500 Broadway,
Suite 2305,
New York, NY 10036
(212) 840–6655

ST. KITTS AND NEVIS

(U.S.)
St. Kitts and Nevis Tourist Board,
650 Fifth Ave.,
New York, NY 10019
(212) 315–1760

(U.K.)
St. Kitts and Nevis,
Rosumonde Vern UK Associates,
15 Wardour Street,
London, W1
(01) 437–9475

ST. LUCIA

(U.S.)
St. Lucia Tourist Board,
41 E. 42nd St.,
New York, NY 10017
(212) 867–2950

(CANADA)
St. Lucia Tourist Board,
151 Bloor St. W.,
Toronto, Ont. M5S 1S4
(416) 961–5606

(UK)
St. Lucia Tourist Office,
1 Collingham Gardens,
London, SW5
(01) 370–0926

ST. MAARTEN

St. Maarten Tourist Board,
275 Seventh Ave.,
New York, NY 10001–6708
(212) 989–0000

ST. VINCENT AND THE GRENADINES (Bequia and Mustique)

(U.S.)
Caribbean Tourism Association,
20 E. 46th St.,
New York, NY 10164
(212) 682–0435

(U.K.)
St. Vincent and the Grenadines Tourist Board,
1 Collingham Gardens,
London, SW5
(01) 370–0925

TRINIDAD & TOBAGO

(U.S.)
Trinidad & Tobago Tourist Board,
400 Madison Ave.,
New York, NY 10017
(212) 838–7750

(CANADA)
Trinidad & Tobago Tourist Board,
145 King St. W.,
Toronto, Ont. M5H 1G8
(416) 367–0390

(UK)
Trinidad and Tobago Tourist Board,
48 Leicester Square,
London, WC2
(01) 839–7155

UNITED STATES VIRGIN ISLANDS

(U.S.)
USVI Division of Tourism,
1270 Avenue of the Americas,
New York, NY 10020
(212) 582–4520

(CANADA)
Earl B. Smith Travel Marketing,
234 Eglington Ave. E., #306,
Toronto, Ont. M4P 1K5
(416) 485–7577

(UK)
United States Virgin Islands,
Div. of Tourism,
25 Bedford Square,
London, WC1
(01) 637–8481

Index

ABOUT THE AUTHOR

JONATHAN RUNGE, a native of Massachusetts, is the co-author of *Ski Party!—The Skier's Guide to the Good Life.* He first visited the Caribbean in 1977 on a spring break and has been hooked on the place ever since. After graduating from Tufts, he moved to New York and spent too many years working for ad agencies but is now a confirmed travel writer. Besides being an avid skier, he is also a USCG-licensed captain and PADI-certified diver.

Jonathan lives in New York City and Sag Harbor, New York.

If you have any comments, suggestions, or information for the next edition, please write me:

JONATHAN RUNGE
RUM AND REGGAE
P.O. BOX 104
SAG HARBOR, NY 11963